The Way We Live Now

The Way We Live Now

AMERICAN PLAYS & THE AIDS CRISIS

Edited by M. Elizabeth Osborn

THEATRE COMMUNICATIONS GROUP   NEW YORK

The Way We Live Now: American Plays and the AIDS Crisis is published by
Theatre Communications Group, Inc., the national organization for the
nonprofit theatre, 355 Lexington Ave., New York, NY 10017.

The Way We Live Now: American Plays and the AIDS Crisis is supported, in part,
by a grant from the New York State Council on the Arts.

Cover photograph: "Calla Lily, 1986" by Robert Mapplethorpe, courtesy of The
Estate of Robert Mapplethorpe, copyright © 1986.

Book design and composition by The Sarabande Press

The Way we live now: American plays and the AIDS crisis/edited by M.
    Elizabeth Osborn.
    ISBN 1-55936-006-2: $24.95—ISBN 1-55936-005-4 (pbk.): $14.95
    1. AIDS (Disease)—Drama. 2. American drama—20th century.
I. Osborn, M. Elizabeth.
PS627.A53W38 1990
812'.54080356—dc20
90-10829
CIP

First Edition: May 1990
Second Printing: March 1993

One-third of the profits from this book will be donated for AIDS research.

*For all the theatre artists
and dear friends we have lost*

Acknowledgments

This book grew out of a brainstorming session with Paula Vogel late in 1987 (before she started her own AIDS play). The process of assembling scripts for consideration was a long one. There are many plays dealing with AIDS out there—and more appearing all the time—but finding out about them, and then actually getting hold of the scripts, is not easy. People across the country supplied me with suggestions, contact information, copies of plays; they include many of the writers who appear in this book, as well as Misha Berson, Michael Dixon, Peter Franklin, Jim Leverett and especially Don Shewey. Eventually, as word spread, quite a few playwrights I did not know sent in their work. I am grateful to them all—and to Michael Feingold, who without hesitation agreed to write what proved to be a wrenching and eloquent introduction.

Some plays we wanted to include were unavailable—most notably Larry Kramer's *The Normal Heart*. Fortunately I had at hand many more worthwhile plays than we had room for. Part of what made selection difficult was the fact that virtually all of them are obviously grounded in personal experience; the writers have come very close to the disease. My own work has also been fueled by rage and grief; the day I learned that John Hirsch was seriously ill with what might be AIDS was the day I restarted work on a stalled project. For me the book has become a tribute to his memory.

—M. Elizabeth Osborn

Contents

CONTENTS

Introduction

BY MICHAEL FEINGOLD

> HAMM *(Violently)*: Use your head, can't you,
> use your head, you're on earth,
> there's no cure for that!
> *Endgame*

Imagine a play with no protagonist. The action proceeds, some characters suffer unimaginably and die, others in their wake are left bereft, crazed, numb with shock. The performance goes on, lasting days, months, years. Uncounted numbers participate. The torment continues without explanation and without letup; alleviations are found, but no solutions. The end of the performance is not yet in sight. The main character is still invisible.

Acquired Immune Deficiency Syndrome—the ponderous name we give to the leading figure in this terrifying and interminable spectacle—has been giving a grand-scale performance on the world's stage for a full decade now. As science has learned more about it, and discovered more ways of temporarily restraining it, its character has changed; so have the statistics of those it strikes. But it is still unpredictable, a congeries of symptoms for which there is neither a cure nor a vaccine, nor even a workable estimate of the incubation period. We have barely glimpsed its face, much less found a way to stop it.

The theatre—the world-scale medieval *Totentanz*—over which this unpredictable actor-manager-playwright-director presides is a tragic theatre in the largest and most metaphysical sense, one in which human beings are forced to confront—there really is no other word for it—Destiny. Though no citizen of fifth-century-B.C. Athens would have had trouble with this concept, it shocks and confuses us; for centuries we have been getting used to the notion that human science and human ingenuity could solve any problem. We can create life in the test tube; we can put it on the Moon; we can freeze-dry it in the event we discover a return from death. But we can't, apparently, stop AIDS. At least not yet.

To confront the unknowable in a generalized, abstract way is easy enough: everybody has to die sooner or later. "Thou know'st 'tis common," &c. When you arrive there individually (after, one hopes, a good fulfilling threescore and ten) it becomes a personal drama, involving self, family, a few intimate friends, humanly possible to play out, with guidance from tradition, religion, the hospital scenes of daytime soaps.

But AIDS deprives us of our roles in the customary death scene, intervenes in any comfortable transaction we might have evolved with Death. It is epidemic, and so can never be quite individual. It comes unjustly before its time, sparing or striking arbitrarily, and so can never be wholly inevitable. Because of its arbitrary choices, too, one can never quite call it a consequence of one's own actions, never entirely take responsibility for it as the hero of a tragic drama ought to be able to do. It simply is *there*, scattering fates this way and that, truncating some lives and leaving others mysteriously carefree, prolonging some torments hideously and cutting others off with the gentle snap of a leaf falling in autumn. Its combination of caprice and control, carried out on so large a scale, undercuts almost any response we can evolve. We react to it with a puzzled, inhibited caution, fearing simultaneously for our lives and the appearance we create—a set of nervous supporting players in a show whose volatile star has unexpectedly come onstage drunk, with a loaded gun.

As it steals the lives of our friends and loved ones, AIDS steals our dialogue, or poisons it with this inhibited self-consciousness. What can you say, for instance, to a casual acquaintance you haven't seen for several years, whom you meet on the street, on a sunny summer afternoon, in a shrunken and twisted condition? Dying lowers the inhibitions; his opening words to you are: "I have locomotor ataxia from creeping paralysis of the spine. I can't wait till it travels all the way up to my brain and I'm finally dead. You don't know how I long for that." I'm sorry to say I did not invent this speech, and even sorrier that I could not think of any decent or articulate response to it at the time. The unforgivable things AIDS does to the dying are made worse by its ability to turn the rest of us into living statues, abashed dumb animals in the presence of some unseen herdsman.

The strange, dispiriting etiquette that we have built up out of our initial numb shock and terror (and where were you on that sunny July weekend when the *New York Times* carried its famous first news story about KS?) is indicative of the consternation into which AIDS throws us. Unlike Albany at the end of *King Lear*, we seem to think we can obey the weight of this sad time by saying what we ought to say rather than what we feel. The question "How are you?," when addressed by heterosexuals to their gay friends in a certain tone, has become an impertinence. (One straight woman I know made a practice of phoning each of her gay friends once a week, inquiring after their health, until they came to her as a group and begged her to stop.) We are asked to regard AIDS patients—mustn't call them victims—as a unified and hopeful group; we are encouraged, at the informal memorial services that have become a prevailing theatrical form in our time, to dwell on the humor and bravery of the deceased, and only peripherally to contemplate their achievements, their suffering, the way the conduct of their lives did or did not encourage the onset of infection.

Most disturbing of all, we are urged, subtly, to view each death as the equivalent of every other, each lost individual as equally irreplaceable. This is no doubt true in the largest philosophical and democratic sense—"thou know'st 'tis common," &c.—but in other senses it is deeply and outrageously untrue, in the first place because, as every death is individual, so each death from AIDS is distinctively unjust: "Why should a dog, a horse, a rat have life / And thou no breath at all?" Secondly, because many of those affected are artists in their creative prime, and what an artist gives the world is not the same as ordinary souls doing their jobs and leading their ordinary lives. I am sorry for the brute fact, but when an accountant dies, there is another accountant; when Mozart dies, there may be Beethoven, but that is something quite different. And the world is not always so lucky as to get Beethoven: after Shakespeare dies, there is only James Shirley. Consider now a world in which fifty to a hundred young Burbages die each year, and talk to me about the state of the theatre in the era of AIDS, if you can.

Perhaps this particular pain is not so significant, not so awful to deal with, as the pain of the man with locomotor ataxia. Or the blind pianist, shriveled to ninety-five pounds, who says, "I just wish my hands weren't paralyzed." Or the friend whose cheery letter, about his good spirits and how well he is being nursed, you receive from Canada after he has been dead two weeks. Or the old schoolmate you don't even know is ill until you find one of his favorite books, with his name on the flyleaf, in a secondhand bookstore . . . . To say some deaths are more important to the world, some griefs as wide as they are deep, is not to depreciate the importance of any death, the depth of any grief. During the 1980s, my grief at the loss of so many artists made me uncomfortably proficient in the writing of obituaries; it was a way, for me, of moving out of the numbness. I began to give it up—I haven't wholly cured myself of the habit yet—when an actress, gifted and much loved in the New York theatrical community, was killed in a car crash, the victim (yes, here it's the right word) of a drunken teenager at a dangerous intersection in a remote part of the South-west. I wrote her obituary, and I was profoundly upset by the number of people who told me it was a relief to read, for a change, a memorial tribute to someone who had not died of AIDS. I didn't know what to say to these people, either, but their attempt to efface a widespread grief with a more local one made me realize that my articulation of sorrow had become a way of distancing myself from it, perhaps unhealthy; since then I have written less on the subject, and mourned more.

Mourning, privately or collectively, is a beginning of action. If I have seemed to say, so far, that the burgeoning of AIDS froze us into a state of inaction, and that the community of artists has been particu-larly devastated by it, I have meant to say something else as well: that artists, having been among the first to feel the numbness descend, were among the first to search for ways out of it. Artists have been in the forefront of the fight for funding of AIDS research and patient care, the fight to stop discrimination against AIDS patients, the fight to disseminate information about AIDS freely.

These fights are not won: as the epidemic goes on, so do the stigma, the fear, the prudery and bigotry and hypocrisy that give it fertile ground to grow in. The deaths of many eminent men, from Cardinal Cooke to William Casey of the CIA, have been alleged to be caused by AIDS, but these rumors have stayed unconfirmed, in the realm of malicious gossip; only an actor, Rock Hudson, has been brave and honest enough to face, in the time before his death, the double burden of fatal disease and worldwide celebrity. The comparison of his conduct with Roy Cohn's (to cite only a case where the rumors have resolved into fact) suggests that our artists, on the whole, are dealing with the matter much more humanely than our worldly powers.

To deal with the epidemic in art is a different matter, though one contiguous to dealing with it in life. The photographer Robert Mapplethorpe may be said to have solved the problem by making both his art and his AIDS such public and confrontational matters that they merged in the popular mind, or at any rate in the backward and bigoted version of it represented by Jesse Helms. This is possible for an artist to whom daring is everything, or one who works in a field where single, rather than sequential, statements are the essence of the work. Even in Naturalism, a play is not a photograph; if Ibsen had died of syphilis after writing *Ghosts*, it would have been his art, and not Victorian morality, that got discredited. (The transactions of nineteenth-century artists with syphilis, by the way, ought to be assembled in dramatic form as a mirror in which we can read some aspects of our own condition: one of many AIDS plays still to be written.)

Plays are first of all models of behavior, imitations of life which reflect back onto it. They give us patterns to follow or to reject, motives and meanings for action, consequences to hope for or to avoid; in their ambiguities they offer alternatives. In this volume you will find a range of human possibilities as wide and complex as the reach of the epidemic itself—as is necessary if we mean to battle it. You will also find a record of the numbness, the shock, the fright, the immobility I have mentioned. There is no way to overcome these things without viewing them straight on.

Notice, too, how many of the plays in this volume deal with tentative, self-conscious gestures, attempts to formulate responses to the devastation: the ceremony and silence of *Andre's Mother*, the verse play and poems embedded in *Zero Positive*, the ritualized action of *Safe Sex*, the montaged "documentary" speeches of *As Is*, the stage-by-stage position-taking of the disembodied voices in *The Way We Live Now*, the fantasy escapes of *The Baltimore Waltz*, the simultaneous speeches of *Jack*. The invisible protagonist cannot be outmaneuvered easily; many stratagems must be tried.

I don't say anything about morality, about ethics, about the politics of choices and of immediate actions. One AIDS play that deals with these matters in the short term, Larry Kramer's *The Normal Heart*, is not in this volume, by its author's request. But just by virtue of its aggressive position-taking on the subject, it's already had many useful effects, among them the gift of provoking censorship battles which have revealed—as if we didn't already know—that the American public, in 1990, remains as confused and uninformed about the nature of art as about that of AIDS.

The hare-brained extremist organizations which have sprung up in attempts to ban *The Normal Heart* (and at times also its kinder, gentler counterweight, William M. Hoffman's *As Is*), have approached the mere mention of homosexuality in a play as if this, in itself, were a form of proselytizing—as if watching young men suffer and die in agony onstage were an automatic inducement to audiences to adopt their sexual practices (the implied assumption, as Pauline Kael pointed out during a similar uproar in the mid-1950s, is that heterosexuality can't hold its own in a free market). The other chief complaint protesting groups have had about these plays is their use of profanity and "vulgar" (meaning sexual) language: the morally relativistic absurdity of complaining about dirty words while babies wither away and die from opportunistic infections does not seem to have occurred to these well-meaning souls, who would rather protect their ears than their grandchildren.

And, of course, in missing the simple point about free speech, they miss the vastly more complex one about art, in which the more stridently you advocate, the more likely you are to provoke a contrary notion in the minds of your audience, which automatically perceives your assertions in their dramatic context. "For the poet," as Sir Philip Sidney succinctly put it, in the most lucid defense of the artist's viewpoint, "he nothing affirms, and therefore never lyeth." The theatre is there to explore these issues, not to decide them for us, just as it can't, being fiction, assuage our grief at the many real losses we've suffered. What it can do best, perhaps, in the long term, is teach us the processes we are likely to go through: not make us cry, but show us the how and why of crying. Not make us grieve, but display the changing nature of grief. Not preach anger or love or despair, but dramatize—*dramatize*—the way we experience these feelings. And when the theatre does this—as the many tentative stances in these plays do, each in its own measure—then something else happens: because of art, our experience of ourselves awakens. We unfreeze. Our sense of shared feelings, shared events, overcomes the numbness. Humanity, and not the syndrome, becomes the protagonist. If we can do that in art, then it can be done in life. Sharing our losses creatively, we can begin to share our hope.

MICHAEL FEINGOLD *is lead theatre critic for* The Village Voice. *His translations and adaptations for the stage range from the* Threepenny Opera *seen on Broadway in 1989 to Copi's AIDS play* Grand Finale, *included in* Gay Plays: An International Anthology.

The Way We Live Now

As Is

BY WILLIAM M. HOFFMAN

The "Red Death" has long devastated the country. No pestilence had ever been so fatal, or so hideous. . . . The scarlet stains upon the body . . . were the pest ban which shut the victim out from the sympathy of his fellow-men. . . . But the Prince Prospero was happy and dauntless and sagacious. When his dominions were half depopulated, he summoned to his presence a thousand hale and light-hearted friends . . . and with these retired to the deep seclusion of one of his castellated abbeys. . . . A strong and lofty wall girdled it in. The wall had gates of iron. The courtiers brought furnaces and massy hammers and welded the bolts. . . . With such precautions the courtiers might bid defiance to contagion. In the meantime it was folly to grieve, or to think. The Prince had provided all the appliances of pleasure. There were buffoons, there were improvisatori, there were ballet-dancers, there were musicians, there was Beauty, there was wine. All these and security were within. Without was the "Red Death."

        —The Masque of the Red Death, *Edgar Allan Poe*

My tale was heard, and yet it was not told;
My fruit is fallen, and yet my leaves are green;
My youth is spent, and yet I am not old;
I saw the world, and yet I was not seen;
My thread is cut, and yet it is not spun;
And now I live, and now my life is done.

        —Elegy, *Chidiock Tichborne*

SAUL

RICH

Depending on the budget and the skills and aptitudes of the performers, at least four other men and two women play the following:

HOSPICE WORKER	MARTY
CHET	VINNIE
BROTHER	CLONES (3)
BUSINESS PARTNER	PEOPLE WITH AIDS (4)
LILY	AVERAGE PEOPLE (6)
TV ANNOUNCER (Prerecorded)	HOTLINE COUNSELORS (2)
DOCTORS (5)	NURSE
BARTENDER	HOSPITAL WORKER
PICKUPS (2)	DRUG DEALERS AND
	CUSTOMERS (5)

TIME The present.

PLACE New York City.

PLAYWRIGHT'S NOTE

Except for short exits, the actors remain onstage for the whole play. There is no intermission.

5

In memory of:

R.A.
S.A.
Fortunato Arico
M.B.
Michael Baseleon
Kenneth Burgess
Francis Brady
Stephen Buker
Phil Carey
Gregory Y. Connell
Daniel Corcoran
Wilfredo Davilla
Arthur Ellenbogen
Bill Elliot
Tom Ellis
Timothy Farrell
Christian Fincke
Neil Flanagan
George Harris
Anthony Holland

Mark Johnson
Charles Loubier
Charles Ludlam
Ed Lynch
André Mathis
J.J. Mitchell
John Murphy
Pierre Murue
Arthur Naftal
Stephen Pender
Glenn Person
Russell Redmond
L.S.
Tony Serchio
Giulio Sorrentino
Larry Stanton
David Summers
Rick Wadsworth
Larry Waurin
Stuart White

Stage right is Saul's fashionable loft space, suggested by a sofa, Barcelona chair, bench and area rug. Upstage center is a bar; stage left, a bench.

The Hospice Worker, a dowdy middle-aged woman, walks downstage center and addresses the audience.

HOSPICE WORKER: Mother Superior always used to say, "Watch out for the religious cranks, Sister Veronica." When I started working for the hospice I had a touch of the crank about me. I think maybe that's why they gave me the old heave-ho from the convent. But I've kept my vow of chastity and I've made a pilgrimage to Lourdes.

My job is to ease the way for those who are dying. I've done this for the last couple of years. I work mainly here at St. Vincent's. During the day I have a boring secretarial job, which is how I support my career as a saint.

I was much more idealistic when I started. I had just left the convent. I guess I thought working with the dying would give me spiritual gold stars. I thought I'd be able to impart my great wisdom to those in need of improvement. I wanted to bear witness to dramatic deathbed conversions, see shafts of light emanating from heaven, multicolored auras hovering above the heads of those in the process of expiring. I always imagined they would go out expressing their gratitude for all I had done.

A quick joke: Did you hear about the man who lost his left side? . . . He's all *right* now. All right now. (*She laughs*) We tell a lot of jokes in my line of work.

She takes her seat. Lights come up on two casually dressed men in their thirties seated in the living area.

7

RICH: You take Henry.

SAUL: Cut him in half.

RICH: You can keep him.

SAUL: What are we going to do about him?

RICH: I said he's yours.

SAUL: You found him.

RICH: I don't want him.

SAUL: Chet doesn't like cats?

RICH: I knew this would happen. Don't start in.

SAUL: We gotta get things settled.

RICH: Then let's. How 'bout if we simplify things: sell everything and split the cash.

SAUL: Even the cobalt glass?

RICH: Yes.

SAUL: And Aunt Billie's hooked rug? Say, how's she doing?

RICH: She's on medication. Sell the rug.

SAUL: I will not sell the manikin heads. I don't care what you say.

RICH: Then take them.

SAUL: And the chromium lamp? I love that lamp.

RICH: Take it.

SAUL: And the Barcelona chair?

RICH: The Barcelona chair is *mine*! (*Beat*) Fuck it. Take it. Take everything. I won't be Jewish about it. (*He rises to go*)

SAUL: Why didn't you warn me we were going to play Christians and Jews today? I would have worn my yellow star.

RICH: I've gotta go. (*He is leaving*)

SAUL: Where're you going?

RICH: I'm not feeling so hot. Let's make it another day.

SAUL (*Blocking his way*): Sit down.

RICH (*Pushing his hand away*): Don't push me.

SAUL: Sorry. I don't like this any more than you, but we gotta do it. It's been six months. (*Lightening things up*) A divorce is not final until the property settlement.

RICH: Saul . . . ? (*He's about to say something important*)

SAUL: What, Rich? (*He waits expectantly*) What?

RICH: Never mind.

SAUL: What? . . . What? . . . You always do that!

RICH: I want the chair.

SAUL: You can have the fucking Barcelona chair if Chet wants it so bad! . . . What about the paintings? Do you want to sell the Paul Cadmus?

RICH: Yes.

SAUL: You love the Cadmus. (*Silence*) And who's going to buy the Burgess drawings? Did you hear that Kenny died?

RICH: We'll donate them to the Metropolitan.

SAUL: Just what they always wanted: the world's largest collection of Magic Marker hustler portraits.

Rich nods.

RICH: They're yours.

SAUL: But you commissioned them. We'll split them up: I get the blonds and you get the blacks—or vice versa.

RICH: All yours.

SAUL: Then you get the Mickey Mouse collection.

RICH: Sell it.

SAUL: You don't sell collectibles. Not right now. What's with this money mania? Between the book and the catering, I thought you were doing well.

RICH: I want to build a swimming pool.

SAUL: You don't swim.

RICH: I want a Mercedes.

SAUL: You don't drive. It's Chet—he'll bankrupt you! (*Beat*) I don't believe I said that . . . (*Sincerely*) Your book is beautiful.

RICH: I never thanked you for the cover photograph.

SAUL (*Shrugging off the compliment*): How's it selling?

RICH: Not bad—for short stories. Everyone mentions your photo. Ed White said—

SAUL: Your book is terrific. Really.

RICH: I'm glad you like it.

SAUL: One minor thing.

RICH: What's that?

SAUL: I thought the dedication was a bit much.

RICH: Why are you doing this?

SAUL: Don't you think quoting Cavafy in Greek is a little coy?

RICH: Please!

SAUL: Why didn't you just say, "To Chet, whose beautiful buns inspired these tales"?

RICH: Jesus Christ!

SAUL: I'm sorry!

Silence.

RICH: I sold the IBM stock. You were right about it. You have always been right about money. (*He hands Saul a check*) This includes the thousand I borrowed for the periodontist.

SAUL: You sure?

RICH: Take it.

SAUL: I'm not desperate for it.

RICH: It's yours.

SAUL: I don't want it.

RICH: Damn it!

SAUL (*Taking the check*): Okay.

RICH: That makes us even now.

SAUL (*Examining the check*): Clouds and trees.

RICH: Let's get on with this.

SAUL: Is he waiting for you downstairs? You could have told him to come up.

RICH: Shit. No! Can it. (*Beat*) I won't be wanting the copper pots.

SAUL: Why not? When you and Chet move to your space you'll want to cook again.

RICH: I just don't want them! People change. (*Silence*) I'm eating out a lot.

SAUL: Chet can't cook?

RICH (*Deciding not to respond with a bitchy comment*): You keep the rowing machine.

SAUL: Have you lost weight?

RICH: And the trampoline.

SAUL: There's some Black Forest cake in the fridge. *(He goes toward the kitchen to get the cake)*
RICH: Stop it.
SAUL: Stop what?
RICH: Just stop.
SAUL: I can't.
RICH: We're almost through.
SAUL: I have feelings.
RICH: You have only one feeling.
SAUL: He won't make you happy.
RICH: Here we go again. *(He gets up to go)*
SAUL: Don't!
RICH: Keep everything.
SAUL: I'm not myself.
RICH: Nothing is worth this.
SAUL: I've been upset.
RICH: I mean it.
SAUL: Don't go. Please.

Rich sits. Long pause.

SAUL: I visited Teddy today at St. Vincent's. It's very depressing . . . .
He's lying there in bed, out of it. He's been out of it since the time
we saw him. He's not in any pain, snorting his imaginary cocaine,
doing his poppers. Sometimes he's washing his mother's floor, and
he's speaking to her in Spanish. Sometimes he's having sex. You
can see him having sex right in front of you. He doesn't even know
you're there.

Pause. Both men look down at their feet.

SAUL: Jimmy died, as you must have heard. I went out to San
Francisco to be with him the last few weeks. You must have heard
that, too. He was in a coma for a month. Everybody wanted to pull
the plug, but they were afraid of legal complications. I held his

11

hand. He couldn't talk, but I could see his eyelids flutter. I swear he knew I was with him.

Pause.

SAUL: Harry has KS, and Matt has trouble breathing. He went for tests today . . . . I haven't slept well for weeks. Every morning I examine my body for swellings, marks. I'm terrified of every pimple, every rash, even though I've tested negative. If I cough I think of Teddy. I wish he would die. He *is* dead. He might as well be. Why can't he die? I feel the disease closing in on me. All my activities are life and death. Keep up my Blue Cross. Up my reps. Eat my vegetables.

    Sometimes I'm so scared I go back on my resolutions: I drink too much, and I smoke a joint, and I find myself at the bars and clubs, where I stand around and watch. They remind me of accounts of Europe during the Black Plague: groping in the dark, dancing till you drop. The New Wave is the corpse look. I'm very frightened and I miss you. Say something, damn it.

Beat.

RICH: I have it.

Immediately the lights come up on the left side of the stage.

CHET (*A handsome, boyish man in his early twenties*): You what?
LILY (*A beautiful woman, thirtyish*): You have what?
BROTHER (*To his wife, whom we don't see*): He has AIDS.
SAUL: I don't think that's funny.
PARTNER: Don't be ridiculous.
RICH: That's the bad news.
PARTNER: You ran the   LILY: Darling!
  goddamned marathon.
RICH: The good news is that I have only the swollen glands.

Two doctors appear in white gowns.

DOCTOR 1: We call it a "pre-AIDS condition."

DOCTOR 2: "AIDS-related complex."

RICH: I've lost some weight.

SAUL: I'm in a state of shock.

LILY: Move in with me. Chet doesn't know how to take care of you.

RICH: I tire easily. My temperature goes up and down.

DOCTOR 1: Your suppressor cells outnumber your helper cells.

BROTHER: I don't care what he has, Betty, he's my brother.

CHET: You're my lover.

LILY: You're my buddy.

PARTNER: Rich and I started the business about a year ago. But now word got out that Rich is ill. I tried to explain: he doesn't touch the food; I do all the cooking. But they won't listen.

BROTHER: I'm not in the habit of kissing my brother. I touched him on the back when I arrived and when I left.

PARTNER: Why would they? I wonder if I'd use a caterer who had AIDS.

SAUL: Doctors make mistakes all the time.

DOCTOR 2: I can put you on AZT.

DOCTOR 1: And pentamidine mist.

LILY: I got this job.

CHET: If you don't mind, I'll sleep on the couch tonight. You've been sweating a lot.

LILY: I can't turn it down. The work is pure dreck, and who wants to tour Canada in January, but they're paying a fortune.

BROTHER: When he offered me a cup of coffee I told him I'd have a can of beer.

LILY: I'll be back in four weeks.

PARTNER: I can understand what he's going through. Myself, I've been wrestling with cancer for a while.

SAUL: Remember when they told my niece she had skin cancer? It turned out to be dry skin.

PARTNER: I'm winning.

CHET: I hope you don't mind, but I'll use the red soap dish and you'll use the blue.

RICH: Christ! I've been putting the blocks to you nightly for months and now you're worried about sharing the fucking soap dish?

BROTHER: Christ, I didn't even use the bathroom, even though I had to take a leak so bad I could taste it. Now, that's paranoid.

PARTNER: I wonder if it's safe to use the same telephone, or whether I'm being paranoid.

CHET: I know I'm being paranoid.

LILY: They're flying me out to the Coast. I hate that place.

RICH: Chet, you've been out every night this week. Do you have to go out again?

BROTHER: I know you're scared, Betty, but I will not tell my own brother he's not welcome in my house.

CHET: Need something from outside?

BROTHER: He's spent every Christmas with us since we got married, and this year will be no exception.

RICH: Forget I said anything: just don't wake me up when you get in.

BROTHER: You're forcing me to choose between you and my brother.

CHET: See you later.

LILY: I've been dating this guy, Mick—can you imagine *me* dating? Well, he's very nice, and he's got a lot of money, and he's not impressed with my life in the theatre, and he's straight— and that's why I haven't been up to see you. Rich?

CHET: You know I'd do anything for you.

RICH: You're walking out on me.

BROTHER: We're going to Betty's mother for Christmas.

CHET: I need more space to get my head together.

SAUL: What did you expect?

RICH: Chet, please, I need you!

Rich tries to put his arms around Chet. Everyone except Saul pulls back terrified.

CHET, BROTHER, LILY, PARTNER, DOCTORS: Don't touch me!

Beat.

LILY: Please forgive me!
CHET: This thing has blown me away.
BROTHER: If it weren't for the kids.
PARTNER: I don't know what the hell we're going to do.
SAUL: Bastards!

Chet, the Brother, the Partner and Lily put on white gowns and become Doctors.

RICH (*To Doctor 1*): Doctor, tell me the truth. What are my chances?
DOCTORS 1 AND 2: We have some highly effective treatments.
RICH (*To Doctor 2*): Doctor, tell me the truth. What are my chances?
DOCTOR 2: The medical advances are astounding.
RICH (*To Doctor 3*): What are my chances.
DOCTOR 3: We're optimistic.
RICH (*To Doctors 4 and 5*): Am I going to make it, doctors, yes or no?!
DOCTOR 4: Just hang in there.
SAUL: Rich?

TV ANNOUNCER (*Pre-recorded*): Scientists tell us that millions of people worldwide are infected. So far, a vast majority of the cases in this country have been homosexual or bisexual men or intravenous drug users of both sexes, but the disease is beginning to make inroads into the general population. When will science conquer this dreaded plague? We don't know. We don't know. We simply don't know. Don't know. (*Etc.*)

15

DOCTORS: We don't know.

SAUL: And for three months you kept this from me.

The Doctors exit. We're back in Saul's apartment.

RICH: I don't want your pity.

SAUL: You're my friend. You'll stay with me till you feel better.

RICH: Aren't you afraid I'll infect you?

SAUL: We'll take reasonable precautions.

RICH: Paper plates, plastic cups, face masks—

SAUL: You have HIV, you're not radioactive.

RICH: I'd prefer to live alone, thank you.

SAUL: You need me.

RICH: Besides, if I live with you, where am I going to bring my tricks?

SAUL: You pick up people?

RICH (*Standing at the bar*): I go to bars . . . I pick up guys . . . but I give them a medical report before we leave . . .

Without a pause, we're in a bar. Rich is talking to a stranger.

RICH: I should tell you something.

PICKUP 1: You like something kinky. Whips? Golden showers? Fist?

RICH: It's not like that.

PICKUP 1: I once picked up a guy liked to be yelled at in German. The only German I know is the "Ode to Joy" from Beethoven's Ninth. (*Yelling like an enraged Nazi*) "O Freude, schöner Götterfunken, Schweinehund, Tochter aus Elysium, Dummkopf!"

RICH: I have a very mild case of lymphadenopathy.

PICKUP 1: What's that?

RICH: An AIDS-related condition.

PICKUP 1: Oh, shit.

RICH: Just the swollen glands—

PICKUP 1: No way. Uh-uh . . . . Good luck . . . . Oh, man . . .

Pickup 1 exits. We're back with Rich and Saul.

RICH: So I stopped telling them.

SAUL: You mean you take them home and don't tell them?

RICH: We do it there in the bar.

SAUL: How can you?

RICH: I lurk in dark corners where they can't see my lumps. I'm like a shark or a barracuda, and I snap them up and infect them.

SAUL: How can you joke about this?

RICH: I don't care. I'm going to die! I'll take as many as I can with me. And I've pissed in the Croton Reservoir. I'm going to infect the whole fucking city! Wheeeee!

SAUL: No fucking around, give me a straight answer. Do you still pick up people?

RICH: Maybe I ought to wear a sign around my neck and ring a bell: "AIDS, I've got AIDS, stand clear!" Would that make you happy? Or maybe I should dig a hole in the ground, douse myself with kerosene, and have a final cigarette. No muss, no fuss. Is that what you want?

SAUL: Forgive me for not trusting you. It's just that I'm frightened of it. I don't know what I'm saying half the time.

RICH: How the fuck do you think I feel? My lover leaves me; my family won't let me near them; I lose my business; I can't pay my rent. How the fuck do you think I feel?

SAUL: You'll stay here with me.

RICH: Till death do us part.

SAUL: I love you.

RICH: I don't want your love!

SAUL: Take what you can . . . [get]! I didn't mean that. I love you. I always have. You have nowhere to go. You've got to stay with me.

RICH: Shit shit shit.

SAUL: You were kidding about picking up people.

RICH: What do you think? What would you do in my place?

SAUL: I wouldn't . . . I'd . . . . Therapy! . . . I don't know what I'd do.

We're back in the bar.

PICKUP 2: Jesus, I've told you all about myself. I've really spilled my guts to you. I *needed* to do that. Maybe I shouldn't say this, but, Christ, you know something? I like you very much. Even though you *are* a writer . . . . Would you like to come home with me?

RICH: I'd like to very much . . . (*He checks his watch*) but I have an appointment.

PICKUP 2: Then tomorrow, how about tomorrow? I don't want to lose track of you. I don't know when I've had such a good time. I can *talk* to you.

RICH: I've enjoyed myself, too.

PICKUP 2: Then maybe we'll have dinner, maybe go to the movies. Do you like movies? There's a Mapplethorpe retrospective at MOMA. Or maybe we could see the new Everett Quinton—

RICH: Thanks, but I have to tell you something. I have—

PICKUP 2: You have a lover. I knew it. You're too nice to be un attached.

RICH: I have . . . I have . . . I have a lover.

We're back with Saul.

SAUL: You have a lover.

RICH: I don't even know where he is.

SAUL: I don't mean Chet. I mean me.

Rich turns away. He's back in the bar with another stranger, Clone 1, who is wearing a leather jacket and reflecting aviator glasses. Saul continues to plead to Rich's back.

SAUL: What about me?

Rich tries in vain to get Clone 1's attention.

RICH: Pardon me.

SAUL: What about me?

RICH: Yo. Yoo-hoo. Hello.

SAUL: What about *me*?!

RICH *(To Clone 1)*: What about me?!

CLONE 1: What about you?

RICH: I'm a very interesting guy. You look like a very interesting guy. Let's talk. And if you don't want to talk, let's go back there and let's . . . *(He stares Clone 1 straight in the face)* I'll do anything you want. Anything.

CLONE 1: I want you to get the fuck out of my face. Can't you see I'm cruising that dude over there?

We notice for the first time an identically dressed man standing across the room.

RICH: Well, fuck you.

CLONE 1: What's that, buddy?

Rich turns his back on Clone 1 and starts talking loudly to the Bartender.

RICH: Gimme a Jack Daniels straight up—*no* ice—make it a double, and a Heinekens chaser.

BARTENDER: Double Jack up, Heinie back.

Clone 2 has moseyed on over to Clone 1. They stand side by side, facing the audience, feigning indifference to each other.

CLONE 2: Your name Chip?

RICH: No ice!

BARTENDER: No ice.

CLONE 1: Chuck.

RICH: Hate ice.

CLONE 2 *(Extending his hand)*: Chad.

The Clones shake hands.

RICH *(To the Bartender)*: Put 'er there, Chet—I mean Chump. You come here often? *(He downs the shot and beer as quickly as he can)*

19

CLONE 2: Thought you were this guy Chip I met here on Jockstrap Night.

CLONE 1: Haven't been here since the Slave Auction.

CLONE 2: Look familiar.

With synchronized actions the Clones turn to look at each other, then turn away.

CLONE 1: Go to the Spike?

CLONE 2: Been there.

RICH (*To the Bartender*): Quiet for a Friday . . .

CLONE 1: I know where.

RICH: Not much action.

CLONE 2: Limelight?

RICH (*Offering his glass*): Same . . .

CLONE 1: Nah.

RICH: They're home watching pornos.

CLONE 1: Bookstore on Christopher. Ever go there?

CLONE 2: Not in years.

CLONE 1: Gotta be real careful.

RICH: Or having sex on the phone.

CLONE 2: Right. Me, I'm HIV negative.

CLONE 1: Can you prove it? (*He punches Clone 2 on the arm*) Kidding.

CLONE 2: Gotta be real careful. Run six miles a day.

RICH: My philosophy is: you've got it, you've got it. Nothing you can do about it. (*He offers his glass*)

Same.

CLONE 1 (*Tweaking Clone 2's nipple*): So what're you up for?

CLONE 2: Come right to the point, don't you?

The Clones perform a macho mating ritual of arm wrestling, punching and ass grabbing to determine who is the "top man."

RICH: Poor bastards that got it: cancer, pneumonia, herpes all over. I mean, I'd kill myself if I had to go through all that shit. Get a gun and perform fellatio on it . . .

CLONE 2: What're you up for, Daddy?

RICH: Slash my wrists *with* the grain . . .

CLONE 1: Me top.

RICH: Subway tracks?

CLONE 1: Got some beautiful . . . *(He snorts deeply to indicate cocaine)*

CLONE 2: Ever do opium?

CLONE 1: I have a water pipe. We'll smoke it through some Southern Comfort.

RICH: Or maybe I'd mix myself a Judy Garland: forty reds and a quart of vodka. *(He hands his glass to the Bartender)* Fuck the beer!

CLONE 1: We're roommates now. What about you?

RICH *(The ecstatic drunken poet)*: "Glory be to God for dappled things . . ."

CLONE 2: I'm free, white, and twenty-four.

RICH: "For skies of couple-colour as a brinded cow . . ."

SAUL: I know it sounds stupid, but take care of your health.

RICH: "For rose-moles all in stipple upon trout that swim . . ."

CLONE 2: In bed, I mean.

RICH: I don't care what anybody says, I believe that somewhere, you know, deep down. *(He holds out his glass)*

CLONE 1: I'll do anything you want.

RICH: Beyond all this incredible pain and confusion, anxiety, fear, terror . . . *(He holds out his glass)*

BARTENDER: No ice.

CLONE 2: Anything?

RICH: I believe that there might be . . . *(Searching for words to describe the Supreme Being)* that there could be . . . that there is—

CLONE 1: Safe sex!

SAUL: You're drinking too much.

RICH: I believe in a perfect . . . *(He is having a booze-fueled vision of the Godhead)*

CLONE 2: Mirrors . . .

RICH: Shining . . .

CLONE 1: Chains . . .

RICH: Powerful . . .

SAUL: Vitamins . . .

RICH: Pure . . .

A third Clone appears.

CLONE 3: Condoms . . .

CLONE 1: Dildo . . .

SAUL: Diet . . .

RICH: Free . . .

CLONE 2: Dungeon . . .

SAUL: Acupuncture . . .

RICH: Truthful . . .

CLONE 3: Ten inches . . .

SAUL: Interferon . . .

RICH: Beautiful . . .

CLONE 3 *(Approaching the bar, to the Bartender)*: Beer! *(He accidentally spills beer on Rich)*

CLONE 2: Watersports.

RICH *(Raging drunkenly)*: Asshole!

CLONE 1: Hey!

RICH: I'll kill ya, faggot!

SAUL *(Intervening)*: Hey! . . . He's been drinking.

BARTENDER: Get that jerk outta here!

RICH: What'sa matter, can't you fight like a man?

SAUL *(Gently but firmly)*: Rich.

RICH: Fuck all that shit!

SAUL: Rich.

RICH: Let Him cure me!

SAUL *(Trying to distract him)*: Did you hear the one about Irving Berlin? What's he doing now?

RICH *(To God in the sky, shaking his fist)*: You hear me, motherfucker?

SAUL: He's decomposing.

RICH: Cure me!

They are out on the street by now.

22

SAUL: C'mon, keep moving.

RICH: I'm a very bad person.

SAUL: You're an asshole.

RICH: I wanted to go to bed with that guy.

SAUL: I practically beg you to move in—

RICH: I wasn't going to tell him about me or anything.

SAUL: And what do you do?

RICH: But you want to know something?

SAUL: You disappear for two weeks.

RICH: I wouldn't do that. I would *never* do that.

SAUL: I almost called the cops.

RICH: You believe me?

SAUL: Believe what?

RICH: I never never never would ever do that.

SAUL: Do you remember the one about the Polish Lesbian?

RICH: Never.

SAUL: She liked men.

The joke pretty much sobers Rich up.

RICH: You asshole.

SAUL: You schmuck.

RICH: You prick.

SAUL: God, I miss talking dirty.

RICH: Talking dirty makes it feel like spring. (*He is the superstud*) Suck my dick, faggot.

SAUL (*Superstud*): Kiss my ass, cocksucker.

RICH: Sit on it, punk.

SAUL: Lick boot, fruit.

RICH: God, how I used to love sleaze: the whining self-pity of a rainy Monday night in a leather bar in early spring; five o'clock in the morning in the Mineshaft, with the bathtubs full of men dying to get pissed on and whipped; a subway john full of horny high school students; Morocco—getting raped on a tombstone in Marrakesh. God, how I miss it.

SAUL: I miss my filthy old ripped-up, patched button-fly jeans that I sun-bleached on myself our first weekend on the Island. Remember? It was Labor Day—

RICH: Memorial Day.

SAUL: And we did blotter acid. Remember acid before they put the speed in it? And we drank muscadet when we got thirsty.

RICH: Which we did a lot.

SAUL: Remember?

RICH: Remember Sunday afternoons blitzed on beer?

SAUL: And suddenly it's Sunday night and you're getting fucked in the second-floor window of the Hotel Christopher and you're being cheered on by a mob of hundreds of men.

RICH: And suddenly it's Friday a week later, and he's moved in, sleeping next to you, and you want him to go because you've met his brother Rod or Lance—

SAUL *(Practically sighing)*: Miles.

RICH: —late of the merchant marines, who's even humpier.

SAUL: Orgies at the baths—

RICH: Afternoons at the Columbus Avenue bookstore.

They are in the back room of a gay porno shop, or "bookstore." They play their favorite bookstore habitués.

RICH: More! *Give* it to me!

SAUL: Give it to *you*? Give it to *me*! Get out of my way, he's mine!

RICH: No, he's mine! Keep your hands off my wallet!

SAUL *(A black queen)*: Sistuhs, theyuh's plenty heah fo' ivrybody.

RICH *(A tough New York queen)*: Hey, Mary, the line forms at the rear.

SAUL: And whose rear might that be, sugar?

Two other men appear in the bookstore.

MARTY: Hey, Vinnie?

VINNIE: Marty?

MARTY: What are you doing here? You said you were gonna buy the papers.

VINNIE: You said you were gonna walk the dogs.

MARTY: You trash!

They exit, bickering.

SAUL: I always knew when you were fucking around.
RICH: You did your share.
SAUL: *Moi?*
RICH: I knew why Grand Union wouldn't deliver to our house.

They have returned to the loft.

SAUL: God, I used to love promiscuous sex.
RICH: Not "promiscuous," Saul, nondirective, noncommitted, non-authoritarian—
SAUL: Free, wild, rampant—
RICH: Hot, sweaty, steamy, smelly—
SAUL: Juicy, funky, hunky—
RICH: Sex.
SAUL: Sex. God, I miss it.

Rich lowers his eyes. Saul nods and goes to Rich. He takes Rich's face in both hands and tries to kiss him square on the mouth. Rich pulls away frantically.

RICH: NO!
SAUL: It's safe!
RICH: You don't know what you're doing!
SAUL: It's my decision!
RICH (*Shaking his head*): No. Uh-uh. NO!

Saul sits on the sofa. Rich tries to take Saul's hand, but Saul pulls it away. Beat.

RICH: The best times for me were going out with you on shoots.
SAUL: I thought you found them boring.
RICH: I enjoyed them.

SAUL: I was always afraid of boring you.

RICH: Remember staying up all night shooting the harvest moon at Jake's place?

SAUL: My fingers got so cold I could barely change film.

RICH: It was almost as bright as daylight. Remember the apple tree stuck out in the middle of the pasture, how the moonlight drained it of color?

SAUL: I remember the smell of the blanket we took from the barn.

RICH: Remember, I bet you I could find five constellations?

SAUL: You found six. . . . I never wanted us to break up.

RICH: Passive aggression.

SAUL: I wanted things to always remain the same. I'm still like that. I even like eating the same things day after day.

RICH: Pork chops, French fries—

SAUL: No change. I used to love our routine together. I'd go to work and then you'd be there when I got home, writing—

RICH: Drinking.

SAUL: I'd do this and you'd do that, and then we'd . . . (*He makes a graceful gesture to indicate making love*) for a while—while *Mission Impossible*'d be on low in the background.

RICH: And then *Star Trek*.

SAUL: I never got tired of the same—

RICH: We were stagnating.

SAUL: —day after day the same, so we'd have a structure to fall back on when life dealt us its wild cards or curve balls. I want to be just half awake, like at the seashore, watching the waves roll in late in the afternoon, hypnotized by the glare of the sun, smelling the sea breeze and suntan lotion.

Beat.

SAUL: Mom is what? She's lying there next to Dad on the Navaho blanket, with white gunk on her nose, and my baby sister has finally stopped screaming and is sucking on the ear of her dollie. And Aunt Ellie—the one who said she thought I had good taste when she met you—is snoring next to husband number three.

Her bazooms are going up and down, up and down, almost popping out of her bathing suit. It's so peaceful.

Long pause.

SAUL: I was at the gym soaking in the hot tub when I first heard about AIDS. It was how many years ago? My friend Brian—remember him?—was soaking, too, and he told me about a mutual friend who had died the week before. It was "bizarre," he said . . .

A group enters, quietly talking.

1ST MAN: The first person I knew who had AIDS was George. I had just seen him at the movies—*Mommie Dearest*—and we had a big laugh together. I remember he had a little cough. I ran into his mother it couldn't have been a week later and she told me he had died. It was absurd. I had just seen George.

1ST WOMAN: The first time it really hit me was when my boss got ill. When Roger got out of the hospital I didn't know what to say. I said, "You look so much taller." He said, "Well, I've lost about forty-five pounds."

2ND WOMAN: The first time I heard about it I was standing in my kitchen.

1ST MAN: It hit home after that.

2ND WOMAN: I was about to go out shopping for my youngest's birthday party.

The phone rang. It was this doctor calling me about my son Bernard. He used all these words I can't pronounce. And then he said, "Do you understand what I've told you?" I said yes. Right before he hung up he said, "So you know he has AIDS." That's the first time I heard that word.

1ST MAN: Do you understand what I've told you?

1ST WOMAN: So you know he has AIDS.

JOHN: The first time I heard about AIDS was in 1981. I was on the seven A.M. shuttle to Boston, trying to make a nine o'clock appointment in Cambridge. I was looking over the shoulder of the man next to me, at his newspaper, and I caught the words "cancer," "promiscuous," "homo-sexual." I turned white.

COP: The word never really registered in my mind until they transferred this guy with AIDS to our unit. The guys on the job were up in arms that they were going to expose us to it. I didn't know what to think. I got used to Kenny though. He wanted to keep working very badly. I think he had a lot of courage.

1ST WOMAN AND JOHN: I think he had a lot of courage.

2ND MAN: The first memorial service I went to was on the set of *Oh! Calcutta!* It was

2ND WOMAN: He was in the theatre.

COP: I couldn't figure it out.

1ST WOMAN: Fortunato . . .

COP: Steve . . .

2ND MAN: Phil . . .

1ST WOMAN: Arthur . . .

JOHN AND COP: Tim . . .

2ND WOMAN: Neil . . .

2ND WOMAN: Glenn . . .

2ND WOMAN: Julie . . .

COP: Luis . . . Larry and his lover Danny . . . Stuart . . . J.J. . . . Maria . . . Jamal . . .

2ND WOMAN: David . . . Stuart . . . J.J. . . . Maria . . . Jamal . . . Tony . . .

for Bill. He was in the theatre. They filled the house. He had hidden the fact that he was ill for a year. A while before he asked me if I wanted his dog—a beautiful husky. I couldn't figure it out. He loved that dog . . . . Since that time I've been to how many memorial services? Seth . . . Robby . . .

2ND WOMAN: Francis . . .

JOHN: Greg . . .

2ND WOMAN: Freddy . . .

1ST MAN: Tom . . .

1ST MAN: Christian . . .

JOHN: Pierre . . .

COP: Stephen . . .

1ST AND 2ND MAN AND 1ST WOMAN: Russell . . . Luis . . . Larry and his lover Danny . . . David . . . Stuart . . . J.J. . . . Maria . . . Jamal . . .

JOHN: Larry . . . David . . . Stuart . . . J.J. . . . Maria . . . Jamal . . . Charles . . . Tony . . .

The group exits.

SAUL: . . . and he told me about a mutual friend who had died the week before. It was "bizarre," he said. Brian died last week of the same thing. And he and I once soaked in the same hot tub, making a kind of human soup . . . . That's all I ever wanted to do was relax. *(Long pause)* You'll stay with me. I won't bother you.

RICH: Just until I feel better.

SAUL: I understand: you're not coming back to be my lover.

RICH: Right. Is that okay?

SAUL: Schmuck. *(Mimicking him)* Is that okay? Is that okay? It's *okay!* Asshole. Who the fuck wants you anyhow? And when I have guests stay the night, you disappear into your room. Right?

RICH: Right. Understood. *(Offhand)* You seeing somebody?

SAUL: I said when I have guests.

RICH: You planning an orgy?

SAUL: Just so we understand each other.

RICH: I should mention one thing.

SAUL: No, you do not have to spend Passover with the tribe.

RICH: I miss your father.

SAUL: Then go live with him. He *likes* you. The two of you could be very happy together.

RICH: One thing.

SAUL: He's never really liked me.

RICH: Saul.

SAUL: He's always been polite but—

RICH: Are you finished?

SAUL: No, I will not bring you coffee in bed. I only do that for lovers. Besides, I broke your blue mug.

RICH: Saul, please.

SAUL: On purpose.

RICH: One thing. I'm embarrassed. I'm just about broke. The doctors. Tests.

SAUL: I thought you were insured.

RICH: They're pulling a fast one.

SAUL: We'll sue. I'll call Craig. He'll know what—

RICH: Craig told me not to have high hopes.

SAUL: We'll get by. You'll see.

RICH: I'll keep track of every cent you spend on me. You'll get it all back when I can work. I swear.

SAUL: Not to worry, I'll take it out in trade.

RICH: Saul, I'm frightened!

Saul takes him in his arms.

SAUL: We'll be okay, we'll be okay . . .

They hold each other. Lily walks into the scene with Chet. She's dressed in evening wear and is carrying a number of accessories, including a mirror and a shawl. Chet is dressed in cutoffs and a sweatshirt. We are in a flashback.

LILY: Rich, congratulations! It's fantastic that they're going to publish your book.

Saul tries to break from the clinch, but Rich holds him back.

RICH: No autographs, please.

LILY: It's wonderful, it really is, but can you guys celebrate later?

SAUL *(To Rich)*: Let me go. *(To Chet)* How do you do? I'm Saul.

LILY: Shit. Saul, Rich—my cousin Chet.

SAUL *(Trying to shake hands)*: Hi, Chet. *(To Rich)* You're strangling me.

CHET: Hi.

RICH *(To Saul)*: It's your last chance to kiss the author before he becomes famous and goes straight.

SAUL: Straight to the bars. *(To Chet)* So how do you like New York?

CHET: I only got here yesterday. Lily's taking me to a show tonight.

RICH: Do you think success will change me?

SAUL: God, I hope so.

LILY: I know I'm being a pig, but I need head shots by six o'clock. *(She lowers a roller of colored background paper)* It's a dazzling role for me

31

and *(To Saul)* you're such an artist.

SAUL: Rich is the "artiste" in the family.

LILY: Chet, be an angel and bring Saul his camera. It's by the bar.

Chet looks for the camera.

SAUL *(To Chet)*: Don't let your cousin push you around the way she does me.

LILY: Come on, Saul, make click-click.

SAUL: Unless you like that sort of thing.

RICH: That's all I get?

LILY *(To Rich, about Saul)*: Leave the boy alone.

RICH: A hug and a bitchy remark?

SAUL *(To Rich)*: That and a subway token.

RICH *(To Saul)*: No "Gee, Rich, I'm so proud of you"?

SAUL *(Smiling falsely)*: Gee, Rich, I'm so proud of you.

RICH: I finally have some good news and he's annoyed.

CHET *(To Lily, holding the camera)*: What should I do with this?

SAUL: Well, your brother called, while you were out guzzling lunch with your agent, Dr. Mengele. Call him back.

RICH: What'd he have to say?

SAUL: Call him and ask him. I'm not your secretary.

RICH *(Imitating him)*: I'm not your—

SAUL: He forgot my fucking name again. How long we been together?

RICH: Too long. Forget my brother. It's my first fucking book. Let's celebrate.

SAUL: You celebrate.

LILY: I'll throw a party.

RICH: What'll you serve, organic cabbage juice?

SAUL *(To Lily)*: His brother's a scumbag.

RICH: He likes you, too.

CHET *(To Saul, still holding the camera)*: Do you want this?

SAUL *(To Chet)*: Thanks, Chuck.

CHET: Chet.

Saul accepts the camera from Chet, but ignores the correction.

32

LILY *(Fondly, to Rich)*: You're such a lush.

RICH: Whatever happened to my old drinking buddy?

LILY: Did you know they have gay A.A. meetings?

Rich makes a face.

SAUL *(To Rich, trying to be nice)*: It's great news, babes, really.

RICH: You really don't give a fuck.

SAUL: Just how many copies you think a book of "fairy tales" will sell?

LILY: I picked a fine day to have my picture taken.

SAUL: If you only knew how much I love doing head shots.

RICH *(To Saul)*: Ah, fuck it, I guess I'm being childish.

SAUL: I shouldn't have said that. I'm thoughtless.

Rich shrugs.

LILY: And I'm Sneezy. No, really, I'm selfish. But I want that role so
    bad. I play the ghost of Marie Antoinette. *(To Saul, throwing the
    scarf around her neck and taking a tits-and-ass pose)* How do you like
    this, hon? "Let them eat . . ."

She drops the pose immediately as Saul starts to photograph her.

SAUL: Move your head a little to the . . .

She moves her head.

SAUL: Good. *(He snaps her)*

RICH *(Going to living area)*: I'm going running. *(He changes into jogging
    clothes)*

CHET *(He has followed Rich)*: How far do you run?

RICH: Depends. I'm in training for the marathon.

CHET: The marathon! Hey, that's great. I run, too.

RICH: Oh, yeah?

Lily and Saul are busy taking pictures in the other side of the loft. They can see Rich and Chet, but they can't easily hear them.

LILY: How's this?

CHET: Congratulations on the book.

RICH: Thanks.

SAUL: That's right.

LILY: I forget the director's name. He's Lithuanian.

CHET: That poem of yours that Lily has hung up in her kitchen, I read it. I think it's great.

SAUL: Great.

RICH: You don't much look like the poetry type.

LILY: Latvian.

CHET: I'm not. I just love your poem.

RICH: Are you a student?

CHET: Just graduated from San Francisco State.

LILY: Everybody in the play is dead.

SAUL: Your cousin's hot. Is he gay?

LILY: I don't know. I'll ask him. *(Yelling to Chet)* Chet, are you gay?

SAUL: Christ.

RICH: That's what I call tact.

LILY: Well?

CHET *(Loud, to Lily)*: Yes.

LILY: Thanks, hon.

SAUL: Give us a little more cheek . . .

CHET: There's a line of your poem I don't understand.

RICH: Only one? I have no idea what any of it means.

CHET: "The final waning moon . . ."

SAUL: Don't smile.

RICH: "And the coming of the light."

CHET: I love the way it sounds.

SAUL: Smile.

CHET: "The final waning moon / And the coming of the light."

SAUL *(Indicating to Lily that he wants a sexy pose)*: He loves you.

CHET: Oh, I get it.

RICH: Lily tells me you're looking for a place to stay.

CHET: New York is so expensive.

SAUL: He lusts for you.

RICH: A friend of mine wants someone to take care of his loft while he's in L.A.

SAUL: He wants to ravage you.

CHET: I'll do it.

RICH: He has eight cats.

CHET: Eight tigers, I don't care.

LILY: I love that play.

RICH: It's in Tribeca.

SAUL (*Yelling to Rich*): I apologize about the book.

Rich and Chet ignore Saul.

CHET: Where's Tribeca?

SAUL: Did you hear me?

RICH: On the isle of Manhattan.

CHET: We're on the isle of Manhattan.

RICH: We are.

LILY: The main characters are all ghosts.

CHET: I know that.

SAUL: I'll throw him a party.

RICH: That's about all you have to know.

SAUL: A big bash.

CHET: Is it?

LILY: We'll do it together.

RICH: I'll tell you a few more things.

CHET: Will you?

SAUL: I'll even invite his brother.

RICH: You bet your ass I will.

SAUL (*Snapping up the roller of background paper*): Finished.

Lily, Rich and Chet leave. Saul goes to the sofa. The Hospice Worker comes forward.

HOSPICE WORKER: A woman is told by her doctor that she has cancer

35

and has only a month to live. "Now wait just one minute," she tells the doctor. "I'll be wanting a second opinion." To which the doctor replies, "Okay, you're ugly, too."

David told me that one. He was an old Jewish man who had survived the Lodz ghetto in World War II. He'd seen everything in his life, and when the time came for him to go, he accepted it. The doctors wanted to go to obscene lengths to keep his body alive, but he refused. I loved him.

But most of my people are more like Margaret. She was in her nineties. She half accepted the fact that she was dying. One moment she'd be talking to you about which nephew she was definitely going to cross out of her will, and the next she'd be telling you about the summer vacation she was planning in Skibbereen. She had terminal cancer! But I always go along with what they have to say. My job is not to bring enlightenment, only comfort.

Which reminds me: Margaret's family saw her as some kind of prophet. The whole clan was in the room waiting to hear her last words. She had developed a distinct dislike for her family, so I was sitting closest to her when she went, and therefore I could hear what the poor soul was whispering. After it was all over, they asked me what prayer she had been uttering. I told them the Lord's Prayer. I didn't have the heart to tell them that what she was saying was "Oh, shit, oh, shit, oh, shit."

I've worked with thirty-five people altogether. About a third of them had AIDS. It *is* the Village.

She exits. Lights come up on left area. An AIDS support group is in session.

PERSON WITH AIDS 1: Funny thing is, I wasn't at all promiscuous.
PWA 4: Oh, please.
PWA 1: I swear. And I never drank much—once in a while a beer with Mexican food—and I don't smoke, and drugs, forget . . . . I met Jerry in my sophomore year—we shared the same dorm room at Hofstra—and we fell in love, and that was it for me. When the

sex-revolution thing happened, I remember I felt retarded. Everybody was doing all those wild things. Me, I was going to the opera a lot. As far as I know, Jerry didn't screw around. He swore he didn't. But then . . . he's not around for me to cross-examine. He left me.

RICH: Well, I . . .

PWA 3: What?

RICH: No.

PWA 2 (*A young housewife, eight months pregnant*): At least when I come here I don't have to lie. Like "Bernie's doing better. I'm fine." I can even crack up if I want to. Don't worry, I won't do it two weeks in a row. I mean, who's there to talk to in Brewster? These things don't happen in Brewster. Police officers don't shoot up heroin, cops don't come down with the "gay plague" — that's what they call it in Brewster. I can't talk to Bernie. I'll never forgive him. Have a chat with the minister? "Well, Reverend Miller, I have this little problem. My husband has AIDS, and I have AIDS, and I'm eight months pregnant, and I . . . ." You guys know what I mean. You're the only people in this world who know what I mean.

PWA 5: I know what you guys are going to tell me: I'm suffering from the homophobia that an oppressive society blah blah blah. I never felt good about being gay.

PWA 4: Oh, Mary.

PWA 5: Gay was grim. It was something I did because I had to. Like a dope fiend needs his fix. It always left me feeling like shit afterward. And that's the truth. I felt guilty. I still feel that way.

PWA 2 leans over to put a consoling hand on PWA 5. He pulls away.

PWA 4: I was part of a team trying to teach robots how to use language. (*He moves and talks like a robot*) "I'm Harris, your android model 3135X. I can vacuum the floors, cook cheeseburgers, play the piano." It's much harder to teach robots to understand. (*Instructing a backward robot*) "Joke." (*The robot responds dutifully*) "Noun: a clash of values or levels of reality, producing laughter. Example:

37

Have you heard about the disease attacking Jewish-American princesses? It's called MAIDS. You die if you *don't* get it. Ha. Ha." My coworkers asked me to leave. They were afraid of contracting AIDS through the air, or by my looking at them. You see, they are scientists. My last act before I left was programming one final robot. *(He behaves like a robot again)* "Good morning. This is Jack— *(He suddenly becomes a flamboyantly gay robot)* but you can call me Jackie—your *fabulous* new android model 1069. If you wish to use me—and I *love* being used—press one of those cunning little buttons on my pecs. Go on, press one— *(He switches from a campy tone to an almost angry, accusatory one)* or are you afraid of me, too?" That was my stab at immortality.

RICH: I'm not sure I have it anymore. I feel guilty saying this, like somehow I'm being disloyal to the group. I'm getting better, I know it. I just have these lumps, which for some reason won't go away, and a loss of weight, which has made me lighter than I've been for years.

PWA 3 *(Like a TV commercial)*: Ladies, see those ugly pounds just melt away.

RICH: But anyway, I feel great. I feel the disease disappearing in me. Only a tiny percentage of those with the swollen glands come down with the rest. I'm going to *not* come here next week. I'm sorry.

PWA 3: Rich?

SAUL *(Calling to Rich as if he were in the next room, while feeling the glands in his neck and armpits)*: Rich?

RICH *(Still to group)*: Why do I keep on apologizing?

SAUL: Rich?

RICH: If I *really* thought that I was coming down with it . . . . We all have *options*.

PWA 4: Rich?

SAUL: Rich.

RICH *(Entering Saul's area)*: What?

SAUL: Here, feel my glands.

RICH: You are such a hypochondriac.

SAUL: Do you think they're swollen?

RICH (*Placing his hands around Saul's neck*): They feel okay to me. (*Transylvanian accent*) But your neck—eet is grotesquely mees-shapen. (*Suddenly mock-strangling Saul*) Here, let me feex it.

They start wrestling on sofa.

SAUL: Not fair!

RICH: You're such a hypochondriac.

SAUL: Ow! *I'm* such a hypochondriac. You and your vitamins!

RICH: You and your yoga!

SAUL: You and your wheat grass!

RICH: It's working. My ratio's up.

SAUL: All right! (*To the tune of "New York, New York"*)
   T-cells up,
   The suppressors are down.
   New York, New York.

RICH: Hey, I love you! You know that?

SAUL: If you love me, get off my chest!

RICH: I don't dare. You'd try and get even. You're that way.

SAUL: We'll call a truce. One, two, three . . .

RICH AND SAUL: Truce.

As Rich climbs off Saul's chest, Saul pulls him down, lifting his shirt, and gets him in a hammerlock.

SAUL: You were right. You never should have trusted me.

RICH: Unfair . . . foul . . . most unfair!

SAUL: Fuck fair. The winner gets his way with the loser.

They tussle until Rich gives up.

SAUL: Having vanquished the good ship *Socrates,* the savage pirate chief Bigmeat takes the first mate as his captive.

RICH (*In falsetto*): No, Captain Bigmeat, no!

SAUL: I've had me eye on ye since that time we met in Bangalore. Ye can't escape me now, matey. I shall ravish ye fer sure.

Saul tickles Rich.

RICH: No! . . . I'm pure of blood and noble born!

Gradually their play turns more and more sexual, which Rich resists at first.

RICH: No! . . . No! . . . (*Relents*) Perhaps . . . . Please!
SAUL: Now I got ye, boy-o . . . boy-o . . . boy-o . . . . Oh, boy!

Finally Rich stops struggling. Rich and Saul are close together, panting, exhausted. Saul is about to make love to Rich when he notices a mark on his back.

RICH: What?

Saul ignores him and looks at the mark carefully.

RICH: What? You seduce me, you finally succeed in getting me hot and bothered, and what do you do as I lie here panting? You look at my birthmark.

Saul looks at Rich's back. He touches some marks.

RICH: What is it?
SAUL: Nothing.
RICH: What is it? Tell me!
SAUL: I'm sure it's nothing!
RICH: What! WHAT! *WHAT!* . . .

Immediately, the Hospice Worker draws a curtain that surrounds the entire living area of Saul's loft, hiding it from view. Overlapping the closing of the curtain, we hear the ringing of two telephones. Lights up on two men sitting side by side, answering multiline telephones.

PAT: Hotline, Pat speaking.

BARNEY: Hotline. This is Barney. *(To Pat, covering the phone)* Oh, no, it's her again.

PAT: Are you a gay man?

BARNEY: Didn't we speak a few days ago? *(To Pat, covering the phone)* She doesn't stop.

PAT: We're all worried.

BARNEY: Is he bisexual?

PAT: Calm down, first of all.

The third line rings.

BARNEY: Is he an IV drug user?

PAT: It's not all that easy to get it—*if* you take a few precautions. *(To Barney, covering the phone)* Okay, I'll get it. *(He speaks into the phone)* Please hold on. *(He presses a button)*

BARNEY: It wasn't my intention to insult you.

PAT: Hotline . . . . Shit. *(To Barney, pressing a button)* Lost him. Fucking phone.

BARNEY: So what makes you think he has AIDS?

PAT *(To phone)*: Hello.

BARNEY: He is what?

PAT: The disease is spread through the blood and the semen.

BARNEY: Samoans are *not* a risk group. *(To Pat, covering the phone)* Samoans?

PAT: So wear a condom.

BARNEY: There's half a zillion diseases he has symptoms of.

PAT: Make *him* wear a condom.

The phone rings.

BARNEY: Please hold. *(He presses a button)*

PAT: Kissing is acceptable.

BARNEY: Hotline . . . *(In response to a hate call)* And your mother eats turds in hell! . . . Thank you. *(He presses a button)*

PAT: Myself, I don't do it on the first date.

BARNEY: I would definitely check it out with a physician.

BARNEY: Spots? I'm not a doctor . . . . Go to a doctor.

PAT: Stroking, holding, rubbing, mirrors, whips, chains, jacking off, porno— use your imagination.

BARNEY: I'm sorry you're lonely.

PAT: Our motto is: "On me, not in me."

BARNEY: Madam, we're busy here. I can't stay on the line with you all day.

PAT: You have a nice voice, too, but I'm seeing someone.

BARNEY: Hello?

PAT: Thanks.

BARNEY (*To Pat*): Thank God.

PAT: Good luck.

They hang up at the same time.

BARNEY: Spots. I love it.

PAT (*To himself*): I am not seeing anyone.

BARNEY: What are you talking about?

PAT: I was saying how much I love being celibate. (*He kisses his palm*) So how the fuck are you?

BARNEY: Tired, broke, depressed, and Tim is moving out this afternoon. Well, you asked. I hear you have a new PWA.

PAT: Sorry about Tim. Yes, I have a new baby, a writer. Why do I get all the tough customers?

BARNEY: Because you're so tough.

PAT: So butch.

BARNEY: So mean.

PAT: Weathered by life like the saddle under a cowboy's ass.

BARNEY: Ooooh. I could never be a CMP [Crisis Management Partner]. Where do you get your energy?

PAT: Drugs. I don't do that anymore either. What *do* I do? I wait tables, answer phones, and work with ingrates like Rich. Boy, is he pissed. He calls me Miss Nightingale or Florence and throws dishes and curses his roommate and won't cooperate with the doctor and won't see his shrink and isn't interested in support groups *and he shit in the fucking bathtub!* He shit—

BARNEY: Is he incontinent?

PAT: Fuck, no. He ain't that sick yet. He said it was "convenient." I don't know why he shit in the tub.

BARNEY: A real sweetheart.

PAT: I'm going out of my mind. Thank God they put him in the hospital.

BARNEY: First time?

PAT: Yep.

BARNEY: I'd probably be a real bastard.

PAT: I wouldn't take it lying down.

BARNEY: You'd take it any way you can get it.

PAT: Go on, girlfriend.

BARNEY: Me, if I got sick I'd shove a time bomb up my tush and drop in on Timmy for tea and meet his new lover: Jimmy.

PAT: Jimmy?

BARNEY: I swear: Jimmy. *(Visiting Timmy and Jimmy for high tea)* "Timmy has told me so much about you. I've been *dying* to meet you." And kaboom! There goes Timmy and Jimmy.

PAT: Timmy and Jimmy?

The telephone rings.

BARNEY: Ain't it a gas?

PAT: Gag me, for sure.

BARNEY: For sure.

PAT *(Answering the phone)*: Hotline. Pat speaking.

BARNEY *(Raging)*: When are we going to get some more help around here??!! I'm going out of my mind! *(Suddenly, sweet and sultry as he answers the phone)* Hotline, Barney speaking.

PAT: Are you a gay man?

BARNEY: Are you a gay man?

The lights quickly fade on the two men. The curtain opens, revealing a hospital room, with bed, chair and bed table. The loft space and bar have disappeared. Rich is in bed. Lily, Saul and a Nurse are standing nearby.

NURSE: Temperature and blood pressure, Mr. Farrell.
LILY: Can you come back later?
SAUL: He's had some bad news.
NURSE: He's last on my rounds.
RICH *(To Saul)*: You lied to me.
SAUL: I didn't know.
LILY: He didn't know. I swear.
NURSE: It'll just take a minute.
RICH: What other little details are you keeping from me? They let him lie there like a dog. What else?

A Hispanic Hospital Worker comes in to empty the wastebasket.

RICH: You! *Váyase!* Get the wetback out of here! *Váyase!*
HOSPITAL WORKER: I not do nothing! He crazy.
RICH: You, get out of here before I breathe on you! *Ahora! Ahora! Váyase!*
NURSE: Mr. Farrell, please.
SAUL: Come back later. *Más tarde, por favor.*
RICH: Go back to your picket line. *(To Saul)* They want a wage hike, no less. He tried to get me to bribe him to clean my room—
HOSPITAL WORKER: *Qué coño estás diciendo?* [What the fuck are you saying?]
NURSE: Please cooperate.
LILY: He didn't say anything.
RICH: He won't go near my bed, but he's not afraid to touch my money.
SAUL: You misunderstood him.
RICH: *El dinero está limpio, ah? Tu madre.* [Money is clean, huh, motherfucker?]
HOSPITAL WORKER: *Maricón.* [Faggot.]
RICH *(To Saul)*: They're unionizing primates now.
LILY *(To Rich)*: Sh!

44

HOSPITAL WORKER: *No entiendo.* [I don't understand.] I going. *(He exits)*

LILY *(Aside to Saul)*: I shouldn't have told him about Chet.

SAUL *(Aside to Lily)*: Better you than someone else.

RICH *(Imitating Lily and Saul)*: Bzzz bzzz bzzz.

NURSE *(Trying to put a blood-pressure cuff on Rich's arm)*: Will you be still a moment so I can check your blood pressure?

RICH: Are you a union member, too?

NURSE *(To Saul)*: What shall I do?

LILY: A good friend of his just passed away.

NURSE: AIDS? *(She resumes struggling with the cuff)*

RICH: The undertakers' union. Go away, I'm on strike, too; I refuse to participate in the documentation of my own demise.

SAUL: She's only trying to help you.

RICH *(To the Nurse, ripping off the cuff)*: Go find another statistic for the Center for Disease Control.

NURSE *(To Saul)*: I'm a patient woman, but he wants me to lose it. I swear that's what he's after.

RICH: Lady, fuck off!

SAUL *(To the Nurse)*: Please. Can't you see he's upset?

NURSE *(To Rich)*: Okay, you win. I'm losing it. Are you happy? I'm *angry,* angry, Mr. Farrell.

LILY: Will you please go!

NURSE: A person can take only so much. I give up. I don't have to put up with this shit. I'm gonna speak to my supervisor. *(She exits)*

RICH *(Applauding)*: Three gold stars for self-assertion!

LILY *(To Saul)*: I should have kept my mouth shut.

RICH: Having brought Romeo the news that Juliet is dead, Balthasar makes a tearful exit.

LILY: I don't know what to say. *(She looks at Rich, then Saul)*

RICH: I said: Balthasar makes a tearful exit.

LILY: I know how you're feeling.

RICH: No matter. Get thee gone and hire those horses.

LILY: I loved Chet, too.

RICH: Tush, thou art deceived.

LILY: He told me he was sorry for the way he treated you.

RICH: Do the thing I bid thee.

LILY: He didn't belong in New York. He thought he was so sophisticated, but he was just a kid from Mendocino. I'm sorry I let him go home.

RICH: The messenger must go. The hero wishes to be alone with his confidant. *(He turns his back on Saul and Lily)*

LILY: I'll be back tomorrow. *(Aside to Saul)* I've got half a crown roast from Margo. She went vegetarian. I'll be up. I have to have a talk with Mick. He's irrational on the subject of AIDS. He can go to hell. If he's so afraid, let him move out. *(To Rich)* I won't let him come between us. You're my buddy.

Saul indicates that Lily should leave. She gathers up her belongings, mimes dialing a telephone, and blows Saul a kiss.

LILY: Rich?

Saul shakes his head no. She leaves. Saul tries to think of something to say to Rich. He abandons the effort and picks up the Sunday New York Times *crossword puzzle.*

SAUL: "African quadruped." *(Writing)* G-N-U. . . . "Hitler's father." *(Counting on his fingers)* One, two . . . five letters. Let's see: Herman? Herman Hitler? *(Counting)* That's six . . . . Otto? . . . Werner? . . . Rudi? . . . Putzi? *(He shrugs)* Fuck. *(He reads on)* Thank God: "Jewish rolls." Starts with a B, six letters: bagels. *(He starts to write it in)* Shit, that won't work. I need a Y.

RICH *(Without turning)*: Bialys.

SAUL: B-I-A-L-Y-S.

RICH: Short for Bialystok, a large industrial city in eastern Poland . . . *(Turning to Saul)* hometown of Ludwig Zamenhof, inventor of Esperanto, an artificial international language. Alois Hitler! A-L-O—

SAUL *(Putting down the puzzle)*: Outclassed again. Why do I bother? He knows everything.

RICH: When I was a kid I used to spend all my time in libraries. My childhood was—

SAUL: If I had a father like yours I would have done the same thing.

RICH: But thanks to that son of a bitch I could tell you how many metric tons of coal the Benelux countries produced per annum, and the capital city of the Grand Duchy of Liechtenstein.

SAUL: I give up.

RICH: Vaduz.

SAUL: Miss Trivial Pursuit.

RICH: I knew to which great linguistic family the Telegu language of South India belongs.

SAUL: Telegu? Isn't that the national dish of Botswana?

RICH (*Ignoring him*): The Dravidian.

Saul straightens up the bed table.

RICH: I've always loved words . . . . I wrote poetry when I was a kid. My brother used to make fun of me . . .

Winter, winter,
How you glinter,
With holiday's array.
And the snow
We all know
Is here all day.

Saul smiles.

RICH: I was eight, nine when I wrote that. I had just come in from sledding down Indian Hill—a steep road that connects Jefferson Heights to the valley.

SAUL: You showed it to me on our grand tour of West Jersey.

RICH: It was a late afternoon just before sundown and the sky was intensely blue and intensely cold and you could see the stars already. For some reason nobody was home when I came back, so I stood there at the stamped enamel-top kitchen table dripping in my frozen corduroys and wrote that poem.

SAUL: Are you comfortable?

Rich shrugs. Saul fixes his pillows.

RICH: I was a good kid, but I was lonely and scared all the time. I was so desperate to find people like myself that I looked for them in the indexes of books—under H. I eventually found them—

SAUL: But not in books.

RICH: The next thing you know I moved to the city and was your typical office-worker-slash-writer. I hated my job, so I grew a beard and wore sandals, hoping they would fire me and give me permanent unemployment. I wanted to stay at home in my rent-controlled apartment and drink bourbon and write poems. I did that for a period. I loved it. The apartment got filthy and I did, too, and I'd go out only at night—to pick up guys. And then I found you—in a porno theatre— *(He takes Saul's hand)* and we semisettled down and you took my picture and I started to jog. We bought a loft—

SAUL: And raised a cat—

RICH: —and loved each other. But that wasn't enough for me. I don't think you ever understood this: you weren't my muse, you were . . . *(He searches for the word)* Saul.

Saul rises and looks out the window.

RICH: I loved you but I wanted someone to write poems to. During our marriage I had almost stopped writing and felt stifled even though our loft had appeared in *New York* magazine. And then I met Chet and left you in the lurch and lived with him at the Chelsea Hotel. He was shallow, callow, and selfish, and I loved him, too.

We did a lot of coke and I wrote a lot of poetry and the catering was booming and *The New Yorker* published a story of mine and I ran in the marathon. I was on a roll. *(With mounting excitement as he relives the experience)* I remember training on the East River Drive for the first time. I didn't realize how narrow and dark the city streets were until I got to the river and all of a sudden there was the fucking river. The sky was the same color as that twilight when I was a kid. I came from the darkness into the light. I'm running downtown and I make this bend and out of nowhere

48

straight up ahead is the Manhattan Bridge and then the Brooklyn Bridge, one after another, and my earphones are playing Handel's *Royal Fireworks Music*. It can't get better than this, I know it. I'm running and crying from gratitude. I came from the darkness into the light. I'm running and telling God I didn't know He was *that* good or *that* big, thank you, Jesus, thanks, thanks . . . *(He slumps back, exhausted from the effort)*

The next morning I woke up with the flu and stayed in bed for a couple of days and felt much better. But my throat stayed a little sore and my glands were a little swollen . . . *(Long silence. Casually)* Saul, I want you to do something for me. Will you do something for me, baby?

SAUL: Sure, babe.

RICH: Now listen. I want you to go out of here and go to the doctor and tell him you aren't sleeping so hot—

SAUL: I'm sleeping okay.

RICH: Sh! Now listen: you tell him you want something to make you sleep and Valium doesn't work on you, but a friend once gave you some Seconal—

SAUL: *No!* I won't do it!

RICH *(Pressuring Saul relentlessly)*: I tried hoarding the pills here, but every night the nurse stays to watch me swallow them down.

SAUL: I can't do that.

RICH: I don't want to end up like Chet.

SAUL: I won't listen.

RICH: If you love me, you'll help me. I have something that's eating me up. I don't want to go on. I'm scared to go on.

SAUL: Don't do this to me! I can't handle it. I'll go out the window, I swear, don't do this—

RICH: Don't you see, it's the only way. Just get the pills.

SAUL: No!

RICH: Just have them around. You'll get used to the idea. And when the lesions spread above my neck so that I don't look the same, you'll want me to have them.

SAUL: Help me, help me!

RICH: It's all right. Not now.

SAUL: No.

RICH: Tomorrow.

SAUL: No.

RICH: The day after.

SAUL: No.

RICH: We'll see.

Rich's Brother, wearing a surgical mask, gown and gloves and carrying a small shopping bag, tiptoes in, stopping when he notices Rich and Saul.

SAUL: Oh, my God. I think it's your brother.

BROTHER: I'll come back later.

SAUL *(Pulling himself together)*: No, I was just going.

BROTHER: It's all right, really.

SAUL: I've been here for a while.

BROTHER: I'm interrupting.

SAUL: Really.

RICH *(To his Brother)*: Unless you're planning to come into intimate contact with me or my body fluids, none of that shit you have on is necessary.

BROTHER: The sign says—

RICH: But please restrain your brotherly affection for my sake; who knows what diseases you might have brought in with you?

The Brother removes the mask, gown and gloves.

SAUL: You two haven't seen each other for a while, so why don't I just—

RICH: By all means. You need a break, kid. Think about what I said.

SAUL: It stopped raining. I'll take a walk.

RICH: Have a nice walk.

BROTHER: Good seeing ya . . . ? *(He has forgotten Saul's name)*

SAUL: Saul. Yeah.

Saul exits. Beat.

50

BROTHER: I owe you an apology . . . *(Rich won't help him)* I was very frightened . . . I'm afraid I panicked . . . . Please forgive me.

RICH: Nothing to forgive.

BROTHER *(Brightly)*: Betty sends her love. She sent along a tin of butter crunch. *(He offers Rich a tin, which Rich ignores)* You're not on any special diet? I told Betty I thought maybe you'd be on one of those macrobiotic diets. I read in the papers that it's helped some people with . . .

RICH: AIDS.

BROTHER: Yes. I keep a file of clippings on all the latest medical developments. *(He takes a clipping out of his wallet)* Looks like they're going to have a vaccine soon. The French—

RICH: That's to *prevent* AIDS. I already *have* AIDS.

BROTHER: They have this new drug, AZT.

RICH: I'm on it.

BROTHER: Right. . . . So how are you doing?

RICH *(Smiling cheerfully)*: I have Kaposi's sarcoma, a hitherto rare form of skin cancer. It's spreading. I have just begun chemotherapy. It nauseates me. I expect my hair will fall out. I also have a fungal infection of the throat called candidiasis, or thrush. My life expectancy is . . . I have a greater chance of winning the lottery. Otherwise I'm fine. How are you?

BROTHER: I'm sorry . . . *(Brightly again, after a long pause)* Mary Pat sends her love. She won her school swimming competition and I registered her for the South Jersey championship. Oh, I forgot, she made this for you . . . *(He takes a large handmade fold-out card from the shopping bag. It opens downward a full two feet)*

RICH: Say, have you heard about the miracle of AIDS?

BROTHER: What?

RICH: It can turn a fruit into a vegetable. What's the worst thing about getting AIDS?

The Brother lets the card fall to the floor.

BROTHER: Stop it!

51

RICH: Trying to convince your parents that you're Haitian. Get it?

BROTHER: I came here to see if I could help you.

RICH: Skip it. So what do you want?

BROTHER: I don't want anything.

RICH: Everything I own is going to Saul—

BROTHER: I don't want anything.

RICH: Except for the stuff Mom left us. I told Saul that it's to go to you. Except for the Barcelona chair—

BROTHER: I don't care about—

RICH: I'm leaving Saul the copyright to my book—

BROTHER: Why are you doing this to me?

RICH: So you don't want my worldly possessions, such as they are; you want me to relieve your guilt.

BROTHER: Stop it.

RICH (*Making the sign of the cross over his Brother, chanting*): I hereby exonerate you of the sin of being ashamed of your queer brother and being a coward in the face of—

BROTHER: Stop! Don't! (*He grabs Rich's hand*)

RICH: No!

BROTHER: Richard, don't! . . .

He attempts to hug Rich, who resists with all his strength.

BROTHER: I don't care . . . I don't care! . . . Rich! . . . Richie . . . Richie . . .

Rich relents. They hug.

RICH: I'm so . . . [frightened]

BROTHER: Forgive me. Forgive me.

RICH: I don't want to . . . [die]

BROTHER: It's all right. I'm here . . . I'm here . . .

They hold each other close for a beat. The Hospital Worker rushes into the room.

HOSPITAL WORKER: Psst. *Oye.* Psst.

Rich and his Brother notice the Worker.

RICH: What do you want now?
HOSPITAL WORKER (*Shakes his head no*): *Viene. Viene.* He come. He come.

He pulls the Brother from Rich.

RICH: Who come?
HOSPITAL WORKER: *Su amigo.* Your freng. He no like.
BROTHER: What's he saying?

Rich starts to laugh. Enter Saul. The Worker starts sweeping and whistling with an air of exuberant nonchalance. The following seven speeches overlap.

RICH (*Laughing*): He . . . He . . .
SAUL: What's going on?
BROTHER: Richie, what's so damned funny?
RICH: He thought we . . . (*He breaks up*) that he and I were cheating on you.
BROTHER: He thought that you and I were . . . (*He laughs*)
RICH: He came in to warn me that you were coming! (*He laughs. To the Worker*) *Gracias! Muchas gracias!*
SAUL: He thought you two were . . . (*He laughs*)
HOSPITAL WORKER (*To Rich*): *De nada.* [You're welcome.] Why you laugh? (*He laughs*) *Como hay maricones.* [What a bunch of faggots.]
RICH: *Es mi hermano.* [He's my brother.]
HOSPITAL WORKER: *Coño.* [Fuck.]
RICH: *Perdona por lo que dije antes. Yo* (*Pointing to himself*) *era mucho estúpido.* [Forgive me for what I said to you before. I was being very stupid.]

HOSPITAL WORKER: *De nada. Somos todas estúpidos, chico.* [We're all stupid, my friend.]

He exits. The giggles subside.

BROTHER *(Checking watch, stiffening his spine)*: I've got to be going now.

RICH: I'm glad you came by.

BROTHER: I'll be back tomorrow with Mary Pat. She's been dying— wanting to come by. She's been writing poetry and—

RICH: I'd love to see her. And tell Betty thanks for the . . . ?

BROTHER: Butter crunch. *(Exiting, shaking hands with Saul)* Good seeing ya . . . ? *(He has forgotten Saul's name again)*

SAUL: Saul.

BROTHER: Sorry. Bye. *(He exits)*

SAUL: I won't get upset. I won't get upset.

RICH: What's the matter?

SAUL: It's *my* problem.

RICH: What?

SAUL: Rich, I've thought about things.

RICH: What?

SAUL *(Suddenly exploding)*: Goddamn it! That prick doesn't know my name after—how many years are we together?

RICH: *Were* together.

SAUL: Pardon me, I forgot we got an annulment from the pope. Fuck it, I won't get upset.

RICH *(Overlapping)*: My brother finds it hard to deal with the fact that—

SAUL: I said fuck it.

RICH: Don't you see, it was a big step for him—

SAUL: Your brother hates my fucking guts. Haven't you ever told him I didn't turn you queer?

RICH: My brother—

SAUL: I didn't give you AIDS either.

RICH: My brother—

SAUL: Why're you always defending him? What about me?

RICH: My brother's got a few feelings, too, even if he isn't a card-carrying member of the lavender elite.

SAUL: Let's hear it for our working-class hero.

RICH: You've never tried talking to him. You're so self-centered that it never occurred to you—

SAUL: I'm self—now wait one minute! I'm so self-centered that I was willing to buy the pills for you.

RICH: You have the pills?

The other actors create the sleazy atmosphere of Christopher Street near the Hudson River.

DEALER 1: Yo, my man.

SAUL: I was willing to go down to Christopher Street, where all the drug dealers hang out.

DEALER 2: What's 'attenin', what's 'attenin'?

Saul turns his back to Rich and immediately he is on Christopher Street.

SAUL *(To Dealer 2)*: Nice night.

RICH: I told you to go to the doctor's.

DEALER 1: Smoke 'n' acid,   DEALER 2: Crack . . . crack
MDA 'n' speed. Smoke 'n'   . . . crack . . .
acid, MDA 'n' speed . . .

SAUL *(To Dealer 1)*: I said, "Nice night."

DEALER 1: Real nice. What's shakin', babe?

RICH: All you would've had to say to the doctor was "My roommate has AIDS and I'm not sleeping well."

SAUL *(To Dealer 1)*: I'm not sleeping well.

DEALER 1: I have just the thing. Step right into my office.

DEALER 3: Speed, acid, mesc, ups, downs . . .

SAUL: I'll take one hundred.

DEALER 1: Two dollars a cap.

RICH: Forty's enough.

SAUL: I wanted enough for both of us.

DEALER 1: You got the cash, I got the stash.

RICH: Tristan and Isolde.

DEALER 1: Hey, man, you want them or not?

SAUL: You don't understand anything!

DEALER 1: Look, man, I can't handle all that emotiating.

SAUL (*Near the breaking point*): You've never understood anything!

DEALER 1: Gimme the greens, I'll give you the reds.

RICH: The widow throws herself on her husband's funeral pyre.

SAUL (*Hitting the bed with his fists—if Rich were the bed he'd be dead*): SHIT! SHIT! SHIT! You selfish bastard!

RICH: What stopped you?

SAUL: From hitting you?

RICH: From buying the pills.

SAUL: The pills? Nothing stopped me. I bought them.

RICH: Thank you. Where are they?

SAUL: I threw them away.

RICH: Why?

SAUL: Let me help you live!

RICH: What's so hot about living when you're covered with lesions and you're coming down with a new infection every day? . . . If it gets too bad, I want to be able to quietly disappear.

SAUL: I won't argue the logic of it. I can't do what you want me to do.

RICH: I just want them around. You keep them for me—just in case.

SAUL: I won't.

RICH: Then I'll get them myself. I'll go out of here and get them. (*He climbs out of bed. He's shaky*)

SAUL: You're crazy.

RICH: I don't need you to do my dirty work. (*He takes a few steps*) Where're my clothes? Where'd they put them?

SAUL: Get back in bed!

RICH: I want to get out of here! (*He puts on his robe*) This place is a death machine! (*He starts to leave but collapses on the floor*)

SAUL (*Rushing to his aid*): You idiot.

56

RICH (*Catching his breath*): Well, here we are again.

Saul tries to help him back to bed.

RICH: No. Let me sit . . . . Fuck . . . (*He sits in chair*) "Dependent":
from the Late Latin "to hang from."

SAUL: I tried to do what you asked me to do. Just like always.

RICH: You don't have to apologize.

SAUL: I want you to understand something.

RICH: I understand.

SAUL: It's important. Listen. I had made up my mind to give you half
of the pills and keep the other half for myself. I was walking past
Sheridan Square. It was starting to drizzle again. You've never
seen Sheridan Square look grungier: a drunk was pissing on the
pathetic little flowers. And that crazy lady—you know the one
that sings off-key at the top of her lungs—she was there, too. And
my favorite, the guy with his stomach out to here—

RICH: I get the picture.

SAUL: There I was walking with the pills in my pocket, contemplating
our suicides. And I was getting wet and cold. As I passed the
square, Seconal seemed too slow to me. You don't have a monopoly
on pain.

RICH: I never thought—

SAUL: Shut up. Anyway, I had stopped in front of the Pleasure Chest.
I looked up and there in the window were sex toys and multicolored jockstraps, lit by a red neon sign. I said, "Help me, God."
Which is funny coming from an atheist, let me tell you. . . . I said
it out loud.

RICH: And you could walk again.

SAUL: Well, it wasn't exactly a miracle.

RICH: Thank God.

SAUL: Anyway, there I was in front of a sex shop, and I looked down
and there was a puddle. Now this'll sound stupid.

RICH: Couldn't sound stupider than the rest.

SAUL: In this dirty little puddle was a reflection of the red neon sign.
It was beautiful. And the whole street was shining with the most

incredible colors. They kept changing as the different signs blinked on and off . . . . I don't know how long I stood there. A phrase came to my head: "The Lord taketh and the Lord giveth."

RICH: You blew your punch line.

SAUL: It's the other way around. Anyway, there went two hundred bucks down the sewer.

RICH: Take it off your taxes.

SAUL: Don't you see, I just don't have the right to take your life or mine.

RICH: The Miracle of the Pleasure Chest.

SAUL: Hang in there, Rich.

RICH: Our Lady of Christopher Street.

SAUL: Maybe I'm being selfish, but I want you here. I need you.

RICH: My future isn't exactly promising.

SAUL: I'll take you as is.

RICH: But what happens when it gets worse? It's gonna get worse.

SAUL: I'll be here for you no matter what happens.

RICH: Will you?

SAUL: I promise.

RICH: Shit.

SAUL: What do you want me to say?

RICH: You're so goddamned noble.

SAUL: How do you want me to be?

RICH: I can't afford to be noble. The only thing holding me together is rage. It's not fair! Why me?

SAUL: Why *not* you? Maybe I'm next. No one knows.

RICH: I reserve the right to put an end to all this shit.

SAUL: All right, but if you kill yourself they won't bury you in hallowed ground and you'll go to hell with all us Jews.

RICH: I bet they have a separate AIDS section in the cemetery so I don't infect the other corpses. (*Beat, then suddenly he speaks fiercely*) Do you promise to stick to me no matter what happens?

SAUL: I do.

RICH: *Do you? (He searches Saul's face for the answer)* I need you. (*Long silence. He releases Saul*) Paradise in a puddle.

SAUL: You couldn't resist that, could you?

RICH: Prodigies and signs, why not? It's the end of an era.

SAUL: What do you think'll come next?

RICH: Next? After I'm gone?

SAUL: Don't be maudlin. You know I didn't mean that.

RICH: I know you didn't . . . . I've been wondering what happens after I die . . . . Do you think things go on and on? I don't know. Is this all the time I have? I hope not . . . . Do you think anywhere out there is a place as sweet as this one? I like it here—even though right now I am going through a lot of . . . (*Searching for the word*) difficulty . . . (*He goes back to bed*) And if we get to come back, where do we get to come back to? I don't feature leaving here and going to a goddamned naphtha swamp in the Z sector of some provincial galaxy to live as some kind of weird insect . . . . But if life is a kind of educational process in which each piece of the universe eventually gets to discover its own true divine nature, if it is, then a methane bog on Jupiter might serve just as well as a meadow in the Berkshires . . . . I want to be cremated and I want my ashes to fertilize the apple tree in the middle of Jake's pasture. When you take a bite of an apple from that tree think of me.

SAUL: You'd be the worm in it.

RICH: Saul?

SAUL: What, Rich?

RICH: There's a café way over by Tompkins Square Park, off of B. It holds maybe ten tables and has the scuzziest art on the walls.

SAUL: What about it?

RICH: I want to read my work there.

SAUL: You turned down the Y.

RICH: People go there, gay, straight, with their weird hair and their ears pierced ninety-nine different ways, they go there late in the evening, and there's a guitarist, and they sit there politely and listen. They look newborn, but slightly depraved. I want to read there when I get out of here. And you'll take pictures. Okay?

SAUL: Sounds okay. Sounds good to me.

RICH: Forgive me for being such a fuck.

SAUL: You really are a fuck.

RICH: I'm a real prick.

SAUL: You're an asshole.

RICH: You're a faggot.

SAUL: You're a fruit.

RICH: You know, if we took precautions . . .

SAUL: If what? What? You always do that.

RICH: I don't know.

SAUL: Would you like to?

RICH: If we're careful. Do you want to?

SAUL: I'd love to. What do you think?

RICH: I think it'd be okay.

SAUL: What'll we do?

RICH: I don't know. Something safe.

SAUL: We'll think of something.

RICH: Close the curtain.

SAUL: Do you think we should?

RICH: Well, we can't do it like this.

SAUL: Right.

RICH: Right.

SAUL: What if someone comes in?

RICH: So what?

SAUL: Right. *(He doesn't move)*

RICH: So what are you waiting for?

SAUL: I'm scared.

RICH: So am I. Do you think we should?

SAUL: God, I want to.

RICH: Well, close the fucking curtain!

The Hospice Worker ends the impasse by closing the curtain.

RICH: Thanks.

SAUL: Thanks.

When the curtain is completely shut, the Hospice Worker walks downstage center.

HOSPICE WORKER: I have a new AIDS patient, Richard. He still has a lot of denial about his condition. Which is normal. I think most of us would go crazy if we had to face our own deaths squarely. He's a wonderful man. He writes extraordinarily funny poems about the ward. His lover's there all the time, and he's got a lot of friends visiting, and both families. I only hope it keeps up. It's only his second time in the hospital. They get a lot of support at first, but as the illness goes on, the visitors stop coming—and they're left with only me.

But something tells me it's not going to happen in his case. You should see how his lover takes care of him. God forbid they treat Rich badly, Saul swoops down and lets them have it. He's making a real pain in the ass of himself, which is sometimes how you have to be in this situation.

Rich should be out of the hospital again in a week or so. For a while. He's a fighter . . . . The angry phase is just about over and the bargaining phase is beginning. If he behaves like a good little boy, God will do what Rich tells Him to do . . . . I certainly hope that God does.

I don't know anymore. Sometimes I think I'm an atheist. No. Not really. It's more that I'm angry at God: how can He do this? (*Pause*) I have a lot of denial, *I* am angry, and *I* bargain with God. I have a long way to go towards acceptance. Maybe it's time for me to resign. Maybe I'm suffering from burnout.

But what would I do if I didn't go to St. Vincent's? And it's a privilege to be with people when they are dying. Sometimes they tell you the most amazing things. The other night Jean-Jacques— he's this real queen, there's no other word for it—he told me what he misses most in the hospital is his corset and high heels. I mean he weighs all of ninety pounds and he's half dead. But I admire his spirit. The way they treat him. Sometimes they won't even bring the food to his bed. And I'm afraid to complain for fear they take it out on him! Damn them! . . . I've lost some of my idealism, as I said. Last night I painted his nails for him. (*She shows the audience her vividly painted fingernails*) Flaming red. He loved it.

END OF PLAY

WILLIAM M. HOFFMAN's As Is *was first presented at New York's Circle Repertory Company on March 10, 1985, and opened on Broadway on May 1 of that year. It received a Drama Desk Award, an Obie Award for Distinguished Playwriting and a Tony nomination. The text published here is the revised 1990 version.*

A Poster of the Cosmos

BY LANFORD WILSON

CHARACTER

TOM is a large, brooding man of 36.

TIME 1987.

PLACE A police station in Manhattan.

For Tom Noonan

Tom, most of the time, sits at an institutional table in an institutional chair. There is a tape recorder on the table. He is in a white pool of light in a black void. He wears a white T-shirt, white work pants and sneakers.

He is addressing a cop who would be at the other end of the table, and another off left or right who would be slouching against a door. When he gets up, something in the cops' posture tells him he'd better sit back down.

When he smokes the smoke rises up in the white downspot like a nebula.

TOM (*He is standing and quite pissed-off*): All right, I'm sitting down and I'm staying down. Okay?

He sits.

Now, are you happy?

He glares at the cops in disgust.

Jesus, you guys slay me with that crap. "You don't look like the kinna guy'd do somethin' like dat." You're a joke. Cops. Jesus. I mean you're some total cliché. I don't have to be here lookin' at you guys, I could turn on the TV. "What's that white stuff on your shirt?" Jesus. I'm a baker, it's flour. You want a sample, take to your lab? (*Shaking his head in wonder*) "You don't look like the kinna guy'd do somethin' like dat." What does dat kinna guy who'd do somethin' like dat look like to a cop, huh? And what kinna

65

thing? You don't know nothin'; you know what you think you know. You seen every kinna dirty business there is every night, lookin' under the covers, spend your workin' day in the fuckin' armpits of the city and still ain't learned shit about people. You're totally fuckin' blind and deaf like fish I heard about, spend their life back in some fuckin' cave.

He looks around, taps the tape recorder, looks at it.

Is this on? You got your video cameras goin'? 'Cause I told you I'd tell you but this is the only time I'm tellin' this. So, you know, get out your proper equipment, I'm not doin' this twice.

He looks around, still disgusted.

"You don't look like the kinna guy'd do somethin' like dat." Johnny said I didn't look like no kinna guy at all. Just a big ugly guy. Said I was like Kurt Vonnegut or somebody. Somebody had the good sense not to look like nobody else. He said that, I read every word Vonnegut wrote. He's good. He's got a perverted point of view, I like that. There was a time I wouldn't of understood that, but we change, which is what I'm sayin' here.

Beat.

"You don't look like the kinna guy'd do dat." What kinna guy is *that*? *What* kinna guy? Oh, well, you're talkin' *dat* kinna guy. The kinna guy'd *do* that. *Dat* kinna guy . . . . Well, I *ain't* dat kinna guy. I'm a kinna guy like *you* kinna guys. That's why you make me want to puke sittin' here lookin' at you. "Hey, guys, dis guy is our kinna guy. I can't believe he's dat kinna guy." Well, I *ain't* that kinna guy.

He is almost saddened by the cops.

You guys move in the dark, inna doorways, if you didn't look right through people 'steada at 'em, you'd maybe know there ain't no *"kinna guys."* You'd maybe know you can't sort guys out like vegetables. This is a potato, it goes wid the potatoes; this is a carrot, this here's celery—we got us an eggplant, goes wid the eggplant. That's vegetables, that ain't people. There's no kinna guys, 'cause *guys,* if you used your *eyes,* you'd know, are V-8 juice, man. You don't know *what* kinna thing's in there.

Tom pauses, takes cigarettes from his pants pocket, puts them on the table with a Zippo lighter, takes one from the pack and lights it. He has a new thought that annoys him lightly.

For all you know Johnny was a junkie. Didn't see you lookin' for tracks, and you'da found 'em by the way, so what kinna guys are we talkin' about here? It depresses people to sit here and talk to this kinna massive stupidity.

Beat.

Johnny'd love it. He'd laugh his ass, man. No shit, he'd wet himself over you guys. And I don't wanna make him sound simple. He was like this anything-but-easy sort of person. He used to, you know, when he was a kid, had this prescription for hypertension medication, but he said he didn't take it 'cause it messed up his bowels so bad. *Thinking* was Johnny's problem. Like 'cause his mind was goin' like on all these tracks, like it had all these connections and he was always repluggin' everything and crossin' over these wires, till you could almost like *see* this complicated mess of lines in his head. Like he'd wait till he was like fuckin' droppin', like his eyes had been closed for an hour before he'd even get in bed at night. And then he'd lay there and in a minute he'd be up again. And like, you know, you'd think, aw, shit, 'cause he's smokin' all these cigarettes and this shit and half the time he don't know if he's sittin' up or layin' down. The whole apartment could go up and he'd never know it. He'd just have to go on repluggin' those wires till finally, sorta totally unannounced, somethin' would short-out in his head. You could almost hear like his whole system shut down, and he'd be out cold somewhere. Maybe ona floor, ina chair.

Maybe a beat, but he continues the same.

Then, you know, he was a twitcher. Like a dog. Even in his sleep, which was something I never saw on a human being while they was sleepin'. Like a dog is chasing maybe a rabbit, or gettin' run after by a wolf, but you'd watch Johnny and say, Johnny what the hell are you dreamin' you're chasin'? Then he'd wake up and keep right on twitchin'. You know, the foot is goin' or the fingers are goin'. He'd be biting at his lip or digging at his cheek like a fuckin' junkie, which I don't think he ever was, 'cause he worked for a hospital, procuring, and coulda brought anythin' home but never did, except stories about the fuckin' nurses and orderlies tryin' to steal him blind, falsifying records on him, but he never said he was, and he'd lie, but his lies was always telling things on himself like he was worse than he was. Like he said he'd left his wife and kid back in Arkansas when he was seventeen, and really missed the little daughter, but like he fuckin' never had no kids. The wife, yeah, but—and a lot of shit like he'd been in jail, which he hadn't and all. But he, you know, used to shoot up but he never worked up a habit, 'cause probably he never, at that time, had the bread for it and you can't imagine a worse thief than Johnny, so he'd never make it as a junkie, 'less he had some john supportin' him in it. But he never said he was even an out-and-out user, so you can be pretty sure he wasn't. Which also he wasn't the type 'cause junkies are zombies even before they get hooked. They're basically lazy people don't want the responsibility of livin'. Anyway, you're not gonna catch no twitcher on the shit, 'cause it'd be like, you know, a waste of good shit. And Johnny was this, you know, he'd get his fingers goin' in his hair, I'd look over and say, "Aww, Jesus, Johnny," 'cause there'd be this like patch of red hair in the middle of all his like dirty blond and he'd say, "What, have I got myself bleedin' again?" And you couldn't figger what a basically nice-lookin' guy was always fuckin' himself over like that, but that was just all those wires he was repluggin' all the time. Like the only reason he had a good body was he had these weights, but he'd use 'em like to work off energy not to build himself up. That's what I say, his mom said he was born with it. But he like burned calories like nothin' I ever saw. Ate more than me and he's what? Five-eight, which he thought was short but it isn't like freakish or nothin' to worry about and weighed maybe a buck forty but he used to say like basically his body was a very inefficient machine. He was like a real gas burner.

Beat. He thinks a minute.

He was gonna open a delivery service. This from a guy who had a money job—and he'd be the only deliverer. On his bike. He used to sit and map out routes one place to another. He called himself the Manhattan Transit. Used to make practice runs; you know, during rush hour. But this was just a way to blow off that nervous stuff he had but it didn't work out 'cause he had no business sense. He could organize anything, but he couldn't start something. He went so far he made up this ad and put it in the *Village Voice* two weeks running with our phone number on it. This was during a two-week vacation he had. We was goin' to go down to St. Pete, then he got this idea. Only the damnedest thing, the phone never rung once. No, that's not true. Once about six months later I picked up the phone, said, hello, this guy says, "Is this the Manhattan Transit?" I said it used to be but they sold their bicycle.

Beat.

He would of been good at it. I said he should work at some place where they use messengers but he wasn't interested in workin' for somebody else. He was already doin' that, he had a regular job you'd think kept him so crazy he wouldn't have time to dream up some schemes, but you got to remember all those wires in his head—and he wasn't meant to work in a office. Twitchers are hell in a office. He was at St. Vincent's first, then up to Doctors Hospital and back to St. Vincent's, runnin' procurements for like the whole hospital. Ordering truckloads of rubbing alcohol and all the prescription stuff, the bedpans and walkers, so you know it wasn't no snap, but one wire in his head was always out in the rain on his bike using this like photographic map of the city: the one-way streets, and places blocked off for school kids at recess time. You probably seen him. He's the guy goin' about five times faster than the traffic. And fightin' everythin'. Nothin' was easy. Went at everythin' crazy. He'd get off work, his face all red, you'd know he'd been diggin' at himself again. That he'd be up all night workin' on the bike. So I don't want to make him sound easy. He was anything butta easy sort of person. I was the easy one.

Pause. He stretches, or even gets up, then sits back down. He looks off, thinking.

I was the easy one. He was always wantin' to change things, I didn't care how things was. Then he was always changin' jobs, or tryin' to. He'd blow up at somebody and walk out, they'd always ask him to come back and I been workin' at the same bakery twenty years. Since I was sixteen. And I like it 'cause they're old fashioned and do it the same way they always did. You'd think bakin' bread is nothin' with the machines they use. Doin' all the measuring and mixin' and kneadin', what's to do but carry the trays to the ovens and back, but yeast is a livin' thing; it can't be taken for granted. One batch ain't like the next, and the humidity and temperature in the room makes a difference. Johnny liked it. I couldn't smell it on me but he liked the smell. He said people take on the character of their work and I figured I was gradually becoming this nice crusty loaf of Italian bread. But the way I think of it it's good, 'cause, like I said, it's nourishing and it's a live thing. Bread. But I wasn't foolin' myself that it was a job that calls for a lot of thinkin'. Like Johnny's. Instinct, maybe. Also the money ain't bad and you always got fresh bread. Only thing I didn't like was I worked nights and he worked days.

Pause. He looks at the cops.

Hell, that got a reaction, didn't it? Now you're thinkin', "He ain't our kinna guy after all. Good, we ain't gotta worry about it." But I was, I used to be, I know all that. But circumstances are crazy things; the things that can happen all of a sudden change everything. Like I'd never thought much of myself as part of anything. I was, you know, I thought I was above everything. I just watched it. But really, I didn't know how to get involved in it.

Beat.

So, I get off work at seven, I'm eatin' at this place I always did, Johnny's havin' breakfast. He's depressed 'cause the Cosmos folded. Soccer team. I think they'd folded about five years back but he'd got to thinkin' about it again. And we're talkin' about atmospheric pressure, which is something it happens I've read a lot about, and we're both readers that only read factual stuff. Only I read slow and forget it and he reads like tearin' through things and remembers. And we'd both been married when we was kids, and had a kid of our own, only, you know, it turned out he didn't. And he said he was gay now and he'd been like fuckin' everythin' in sight for five years only he'd got frustrated with it and hadn't been laid in a month, and we're bitchin' our jobs and he got up and goes off for a minute and comes back and says why don't we go around the corner to his apartment 'cause we're takin' up two seats at the counter and this is a business based on volume and I said, no, you got to go to work and he said . . . "I just called in sick."

He smiles, then thinks about it. A frown, a troubled pause.

That's funny. He really did, first time I met him, called in sick. I never thought about that till right now.

Beat.

71

Jesus, all that talkin' about food makes me realize I ain't eaten in two days.

A beat. He looks at the cops expectantly. Apparently there is no reaction.

Fuck it, skip it. So anyway, if you'da said I'd be livin' wid a guy I'da said, you know, go fuck yourself. And it stayed like that. It was somethin' that always surprised me, you know? Well, of course you don't. Assholes. But I'd wake up, go in the livin' room, he'd be in a chair or somethin', you know, twitchin' like he was deliverin' somethin' somewhere. Or actually sometimes he'd be in bed there. And it always like surprised me. I'd think, what the hell do you know about this? If he'd been like a big old hairy guy or something probably nothing would have happened, but Johnny didn't have hair on his body, he had like this peach fuzz all over him that make him feel like . . . skip it. I'm your kinna guy, right? I don't think. I don't analyze. So you know . . . we had like . . . three years. We did go down to St. Pete. He'd heard about it, he'd always wanted to go. We didn't like it. We went on down to Key West, he'd heard about that, too. That was worse. We come back, rented a car, went up to Vermont. And that was good. Except for Johnny drivin', I couldn't let him drive 'cause he'd go crazy. We'd get behind a tractor or somethin', he'd go ape. Also I'd get dizzy on the roads all up and down and curvin' and Johnny being this like aerobic driver.

Pause.

So after three years, when he started gettin' sick—they was very good about it at the hospital. They let him come to work for a while. Then, you know, like I said, he'd dig at himself and bleed, so that wasn't possible. That'd be real bad. So then I started being the one that was crazy all the time and I'd get off and come home in the morning, he'd be starin' out the window or somethin'. He'd say, "I slept fourteen hours." It was like this blessing for him; like

72

this miracle, he couldn't believe it. I guess everything that was goin' on in him, I guess was interesting to him. He was like studying it. I'd say, "What?" And he'd hold up his hand for me to be quiet for a long time and then he'd say, "I'd never have believed pain could be that bad. This is amazing." You know, he had like his intestines all eaten out and that and he had insurance and the hospital was good to him. They all visited him, but he didn't take the painkillers. He was curious about it.

He looks around, then goes on rather flatly.

Then he got worse and started takin' 'em.

Beat.

You could see by his expression that he hadn't thought he was gonna do that. The staff, the nurses and you know the volunteers, the ghouls that get off on that, they were okay. They didn't get in our way much. (*Searching, becoming frustrated*) What I couldn't believe was that I didn't have it. I got the fuckin' test, it was negative. I couldn't believe that. Twice. I couldn't figger that, 'cause like the first time I was with him, I just fucked him and he like laid up against me and jerked off. And that was sorta what we did for a while. That was our pattern; you know, you fall into routines. But after a while, you get familiar with someone, I was all over him. No way I wasn't exposed to that like three times a week for three years. What the hell was goin' on? I got to thinkin' maybe he didn't have it, maybe it was somethin' else, but . . .

He settles down, pauses, thinks of something else.

He had these friends at the hospital, offered him somethin', I don't know what, take him out of his misery, he didn't take it, he wanted to see it through to the end like. (*A little frustration creeps back*) See, my problem was I didn't really know what he was goin' through. You help and you watch and it tears you up, sure, but you don't know *what*, you know, whatta you know?

Beat.

He wanted to come home, but . . . uh . . .

Pause. He regards the cops.

This is the only part you fucks care about, so listen up. We wanted him to be home for the end, but it slipped up on us. We thought he'd come home another time but he went into this like semicoma and just went right outta sight, he just sank. I didn't know if he recognized me or not. I got this old poster of the Cosmos and put it up on the wall across from the bed. They had him propped up in bed, but he just looked scared. He saw it and he said, "What's that?" You know, you know you know everythin' in the room and it's all familiar, and he hadn't seen that before. Probably it was just this big dark thing in front of him that he couldn't tell what it was and it scared him. He didn't understand it. (*Looking around*) This gets bloody, so if you're faint of heart or anything . . . (*Looking up*) All you fuckers out in TV land, recordin' this shit for fuckin' posterity; check your focus, this is hot shit, they're gonna wanna know this.

Pause.

So the nurse comes by, I said he's restin'. She was glad to skip him. And I took off my clothes and held him. He was sayin', it sounded like, "This is curious." And there was just like nothin' to him.

Pause.

See the problem is, like I said, I was the one who was crazy now. And, uh, well, to hell with it. I'm your kinna guy, fellas, I won't think about it. We do what we do, we do what's gotta be done. (*And rather coldly, or that is what he tries for*) So he died in my arms

74

and I held him a long time and then I cut a place on his cheek where he used to dig and on his chest where he used to gouge out these red marks and in his hair. And when the blood came I licked it off him. Cleaned him up. So then the nurse come, you know, and shit a brick and called you guys. But they let me hold him till you come. I guess they was afraid of me. Or maybe of all the blood. Then they knew I had to be crazy, 'cause like we agreed, I'm not the kinna guy'd do somethin' like dat. What they thought, I think, was that I'd killed him, but that wasn't what he wanted and what I had to consider now was myself. And what I wanted.

Pause.

So if it don't take again, then I'm like fucked, which wouldn't be the first time. I guess there's gonna be maybe some compensation in knowin' I did what I could.

A *long wandering pause, then he looks at the cops.*

So. Are you happy now?

A *pause. Eight counts. Blackout.*

THE END

LANFORD WILSON's *plays include* Lemon Sky, *the Pulitzer Prize-winning* Talley's Folley *and* Burn This. A Poster of the Cosmos *was first presented on June 8, 1988 in New York City, as part of Ensemble Studio Theatre's annual one-act play marathon. It was included in* The Best Short Plays 1989.

Safe Sex

by Harvey Fierstein

PLAYWRIGHT'S NOTE

Never lose your sense of humor.

For my darling Court Miller

As the houselights dim we hear the crashing of waves on a beach. As the darkness grows so do the sounds. The waves are joined by the breathing and guttural whispers of two people making love. The sounds slowly become words.

GHEE: Oh.
MEAD: Hah.
GHEE: Ho.
MEAD: Ah.
GHEE: No.
MEAD: Wha?
GHEE: No.
MEAD: Ya.
GHEE: Oh!
MEAD: Yeah.
GHEE: No!
MEAD: Why?
GHEE: Stop.
MEAD: No!
GHEE: No!
MEAD: Come on.
GHEE: You can't do that.
MEAD: It's all right.
GHEE: It's not.
MEAD: Don't stop.
GHEE: You can't do that.
MEAD: It's all right.
GHEE: It's not on the list.

MEAD: I need you.
GHEE: Check the list.
MEAD: Please.
GHEE: Where's the list?
MEAD: Don't.
GHEE: I'm checking the list.
MEAD: It's all right.
GHEE: Where's the light?
MEAD: Come on.
GHEE: I can't find the light.
MEAD: Come back here.
GHEE (*Yelling*): It's not safe. Stop!

The lights pop on brightly. The waves and all other sound ends abruptly as we stare at a bright white lit stage that is bare except for a giant fire-engine red seesaw (teeter-totter). As simply designed as possible, the balancing board has no handles; the base is triangular. Ghee and Mead lie flat on the plank, facing up, their bare feet touching in the center, their heads at opposite ends. They are clothed in the sheerest of fabrics, the palest of pastels. They are perfectly balanced; the plank is perfectly horizontal. They both pant, out of breath, from the struggle.

GHEE (*Slow and definite*): Don't touch me.

Mead does not move or react.

GHEE: Did you hear what I said?

No reaction.

GHEE: I'll get the list.
MEAD: Don't bother.
GHEE: I'm sure it wasn't safe.
MEAD: Sure.
GHEE: I'll show you right on the list. (*Pause*) You want to see it on the list?

MEAD: Forget it.

GHEE: 'Cause you know I'm right and you know that if I show it to you right on the list in black-and-white then you'll have to admit that I'm right. Right?

MEAD: Right.

GHEE: You don't believe me. I'll get the list.

MEAD (*Covering his face with his hands*): Forget it. Just forget it. It doesn't matter. It's over.

Silence between them.

GHEE: There aren't many things that I know a lot about, but on "Safe Sex" I happen to be an expert.

Another silence.

GHEE: Did you say something?

MEAD: No.

GHEE: I hate when you get like this. Now you're mad at me when all I was trying to do was protect us both.

No response.

GHEE: Why can't you stop when I ask you to? Huh?

No response.

GHEE: Why does it always have to come to hurt feelings?

Ghee sits up straight. He sees that Mead is withdrawn. He drops his head.

GHEE: I'm scared, all right? What's so hard to understand? I'm scared!

No response.

81

GHEE: Being scared is smart. You have to be scared. You're supposed to be scared. You're not normal if you're not scared. Everyone's scared.

No response.

GHEE: And I suppose you're not scared?
MEAD: I'm concerned.
GHEE: You're scared.
MEAD: I'm tired.
GHEE: You're angry.
MEAD: Don't tell me what I am.
GHEE: Don't yell at me.
MEAD: Don't tell me what to do.
GHEE: Don't touch me!

They turn their backs to each other, their legs hanging off the ends of the board. Balanced.

GHEE: The honeymoon is over. (*Pause*) Would you say that was a safe assessment?

No response.

GHEE: Lovers for five-and-a-half years, separated for nearly two years, back together for less than a week and already the honeymoon is over.
MEAD (*Under his breath*): Jerk.
GHEE: Fine. It's all my fault. Dump the blame on me. Like I don't feel guilty enough as is.
MEAD: I said you were a jerk. I wasn't blaming you for being a jerk. I didn't say that being a jerk was your fault. Nor was I attempting to make you feel guilty for being a jerk. I made a simple observation. You're a jerk. Now just drop it.
GHEE: I'm a jerk because in the face of this devastating epidemic I insist we take a few precautions?

MEAD: No. You're just a jerk.

GHEE: Well, that's obvious. Who else but a jerk would want you back? Who else but a jerk would *take* you back? Who else but a jerk would fall in love with you in the first place?

MEAD: Want to see a list?

Ghee spins around and bounces on his end of the seesaw, throwing Mead up into the air.

MEAD: Damn!

Ghee, enjoying the advantage of having Mead at his mercy, bounces the board for emphasis as he speaks.

GHEE: Well, come on. I'm waiting. Let's hear the list. How many?

MEAD: You know.

GHEE: No, you see, I only know about your little Larry. But you said that there's a whole list. And much as you cared for him, I'd hardly call little Larry a list.

MEAD: You want to stop?

GHEE: I want to know how many. Larry and who else?

MEAD: Someone else.

GHEE: Who?

MEAD: You wouldn't know them.

GHEE: Them? How many of "them," Casanova?

MEAD: A few. All right?

GHEE: Fine with me, but I wonder how little Larry felt about your "thems."

MEAD: Once I met Larry there was no one.

GHEE: No one?

MEAD: No one!

Mead bounces hard on the board, tossing Ghee off the ground, restoring the balance.

MEAD: He left me. I didn't leave him.

GHEE: And you came crawling back to me.

MEAD: You begged me to come back.

GHEE: I never begged!

MEAD: I never crawled!

They face off, staring each other down. Mead breaks it.

MEAD: I hate when you do this! You're not happy unless you've got me bashing your head into a wall.

Ghee lies back glamorously.

GHEE: I'm horny.

No response.

GHEE: There's definitely something wrong with me. All I have to do is think about you with someone else and I get crazy. What's that: love?

MEAD: Jealousy.

GHEE: No. You think? No! Well . . . . Yeah. Maybe. But if that's jealousy why does everyone put it down?

MEAD: It's an immature emotion. As irrational as it is insulting. It puts an object value on pure emotion and reduces what should be a free partnership into possessor and possessed.

GHEE: I love it. *(Pause)* Whenever I remember your first telling me that you had slept with someone else, all I can think about is the incredible sex we had that night. *(Giggles)* I don't remember pain, though I know there was. I don't remember anger, though there certainly was some of that. Just this overwhelming burning that flamed into the most intense passion I had ever felt. *(Pause)* Remember?

MEAD: I remember waiting for you to scream. Guilt. I remember waiting to be punished. Hurt. I remember lying next to you after you'd fallen asleep and thinking about the sex we had just had.

GHEE: It was great, wasn't it?

84

MEAD: Could have been. That wasn't important. All I remember is that that was the first time you had touched me, let alone made love to me, in over three months.

GHEE *(Angry)*: That's a lie.

MEAD: True.

GHEE: *(Bolting up to look at him)*: It wasn't three months.

Mead stares Ghee down.

GHEE: Maybe three days. Or maybe three weeks.

Mead just stares. Ghee submits. They both lie back once again. Silence. Balance.

GHEE: I was scared. *(Pause)* It was a bad time for me. All you read about, every headline, the only thing on TV, was AIDS. Joey had already died. Tommy was in the hospital. And how many other friends did we have who had it? How many others did we think might?

MEAD: So, I got locked out.

GHEE: I was scared.

MEAD: Of what? We'd been together for five years. We'd already done everything they said you shouldn't. If one of us did have it, if one of us was going to infect the other, it was already done.

GHEE: I was in a panic. I wasn't thinking.

MEAD: You were thinking. About yourself.

GHEE: And you. Before we met I was pretty wild. You talk about your lists? Boy if I had to, I don't think I could ever remember all the guys I had sex with.

MEAD: You didn't have sex with anyone. Trust me, I laid next to you all those years. Sex is something you don't have. Oh, you fiddle and diddle, but sex? Real sex?

GHEE: I don't remember getting any complaints.

MEAD: You never hung around long enough to hear them.

GHEE: That's bull.

MEAD: Think so?

GHEE: What about us our first year? We never got out of bed.

MEAD: I don't remember.

GHEE: You couldn't keep your hands off me.

MEAD: That so?

GHEE: I used to have to beg for dinner breaks.

MEAD: That was years ago.

GHEE: Years before AIDS.

MEAD: Our problems started years before AIDS. AIDS was your salvation.

GHEE: That's sick.

MEAD: You ran right out, got your list of Do's and Don'ts and embraced it like a priest takes his vows. Safe Sex, there in black-and-white you finally had what you always wanted: a concrete, board-certified, actual, purposeful excuse to avoid intimacy. God, you were in your glory! You waved it in my face with one hand and shoved me across the bed with the other. You took your list and nailed it to the headboard like the goddamned sexual command-ments: "Thou shalt not . . . . Thou shalt not . . . . Thou shalt not . . . ." You're not scared of AIDS, you're scared of sex.

GHEE: Me?

MEAD: Or me.

GHEE: You're scared of sex?

MEAD: You're scared of me.

GHEE: Me scared of you? Don't flatter yourself.

MEAD: When I first started fooling around I reasoned that I was justified. I certainly wasn't getting anything at home. I had a right to look elsewhere. But my lies were so blatant, my excuses so lame . . . . I wanted you to catch me. I wanted you to know that you could lose, actually lose, me. I did it right under your nose, right in your bed . . . . I left phone numbers around, and clothing . . . . And nothing!

GHEE: I suspected.

MEAD: You hoped. Wished even. One more excuse to push me away.

GHEE: And what were you doing? Your fooling around was supposed to make me feel safer? What are you, out of your mind?

MEAD: Didn't it? You just said that the best sex we ever had was after you found out about Larry. When there actually was danger. When I actually could have been infected.

GHEE: That was different. We had Safe Sex.

MEAD: We had Safe Distance, and that's all you've ever wanted.

Silence. Both consider what has been said. Ghee sits up, cross-legged, and looks at Mead.

GHEE: So what're you saying; that I'm a lousy lay?

Mead covers his head in frustration.

GHEE: That your complaint, dearie? That you got stuck with a lukewarm lover? Well, fill your ears with this, buddy: I've got two faucets, hot and cold, and if you were getting lukewarm loving then maybe it's because that's what you dialed.

MEAD: Fine. It's all my fault.

GHEE: Hey, don't try and shut me off. You ran this shower, now stand under it. (*Deep breath*) So, you laid alone in bed, did ya? You were forced to walk the streets for affection, eh? Let me tell you something, Samantha, you could have had all the sex you wanted. You could've had intimacy pouring out your eyeballs. All you had to do was wash up.

MEAD: Cheese and crackers!

GHEE: Shut up! You had your chance to mouth your neo-Nietzsche nonsense, now it's my turn at bat.

Ghee and Mead now sit up fully, legs dangling from the board. They balance.

GHEE: You'd come home to me night after night all hot and sweaty from a hard day's work. You'd drift through the door after stopping for a few brews with the boys, reeking of beer, clothes soaked through, hair as greasy as a used-up peanut butter jar, and you'd throw your arms out to me and say, "Baby, I need your lovin'," and expect me to swoon. I swooned all right!

87

Mead opens his mouth to protest.

GHEE: I said shut up!

Mead shakes his head and remains silent.

GHEE: Now, I will admit to finding the air pretty sexy for the first year. It was like living in a John Garfield fantasy, my very own hot blue-collared lover leaving armpit stains on my settee; but after a year? But I figured it was a stage, a phase. After all, when we were first dating you'd show up perfectly coiffed and cologned, and it was a chore and challenge to melt you down. But here we were, fairly crossing the threshold, and I'd traded my Arthurian knight in for his white horse.

   I will grant you, there are those with penchants for farm follies. I do not, however, happen to march in their number. And I'd say, "Baby, wouldn't you like to clean up first?"

   And you'd say, "No."

   And I'd say, "Darling, how about we take a shower together?"

   And you'd say, "How 'bout we don't?" and laugh a laugh as soiled as your sweat socks.

MEAD: Have you no shame?

GHEE: My sex and sensuality have been attacked. There's no time for illusions. You'd strip down and crawl all filthified into my beautiful crisp clean bed and lie there with a beer in one hand, the remote control in the other, watching some ball game or other . . .

MEAD *(Pushing off the ground with his feet)*: I was waiting for you to come to bed, but you were always off somewhere messing around with who knows what.

GHEE *(Pushing off with his feet as well)*: I was throwing in a wash. I was scared what would happen if I left your clothes in the hamper overnight.

Now, with each countering point, Ghee and Mead push the ground with their feet so that they are soon seesawing like mad.

MEAD: You really stink.

GHEE: I? I!?!?! Now let's talk about your feet. I've seen dogs fall in love with spots of grass where you'd walked barefoot.

MEAD: Now I've heard everything.

GHEE: Not by a long shot.

MEAD: I showered every morning.

GHEE: You'd never know it at night.

MEAD: If I wash my hair at night it stands up funny in the morning.

GHEE: Wash it again.

MEAD: I'd be bald!

GHEE: You'd be happy!

MEAD: *You'd* be happy!

GHEE: And that's bad? You knew how I felt. I told you often enough.

MEAD: You never told me, you nagged.

GHEE: So, you knew. You couldn't make the effort.

MEAD: You're still avoiding the real issue.

GHEE: What's the real issue? That I pushed you away?

MEAD: That you couldn't be with me.

GHEE: I couldn't *breathe* with you.

MEAD: You're impossible!

GHEE: God, I feel great! *(He begins to laugh with excitement)* It feels so good to finally get that said.

Mead stops the seesaw abruptly. His feet on the ground, he has Ghee in his power, up in the air. They face off again, only now it is with sexual excitement.

MEAD: You love the way I smell.

GHEE *(Taunting him)*: That so?

MEAD: You missed me when I wasn't there.

GHEE: Says you.

MEAD: When I'd stay out all night I'd come home and find you in bed with one of my jackets or shirts.

GHEE *(Lying back sexily)*: Maybe I was cold.

Mead begins to bounce the board gently, sensuously.

MEAD: Maybe you was gettin' hot. You always smelled of soap. You showered in the morning, showered before bed, showered after sex . . .

GHEE: I was just trying to keep your stink offa me. I was bathing for two. (*He begins to giggle*)

MEAD: What? Come on, what?

GHEE: Ever notice how pruney my skin was?

MEAD: No. It was soft.

GHEE: My fingertips always looked like something you'd pull out of a box of health-food cereal.

Ghee begins to slowly slide down the board toward Mead. Mead continues to pump the board.

MEAD: Your skin was always cool and lightly moist. I remember powder.

GHEE: I use cornstarch.

MEAD: Silky.

GHEE: Smoother.

MEAD: I'd nustle up against you.

GHEE: Your hands were always dry and rough.

MEAD: I'd pull as close against you as I could.

GHEE: I'd turn my head into the pillow.

MEAD: I couldn't get close enough.

GHEE: I couldn't get far enough away.

MEAD: I rubbed against your back.

GHEE: I'd pull the covers over my head.

MEAD: I kissed your neck.

GHEE: I bit the pillow.

Ghee is almost in his arms. Mead reaches out.

MEAD: I wanted you so badly.

GHEE (*Suddenly jumping up and yelling*): Not bad enough to wash!

MEAD: All right, you win! Let's wash!

GHEE: Now?

MEAD: Together.

GHEE: You mean it?

MEAD: I mean it.

GHEE: I love you.

MEAD (*Arms around him*): Let's go.

GHEE (*Stopping everything*): But is it safe? I'd better check the list.

Mead lies straight back in acute frustration and moans.

GHEE: What's the big deal? It'll take me two seconds and this way we can be sure.

Mead simply moans, shaking his head and covering his face with his arms.

MEAD: No. No. No. No . . .

GHEE: On second thought I'm sure it's safe. No, it's safe. In fact I'm positive it's safe. As a matter of record it is not only safe *but* I believe it is highly recommended. It is, as I now recall, the very first rule on the list. The very cornerstone on which Safe Sex is built. So, let's go for it!

Ghee starts to move. Mead does not.

GHEE: Okay? Let's go!

No movement.

GHEE: All right, we're moving now!

Ghee starts to move. Mead remains still.

GHEE: Okay. GO!!!

Still Mead remains. Ghee looks at him unhappily. He reaches out and lifts one of Mead's legs. He lets go of it and it drops lifelessly. Ghee

91

backs away from Mead and begins to rock the board gently as you would a carriage.

GHEE: You okay? *(A pause)* I did this, didn't I?

No response.

GHEE: Whatever happened to sex being fun?
    Whatever happened to sex being dirty?
    Whatever happened to sex being something we did?
    (Studies Mead) I hope you don't think that I was trying to insult you before. Because I wasn't. Are you insulted?
MEAD: Frustrated.
GHEE: But not insulted.
MEAD: No.
GHEE: Good. *(He lies down flat on his back. Pause)* You wanna play Yahtzee?
MEAD: No.
GHEE: C'mon. Let's play a game. How about Monopoly?
MEAD: No.
GHEE: Scrabble?
MEAD: No.
GHEE: Risk!

Mead jumps with excitement. Ghee quickly pulls away.

GHEE: No! I don't want to play Risk.

Mead lies back down in frustration. Ghee thinks.

GHEE: Can I tell you how I felt about you when we first met? How I felt about us?
MEAD: Be my guest.
GHEE: You won't be insulted.
MEAD: No. Probably just frustrated.
GHEE: Good. *(Fresh start)* You know that you were my first love. My

only love. Except if you count you then and you now. But then you'd have to count me then and me now, so I guess "only" still goes.

You was a baby. I was all growed up. You practically lost your virginity. I'd practically lost count.

I tiptoed through your life, living on the edges, covering my tracks, remaining secret and quiet, and was quite happy. They were different times.

Is it enough to say that they were different times? I mean, I had a life, you had a life and we had a life. I lived in my world, you lived in your world and then we shared a bed. We had great sex, but argued politics: to be or not to be in the closet, separatism, legalization, legislation . . . . Politics were argued, sex was great. Different times.

I believe there were fewer Nautilus machines then. There certainly were fewer gyms. We were certainly happier with ourselves. And we loved each other. We shared what we could when we could and our fear was of them that would not let us be. Our anger was for them that would not let us be. Our comfort was being with each other.

Not so different. But different enough.

When I picture you then, I see a man prone in my bed and waiting. No expectations or demands. Just a man, waiting to be with another man, where he was happy and belonged. A nervous smile, an unassumed pose, patient, excited, warm and delicious.

And we were together without question. There at that moment, in the present, together. Perfectly balanced: need and satisfaction. Evenly matched. We soared. And sex was unimportant like air and water.

We had no lists of Do's and Don'ts. There was no death count. The worst you could get from loving was a broken heart. Which you gave me! And I lived. Remember herpes? Remember crabs? Remember worrying about the clap?

And we were invisible. Nobody knew who we were for sure. We were the great chic mysterious underground and I loved every minute!

And then came now.

Different times. Now we enjoy politics and argue sex. Now they know who we are. We're counted in their surveys. We're numbered in their watchfulness. We're powered in their press. We're courted, polled, placated . . . . The myths slowly peel away and the mysteries fade. Now they know that we're teachers and doctors and lawyers and priests and mothers and babies. Now they see us everywhere: hospitals, classrooms, theatres, obituaries . . . . Now when they tell lies about us we answer back. We've found our voices. We know who we are. They know who we are. And they know that we care what they think.

And all because of a disease. A virus. A virus that you don't get because you're Gay, just because you're human. We were Gay. Now we're human.

Y'know, if anyone had ever tried to tell me that one day I would push you across the bed . . . . But I did. I did because it wasn't safe for one person to love another person as much as I loved you. And that was *then*!

(Fondly looking at Mead; it is as if they were renewing their wedding vows) Now? I love you more now than I did on our most carefree day. I trust you more now than before you renounced our commitment. I need you more now than when you were away from me. I want you more now . . . .

And it's impossible. Even if you fought me and won. Even if you broke through and got me to admit who you truly are to me . . .

We can never touch as before. We can never be as before. "Now" will always define us. Different times. Too late.

(The anger builds inside of him) At last we have Safe Sex.

(Turning accusingly to the audience) Safe for them!

(Pulling back into himself) I'm angry.

I'm frightened.

I'm alone.

MEAD: You're not alone.

GHEE: I feel alone.

Mead jumps to his feet and stands on the very end of his side of the board.

94

MEAD: Well, you're not.

GHEE (*Clutching the board for safety*): What're you doing?

MEAD: I love you.

GHEE: I love you too, now sit down.

MEAD (*Motioning*): Come on then, get up.

GHEE: You're out of your mind.

MEAD: After five years with you, who wouldn't be. Get up.

GHEE: You're going to kill yourself.

MEAD: What're you, scared?

GHEE: It's not safe.

MEAD: Then check your list first and then get up.

GHEE: For this I don't have to check no list.

MEAD: Then come on.

GHEE: No.

MEAD: You want to be alone the rest of your life? I came back once. Want to bet if I come back again?

GHEE (*Starting to stand*): Can't we shower first?

MEAD: Later. Come on, you're doing great.

GHEE (*Almost standing*): I'm scared.

MEAD: This is dangerous. You're supposed to be.

Ghee stands up fully and the board balances once again. They stand at opposite ends, facing each other. Ghee is frightened, Mead is proud of him.

MEAD: These are different times with different rules, but some things never change.

GHEE: What are you talking about?

MEAD: Do you trust me?

GHEE: Yes. Can I get down now?

MEAD: Do you believe in me?

GHEE: I told you I did.

MEAD: And you believe I love you?

GHEE: Whatever you say.

Mead stares.

GHEE: All right. Yes.

Mead takes a step toward Ghee. The board remains perfectly balanced. Ghee is terrified.

MEAD: Do you believe in miracles?
GHEE: I don't know. I guess so.

Mead takes another step toward Ghee. Ghee waves his arms wildly to keep balance but there's no need, the board remains perfectly balanced.

GHEE: I love when you take charge.

Mead takes another step toward Ghee. Ghee begins to relax.

MEAD: I love you.

Mead walks to the exact center of the board. Ghee remains still, hanging in space.

GHEE: I love you too.
MEAD: That's all that matters.

Mead holds out his hands to have Ghee join him in the center. Ghee walks toward him.

MEAD: The rest is a piece of cake.
GHEE *(Reaching him)*: Promise?
MEAD *(Arms around Ghee)*: Promise.
GHEE *(Melting in the embrace)*: Let's shower.

Blackout.

THE END

HARVEY FIERSTEIN *is the Tony award-winning author of* Torch Song Trilogy *and* La Cage aux Folles. Safe Sex *is the umbrella title of three one-act plays that premiered on January 8, 1987 at La Mama in New York, and moved to Broadway on March 19.* Safe Sex *is also the title of the middle one-act; Fierstein himself was the first Ghee.*

The Way We Live Now

A SHORT STORY BY SUSAN SONTAG

ARRANGED FOR THE STAGE BY EDWARD PARONE

A story, a poem, should invent the language in which to tell itself. And the language, the *way* of telling, Susan Sontag has chosen to reveal *The Way We Live Now* is what makes her good "story" memorable: a second-, third- and fourth-hand reporting of facts, events and feelings in witty, unsentimental, often hilarious detail by and/or about twenty-six people (one for every letter of the alphabet) gathered around a mutual friend who has AIDS (although the term is never used).

When the Mark Taper Forum asked me to direct a reading in their Literary Cabaret Series I immediately suggested this story, still fresh in my memory more than a year after I read it in *The New Yorker*.

But *how* to read it?

There was never any question in my mind that the story should be read exactly as written, right down to the last comma (it's a punctuator's nightmare that must have tested even *The New Yorker*'s expert staff); I did not want to "dramatize" or adapt it. But after a dozen or so readings everything fell into place when I realized I was thinking of this as a musical piece, chamber music for winds or strings, virtuosic voices all serving, alone or in combination, a single work. This tactic also provided the feeling of *gathering*—friends at a bedside, friends in hallways, each other's rooms, on telephones—and all focused toward one person, going toward one place, the dozen notes in a single sound.

And so it became "A Reading for Five Voices"—with emphasis on the word *reading*. It's the first time in my life as a director when I felt I had to instruct, sometimes implore, actors to, above all, *not* act. We were there to read, seamlessly, Ms. Sontag's story, albeit in a public, entertaining way, and to try to achieve that curious blend of involvement and removal that is one of the story's distinctions. And an important part of the rehearsal process was spent avoiding the temptation to act or to "do" character voices (which could quickly come to sound like a Magoo cartoon).

The thing to remember about a reading is that it's the *voice* in which the writer chose to write that matters. Perhaps the best way to read this, or any, story is to imagine yourself the writer. And if there is any "role" to play, it's that.

For the Mark Taper Forum reading we used three women and two men, although I think any combination of men and women could work as well. It's the pitch and timbre of the voices that should be considered. Susan Sontag has provided the key.

—Edward Parone

A *Reading for Five Voices*

VOICE 1: At first he was just losing weight, he felt only a little ill, Max said to Ellen,

VOICE 2: and he didn't call for an appointment with his doctor, according to Greg, because he was managing to keep on working at more or less the same rhythm,

VOICE 3: but he did stop smoking, Tanya pointed out, which suggests he was frightened, but also that he wanted, even more than he knew, to be healthy, or healthier,

VOICE 4: or maybe just to gain back a few pounds, said Orson,

VOICE 5: for he told her, Tanya went on, that he expected to be climbing the walls (isn't that what people say?) and found, to his surprise, that he didn't miss cigarettes at all and reveled in the sensation of his lungs' being ache-free for the first time in years.

VOICE 4: But did he have a good doctor, Stephen wanted to know, since it would have been crazy not to go for a checkup after the pressure was off and he was back from the conference in Helsinki, even if by then he was feeling better.

VOICE 1: And he said, to Frank, that he would go,

VOICE 3: even though he was indeed frightened, as he admitted to Jan, but who wouldn't be frightened now,

VOICE 2: though, odd as that might seem, he hadn't been worrying until recently, he avowed to Quentin, it was only in the last six months that he had the metallic taste of panic in his mouth, because becoming seriously ill was something that happened to other people,

103

VOICE 4: a normal delusion, he observed to Paolo, if one was thirty-eight and had never had a serious illness;

VOICE 3: he wasn't, as Jan confirmed, a hypochondriac. Of course, it was hard not to worry, everyone was worried,

VOICE 5: but it wouldn't do to panic, because, as Max pointed out to Quentin, there wasn't anything one could do except wait and hope, wait and start being careful, be careful, and hope. And even if one did prove to be ill, one shouldn't give up, they had new treatments that promised an arrest of the disease's inexorable course, research was progressing.

VOICE 1: It seemed that everyone was in touch with everyone else several times a week, checking in,

VOICE 4: I've never spent so many hours at a time on the phone, Stephen said to Kate, and when I'm exhausted after the two or three calls made to me, giving me the latest, instead of switching off the phone to give myself a respite I tap out the number of another friend or acquaintance, to pass on the news.

VOICE 5: I'm not sure I can afford to think so much about it, Ellen said, and I suspect my own motives, there's something morbid I'm getting used to, getting excited by, this must be like what people felt in London during the Blitz.

VOICE 3: As far as I know, I'm not at risk, but you never know, said Aileen.

VOICE 2: This thing is totally unprecedented, said Frank.

VOICE 4: But don't you think he ought to see a doctor, Stephen insisted.

VOICE 2: Listen, said Orson, you can't force people to take care of themselves, and what makes you think the worst, he could be just run down, people still do get ordinary illnesses, awful ones, why are you assuming it has to be *that*.

VOICE 4: But all I want to be sure, said Stephen, is that he understands the options, because most people don't, that's why they won't see a doctor or have the test, they think there's nothing one can do.

VOICE 1: But is there anything one can do, he said to Tanya (according to Greg), I mean what do I gain if I go to the doctor; if I'm really ill, he's reported to have said, I'll find out soon enough.

SCENE TWO

VOICE 3: And when he was in the hospital, his spirits seemed to lighten, according to Donny.

VOICE 5: He seemed more cheerful than he had been in the last months, Ursula said,

VOICE 4: and the bad news seemed to come almost as a relief, according to Ira,

VOICE 2: as a truly unexpected blow, according to Quentin,

VOICE 1: but you'd hardly expect him to have said the same thing to all his friends, because his relation to Ira was so different from his relation to Quentin (this according to Quentin, who was proud of their friendship), and perhaps he thought Quentin wouldn't be undone by seeing him weep, but Ira insisted that couldn't be the reason he behaved so differently with each, and that maybe he was feeling less shocked, mobilizing his strength to fight for his life, at the moment he saw Ira but overcome by feelings of hopelessness when Quentin arrived with flowers,

VOICE 2: because anyway the flowers threw him into a bad mood, as Quentin told Kate, since the hospital room was choked with flowers, you couldn't have crammed another flower into that room,

VOICE 5: but surely you're exaggerating, Kate said, smiling, everybody likes flowers.

VOICE 2: Well, who wouldn't exaggerate at a time like this, Quentin said sharply. Don't you think *this* is an exaggeration.

VOICE 5: Of course I do, said Kate gently, I was only teasing, I mean I didn't mean to tease.

VOICE 2: I know that, Quentin said, with tears in his eyes,

VOICE 5: and Kate hugged him and said well, when I go this evening I guess I won't bring flowers, what does he want,

VOICE 1: and Quentin said, according to Max,

VOICE 2: what he likes best is chocolate.

VOICE 5: Is there anything else, asked Kate, I mean like chocolate but not chocolate.

VOICE 2: Licorice, said Quentin, blowing his nose. And besides that. Aren't *you* exaggerating now, Quentin said, smiling.

VOICE 5: Right, said Kate, so if I want to bring him a whole raft of stuff, besides chocolate and licorice, what else.

VOICE 2: Jelly beans, Quentin said.

SCENE THREE

VOICE 4: He didn't want to be alone, according to Paolo, and lots of people came in the first week,

VOICE 1: and the Jamaican nurse said there were other patients on the floor who would be glad to have the surplus flowers, and people weren't afraid to visit,

VOICE 5: it wasn't like the old days, as Kate pointed out to Aileen,

VOICE 3: they're not even segregated in the hospital anymore, as Hilda observed, there's nothing on the door of his room warning visitors of the possibility of contagion, as there was a few years ago; in fact, he's in a double room

VOICE 2: and, as he told Orson, the old guy on the far side of the curtain

VOICE 4: (who's clearly on the way out, said Stephen)

VOICE 2: doesn't even have the disease,

VOICE 5: so, as Kate went on, you really should go and see him, he'd be happy to see you, he likes having people visit, you aren't not going because you're afraid, are you.

VOICE 3: Of course not, Aileen said, but I don't know what to say, I think I'll feel awkward, which he's bound to notice, and that will make him feel worse, so I won't be doing him any good, will I.

VOICE 5: But he won't notice anything, Kate said, patting Aileen's hand, it's not like that, it's not the way you imagine, he's not judging people or wondering about their motives, he's just happy to see his friends.

VOICE 3: But I never was really a friend of his, Aileen said, you're a friend, he's always liked you, you told me he talks about Nora with you, I know he likes me, he's even attracted to me, but he respects you.

VOICE 2: But, according to Wesley, the reason Aileen was so stingy with her visits was that she could never have him to herself, there were always others there already and by the time they left still others had arrived, she'd been in love with him for years,

VOICE 4: and I can understand, said Donny, that Aileen should feel bitter that if there could have been a woman friend he did more than occasionally bed, a woman he really loved,

VOICE 2: and my God, Victor said, who had known him in those years, he was crazy about Nora, what a heartrending couple they were, two surly angels,

VOICE 4: then it couldn't have been she.

SCENE FOUR

VOICE 1: And when some of the friends, the ones who came every day, waylaid the doctor in the corridor,

VOICE 4: Stephen was the one who asked the most informed questions, who'd been keeping up not just with stories that appeared several times a week in the *Times*

VOICE 2: (which Greg confessed to have stopped reading, unable to stand it anymore)

VOICE 4: but with articles in the medical journals published here and in England and France, and who knew socially one of the principal doctors in Paris who was doing some much-publicized research on the disease,

VOICE 1: but his doctor said little more than that the pneumonia was not life-threatening, the fever was subsiding, of course he was still weak but he was responding well to the antibiotics, that he'd have to complete his stay in the hospital, which entailed a minimum of twenty-one days on the IV, before she could start him on the new drug, for she was optimistic about the possibility of getting him into the protocol;

VOICE 5: and when Victor said that if he had so much trouble eating

VOICE 3: (he'd say to everyone, when they coaxed him to eat some of the hospital meals, that food didn't taste right, that he had a funny metallic taste in his mouth)

VOICE 5: it couldn't be good that friends were bringing him all that chocolate,

VOICE 1: the doctor just smiled and said that in these cases the patient's morale was also an important factor, and if chocolate made him feel better she saw no harm in it, which worried Stephen, as Stephen said later to Donny, because they wanted to believe in the promises and taboos of today's high-tech medicine

VOICE 4: but here this reassuringly curt and silver-haired specialist in the disease, someone quoted frequently in the papers, was talking like some oldfangled country G.P. who tells the family that tea with honey or chicken soup may do as much for the patient as penicillin,

VOICE 2: which might mean, as Max said, that they were just going through the motions of treating him, that they were not sure about what to do,

VOICE 4: or rather, as Xavier interjected, that they didn't know what the hell they were doing,

VOICE 3: that the truth, the real truth, as Hilda said, upping the ante, was that they didn't, the doctors, really have any hope.

SCENE FIVE

VOICE 4: Oh, no, said Lewis, I can't stand it, wait a minute, I can't believe it, are you sure, I mean are they sure, have they done all the tests, it's getting so when the phone rings I'm scared to answer because I think it will be someone telling me someone else is ill;

VOICE 2: but did Lewis really not know until yesterday, Robert said testily, I find that hard to believe, everybody is talking about it, it seems impossible that someone wouldn't have called Lewis;

VOICE 1: and perhaps Lewis did know, was for some reason pretending not to know already, because, Jan recalled,

VOICE 5: didn't Lewis say something months ago to Greg,

VOICE 1: and not only to Greg,

VOICE 5: about his not looking well,

VOICE 3: losing weight,

VOICE 2: and being worried about him

VOICE 5: and wishing he'd see a doctor,

VOICE 1: so it couldn't come as a total surprise.

VOICE 5: Well, everybody is worried about everybody now, said Betsy, that seems to be the way we live, the way we live now. And, after all, they were once very close, doesn't Lewis still have the keys to his apartment, you know the way you let someone keep the keys after you've broken up, only a little because you hope the person might just saunter in, drunk or high, late some evening, but mainly because it's wise to have a few sets of keys strewn around town, if you live alone, at the top of a former commercial building that, pretentious as it is, will never acquire a doorman or even a resident superintendent, someone whom you can call on for the keys late one night if you find you've lost yours or have locked yourself out.

VOICE 3: Who else has keys, Tanya inquired, I was thinking somebody might drop by tomorrow before coming to the hospital and bring some treasures,

VOICE 4: because the other day, Ira said, he was complaining about how dreary the hospital room was, and how it was like being locked up in a motel room,

VOICE 1: which got everybody started telling funny stories about motel rooms they'd known, and at Ursula's story,

VOICE 5: about the Luxury Budget Inn in Schenectady,

VOICE 1: there was an uproar of laughter around his bed, while he watched them in silence, eyes bright with fever, all the while, as Victor recalled,

VOICE 2: gobbling that damn chocolate.

VOICE 3: But, according to Jan, whom Lewis's keys enabled to tour the swank of his bachelor lair with an eye to bringing over some art consolation to brighten up the hospital room, the Byzantine icon wasn't on the wall over his bed,

VOICE 1: and that was a puzzle until Orson remembered that he'd recounted without seeming upset

VOICE 2: (this disputed by Greg)

VOICE 4: that the boy he'd recently gotten rid of had stolen it, along with four of the *maki-e* lacquer boxes, as if these were objects as easy to sell on the street as a TV or a stereo.

VOICE 5: But he's always been very generous, Kate said quietly,

VOICE 4: and though he loves beautiful things isn't really attached to them, to things, as Orson said,

VOICE 2: which is unusual in a collector, as Frank commented,

VOICE 5: and when Kate shuddered and tears sprang to her eyes

VOICE 4: and Orson inquired anxiously if he, Orson, had said something wrong,

VOICE 1: she pointed out that they'd begun talking about him in a retrospective mode, summing up what he was like, what made them fond of him,

VOICE 5: as if he were finished, completed, already a part of the past.

SCENE SIX

VOICE 2: Perhaps he was getting tired of having so many visitors, said Robert,

VOICE 5: who was, as Ellen couldn't help mentioning, someone who had come only twice and was probably looking for a reason not to be in regular attendance,

VOICE 3: but there could be no doubt, according to Ursula, that his spirits had dipped, not that there was any discouraging news from the doctors,

VOICE 1: and he seemed now to prefer being alone a few hours of the day; and he told Donny that he'd begun keeping a diary for the first time in his life, because he wanted to record the course of his mental reactions to this astonishing turn of events, to do something parallel to what the doctors were doing, who came every morning and conferred at his bedside about his body, and that perhaps it wasn't so important what he wrote in it,

VOICE 2: which amounted, as he said wryly to Quentin, to little more than the usual banalities about terror and amazement that this was happening to him, to him also,

VOICE 1: plus the usual remorseful assessments of his past life, his pardonable superficialities, capped by resolves to live better, more deeply, more in touch with his work and his friends, and not to care so passionately about what people thought of him, interspersed with admonitions to himself that in this situation his will to live counted more than anything else and that if he really wanted to live, and trusted life, and liked himself well enough

VOICE 2: (down, ol' debbil Thanatos!),

VOICE 1: he *would* live, he would be an exception;

VOICE 2: but perhaps all this, as Quentin ruminated, talking on the phone to Kate, wasn't the point, the point was that by the very keeping of the diary he was accumulating something to reread one day, slyly staking out his claim to a future time, in which the diary would be an object, a relic, in which he might not actually reread it, because he would want to have put this ordeal behind him, but the diary would be there in the drawer of his stupendous Majorelle desk,

VOICE 1: and he could already, he did actually say to Quentin one late sunny afternoon, propped up in the hospital bed, with the stain of chocolate framing one corner of a heartbreaking smile, see himself in the penthouse, the October sun streaming through those clear windows instead of this streaked one, and the diary, the pathetic diary, safe inside the drawer.

SCENE SEVEN

VOICE 4: It doesn't matter about the treatment's side effects, Stephen said (when talking to Max), I don't know why you're so worried about that, every strong treatment has some dangerous side effects, it's inevitable,

VOICE 3: you mean otherwise the treatment wouldn't be effective, Hilda interjected,

VOICE 4: and anyway, Stephen went on doggedly, just because there *are* side effects it doesn't mean he has to get them, or all of them, each one, or even some of them. That's just a list of all the possible

111

things that could go wrong, because the doctors have to cover themselves, so they make up a worst-case scenario,

VOICE 5: but isn't what's happening to him, and to so many other people, Tanya interrupted, a worst-case scenario, a catastrophe no one could have imagined, it's too cruel,

VOICE 4: and isn't everything a side effect, quipped Ira, even *we* are all side effects,

VOICE 2: but we're not bad side effects, Frank said, he likes having his friends around, and we're helping each other, too;

VOICE 4: because his illness sticks us all in the same glue, mused Xavier, and, whatever the jealousies and grievances from the past that have made us wary and cranky with each other, when something like this happens (the sky is falling, the sky is falling!) you understand what's really important.

VOICE 1: I agree, Chicken Little, he is reported to have said.

VOICE 2: But don't you think, Quentin observed to Max, that being as close to him as we are, making time to drop by the hospital every day, is a way of our trying to define ourselves more firmly and irrevocably as the well, those who aren't ill, who aren't going to fall ill, as if what's happened to him couldn't happen to us, when in fact the chances are that before long one of us will end up where he is, which is probably what he felt when he was one of the cohort visiting Zack in the spring (you never knew Zack, did you?), and, according to Clarice, Zack's widow, he didn't come very often, he said he hated hospitals, and didn't feel he was doing Zack any good, that Zack would see on his face how uncomfortable he was.

VOICE 3: Oh, he was one of those, Aileen said. A coward. Like me.

SCENE EIGHT

VOICE 1: And after he was sent home from the hospital, and Quentin had volunteered to move in and was cooking meals and taking telephone messages and keeping the mother in Mississippi informed,

VOICE 2: well, mainly keeping her from flying to New York and

112

heaping her grief on her son and confusing the household routine with her oppressive ministrations,

VOICE 1: he was able to work an hour or two in his study, on days he didn't insist on going out, for a meal or a movie, which tired him.

VOICE 5: He seemed optimistic, Kate thought, his appetite was good,

VOICE 2: and what he said, Orson reported, was that he agreed when Stephen advised him that the main thing was to keep in shape, he was a fighter, right, he wouldn't be who he was if he weren't,

VOICE 4: and was he ready for the big fight, Stephen asked rhetorically (as Max told it to Donny), and he said you bet, and Stephen added it could be a lot worse, you could have gotten the disease two years ago, but now so many scientists are working on it, the American team and the French team, everyone bucking for that Nobel Prize a few years down the road, that all you have to do is stay healthy for another year or two and then there will be good treatment, real treatment.

VOICE 1: Yes, he said, Stephen said, my timing is good.

VOICE 5: And Betsy, who had been climbing on and rolling off macrobiotic diets for a decade, came up with a Japanese specialist she wanted him to see

VOICE 4: but thank God, Donny reported, he'd had the sense to refuse,

VOICE 1: but he did agree to see Victor's visualization therapist,

VOICE 3: although what could one possibly visualize, said Hilda, when the point of visualizing disease was to see it as an entity with contours, borders, here rather than there, something limited, something you were the host of, in the sense that you could disinvite the disease, while this was so total;

VOICE 4: or would be, Max said.

VOICE 2: But the main thing, said Greg, was to see that he didn't go the macrobiotic route, which might be harmless for plump Betsy but could only be devastating for him, lean as he'd always been, with all the cigarettes and other appetite-suppressing chemicals he'd been welcoming into his body for years;

VOICE 4: and now was hardly the time, as Stephen pointed out, to be worried about cleaning up his act, and eliminating the chemical

additives and other pollutants that we're all blithely or not so
blithely feasting on, blithely since we're healthy, healthy as we
can be;

VOICE 2: so far, Ira said.

VOICE 5: Meat and potatoes is what I'd be happy to see him eating,
Ursula said wistfully.

VOICE 2: And spaghetti and clam sauce, Greg added.

VOICE 3: And thick cholesterol-rich omelets with smoked mozzarella,
suggested Yvonne, who had flown from London for the weekend
to see him.

VOICE 2: Chocolate cake, said Frank.

VOICE 5: Maybe not chocolate cake, Ursula said, he's already eating so
much chocolate.

SCENE NINE

VOICE 1: And when, not right away but still only three weeks later, he
was accepted into the protocol for the new drug, which took
considerable behind-the-scenes lobbying with the doctors,

VOICE 4: he talked less about being ill, according to Donny,

VOICE 5: which seemed like a good sign, Kate felt, a sign that he was
not feeling like a victim, feeling not that he *had* a disease but,
rather, was living *with* a disease (that was the right cliché, wasn't
it?),

VOICE 3: a more hospitable arrangement, said Jan, a kind of cohabita-
tion which implied that it was something temporary, that it could
be terminated,

VOICE 5: but terminated how, said Hilda, and when you say hospitable, Jan, I hear hospital.

VOICE 4: And it was encouraging, Stephen insisted, that from the
start, at least from the time he was finally persuaded to make the
telephone call to his doctor, he was willing to say the name of the
disease, pronounce it often and easily, as if it were just another
word, like boy or gallery or cigarette or money or deal,

VOICE 2: as in no big deal, Paolo interjected,

VOICE 4: because, as Stephen continued, to utter the name is a sign of health, a sign that one has accepted being who one is, mortal, vulnerable, not exempt, not an exception after all, it's a sign that one is willing, truly willing, to fight for one's life.

VOICE 3: And we must say the name, too, and often, Tanya added, we mustn't lag behind him in honesty, or let him feel that, the effort of honesty having been made, it's something done with and he can go on to other things.

VOICE 2: One is so much better prepared to help him, Wesley replied.

VOICE 3: In a way he's fortunate, said Yvonne, who had taken care of a problem at the New York store and was flying back to London this evening,

VOICE 2: sure, fortunate, said Wesley,

VOICE 3: no one is shunning him, Yvonne went on, no one's afraid to hug him or kiss him lightly on the mouth, in London we are, as usual, a few years behind you, people I know, people who would seem to be not even remotely at risk, are just terrified, but I'm impressed by how cool and rational you all are;

VOICE 2: you find us cool, asked Quentin.

VOICE 1: But I have to say, he's reported to have said, I'm terrified, I find it very hard to read

VOICE 2: (and you know how he loves to read, said Greg;

VOICE 4: yes, reading is his television, said Paolo)

VOICE 1: or to think, but I don't feel hysterical.

VOICE 4: I feel quite hysterical, Lewis said to Yvonne.

VOICE 3: But you're able to *do* something for him, that's wonderful, how I wish I could stay longer, Yvonne answered, it's rather beautiful, I can't help thinking, this utopia of friendship you've assembled around him

VOICE 5: (this pathetic utopia, said Kate),

VOICE 3: so that the disease, Yvonne concluded, is not, anymore, out there.

VOICE 5: Yes, don't you think we're more at home here, with him, with the disease, said Tanya, because the imagined disease is so much worse than the reality of him, whom we all love, each in our fashion, having it.

VOICE 3: I know for me his getting it has quite demystified the disease, said Jan, I don't feel afraid, spooked, as I did before he became ill, when it was only news about remote acquaintances, whom I never saw again after they became ill.

VOICE 2: But you know you're not going to come down with the disease, Quentin said,

VOICE 5: to which Ellen replied, on her behalf, that's not the point, and possibly untrue, my gynecologist says that everyone is at risk, everyone who has a sexual life, because sexuality is a chain that links each of us to many others, unknown others, and now the great chain of being has become a chain of death as well.

VOICE 2: It's not the same for you, Quentin insisted, it's not the same for you as it is for me or Lewis or Frank or Paolo or Max, I'm more and more frightened, and I have every reason to be.

VOICE 3: I don't think about whether I'm at risk or not, said Hilda, I know that I was afraid to know someone with the disease, afraid of what I'd see, what I'd feel, and after the first day I came to the hospital I felt so relieved. I'll never feel that way, that fear, again; he doesn't seem different from me.

VOICE 2: He's not, Quentin said.

SCENE TEN

VOICE 4: According to Lewis, he talked more often about those who visited more often,

VOICE 5: which is natural, said Betsy, I think he's even keeping a tally.

VOICE 1: And among those who came or checked in by phone every day, the inner circle as it were, those who were getting more points, there was still a further competition, which was what was getting on Betsy's nerves, she confessed to Jan;

VOICE 5: there's always that vulgar jockeying for position around the bedside of the gravely ill, and though we all feel suffused with virtue at our loyalty to him

VOICE 3: (speak for yourself, said Jan),

VOICE 5: to the extent that we're carving time out of every day,

116

or almost every day, though some of us are dropping out, as Xavier pointed out, aren't we getting at least as much out of this as he is.

VOICE 3: Are we, said Jan.

VOICE 5: We're rivals for a sign from him of special pleasure over a visit, each stretching for the brass ring of his favor, wanting to feel the most wanted, the true nearest and dearest, which is inevitable with someone who doesn't have a spouse and children or an official in-house lover, hierarchies that no one would dare contest, Betsy went on, so we are the family he's founded, without meaning to, without official titles and ranks

VOICE 1: (we, we, snarled Quentin);

VOICE 2: and is it so clear, though some of us, Lewis and Quentin and Tanya and Paolo, among others, are ex-lovers and all of us more or less than friends, which one of us he prefers, Victor said

VOICE 1: (now it's us, raged Quentin),

VOICE 2: because sometimes I think he looks forward more to seeing Aileen, who has visited only three times, twice at the hospital and once since he's been home, than he does you or me;

VOICE 3: but, according to Tanya, after being very disappointed that Aileen hadn't come, now he was angry,

VOICE 4: while, according to Xavier, he was not really hurt but touchingly passive, accepting Aileen's absence as something he somehow deserved.

VOICE 2: But he's happy to have people around, said Lewis; he says when he doesn't have company he gets very sleepy,

VOICE 1: he sleeps (according to Quentin), and then perks up when someone arrives, it's important that he not feel ever alone.

VOICE 2: But, said Victor, there's one person he hasn't heard from, whom he'd probably like to hear from more than most of us;

VOICE 5: but she didn't just vanish, even right after she broke away from him, and he knows exactly where she lives now, said Kate, he told me he put in a call to her last Christmas Eve, and she said it's nice to hear from you and Merry Christmas,

VOICE 4: and he was shattered, according to Orson,

VOICE 3: and furious and disdainful, according to Ellen

117

VOICE 2: (what do you expect of her, said Wesley, she was burned out),

VOICE 5: but Kate wondered if maybe he hadn't phoned Nora in the middle of a sleepless night, what's the time difference,

VOICE 2: and Quentin said no, I don't think so, I think he wouldn't want her to know.

SCENE ELEVEN

VOICE 1: And when he was feeling even better and had regained the pounds he'd shed right away in the hospital, though the refrigerator started to fill up with organic wheat germ and grapefruit and skimmed milk

VOICE 2: (he's worried about his cholesterol count, Stephen lamented),

VOICE 1: and told Quentin he could manage by himself now, and did, he started asking everyone who visited how he looked, and everyone said

VOICE 3: he looked great,

VOICE 4: so much better than a few weeks ago,

VOICE 1: which didn't jibe with what anyone had told him at that time; but then it was getting harder and harder to know how he looked, to answer such a question honestly when among themselves they wanted to be honest, both for honesty's sake and (as Donny thought) to prepare for the worst, because he'd been looking like *this* for so long, at least it seemed so long, that it was as if he'd always been like this, how did he look before, but it was only a few months, and those words,

VOICE 5: pale

VOICE 3: and wan-looking

VOICE 4: and fragile,

VOICE 1: hadn't they always applied? And one Thursday Ellen, meeting Lewis at the door of the building, said, as they rode up together in the elevator,

VOICE 5: how is he *really*?

VOICE 4: But you see how he is, Lewis said tartly, he's fine, he's perfectly healthy,

VOICE 5: and Ellen understood that of course Lewis didn't think he was perfectly healthy but that he wasn't worse, and that was true, but wasn't it, well, almost heartless to talk like that.

VOICE 2: Seems inoffensive to me, Quentin said, but I know what you mean, I remember once talking to Frank, somebody, after all, who has volunteered to do five hours a week of office work at the Crisis Center

VOICE 5: (I know, said Ellen),

VOICE 2: and Frank was going on about this guy, diagnosed almost a year ago, and so much further along, who'd been complaining to Frank on the phone about the indifference of some doctor, and had gotten quite abusive about the doctor, and Frank was saying there was no reason to be so upset, the implication being that *he,* Frank, wouldn't behave so irrationally, and I said, barely able to control my scorn, but Frank, Frank, he has every reason to be upset, he's dying, and Frank said,

VOICE 1: said according to Quentin,

VOICE 2: oh, I don't like to think about it that way.

SCENE TWELVE

VOICE 1: And it was while he was still home, recuperating, getting his weekly treatment, still not able to do much work, he complained, but, according to Quentin,

VOICE 2: up and about most of the time and turning up at the office several days a week,

VOICE 1: that bad news came about two remote acquaintances, one in Houston and one in Paris, news that was intercepted by Quentin on the ground that it could only depress him,

VOICE 4: but Stephen contended that it was wrong to lie to him, it was so important for him to live in the truth; that had been one of his first victories, that he was candid, that he was even willing to crack jokes about the disease,

119

VOICE 5: but Ellen said it wasn't good to give him this end-of-the-world feeling, too many people were getting ill, it was becoming such a common destiny that maybe some of the will to fight for his life would be drained out of him if it seemed to be as natural as, well, death.

VOICE 3: Oh, Hilda said, who didn't know personally either the one in Houston or the one in Paris, but knew *of* the one in Paris, a pianist who specialized in twentieth-century Czech and Polish music, I have his records, he's such a valuable person,

VOICE 5: and, when Kate glared at her, continued defensively,

VOICE 3: I know every life is equally sacred, but that *is* a thought, another thought, I mean, all these valuable people who aren't going to have their normal four-score as it is now, these people aren't going to be replaced, and it's such a loss to the culture.

VOICE 2: But this isn't going to go on forever, Wesley said, it can't, they're bound to come up with something

VOICE 4: (they, they, muttered Stephen),

VOICE 2: but did you ever think, Greg said, that if some people don't die, I mean even if they can keep them alive

VOICE 5: (they, they, muttered Kate),

VOICE 2: they continue to be carriers, and that means, if you have a conscience, that you can never make love, make love fully, as you'd been wont—

VOICE 4: wantonly, Ira said—

VOICE 2: to do.

VOICE 4: But it's better than dying, said Frank.

VOICE 1: And in all his talk about the future, when he allowed himself to be hopeful, according to Quentin,

VOICE 2: he never mentioned the prospect that even if he didn't die, if he were so fortunate as to be among the first generation of the disease's survivors,

VOICE 5: never mentioned, Kate confirmed, that whatever happened it was over, the way he had lived until now,

VOICE 4: but, according to Ira, he did think about it, the end of bravado, the end of folly, the end of trusting life, the end of taking

120

life for granted, and of treating life as something that, samurai-like, he thought himself ready to throw away lightly, impudently;

VOICE 1: and Kate recalled, sighing, a brief exchange she'd insisted on having as long as two years ago, huddling on a banquette covered with steel-gray industrial carpet on an upper level of The Prophet and toking up for their next foray onto the dance floor: she'd said hesitantly, for it felt foolish asking a prince of debauchery to, well, take it easy, and she wasn't keen on playing big sister, a role, as Hilda confirmed, he inspired in many women,

VOICE 5: are you being careful, honey, you know what I mean.

VOICE 1: And he replied, Kate went on,

VOICE 5: no, I'm not, listen, I can't, I just can't, sex is too important to me, always has been

VOICE 2: (he started talking like that, according to Victor, after Nora left him),

VOICE 5: and if I get it, well, I get it.

VOICE 2: But he wouldn't talk like that now, would he, said Greg;

VOICE 5: he must feel awfully foolish now, said Betsy, like someone who went on smoking, saying I can't give up cigarettes, but when the bad X-ray is taken even the most besotted nicotine addict can stop on a dime.

VOICE 2: But sex isn't like cigarettes, is it, said Frank,

VOICE 4: and, besides, what good does it do to remember that he was reckless, said Lewis angrily, the appalling thing is that you just have to be unlucky once, and wouldn't he feel even worse if he'd stopped three years ago and had come down with it anyway, since one of the most terrifying features of the disease is that you don't know when you contracted it, it could have been ten years ago, because surely this disease has existed for years and years, long before it was recognized; that is, named. Who knows how long

VOICE 2: (I think a lot about that, said Max)

VOICE 4: and who knows

VOICE 2: (I know what you're going to say, Stephen interrupted)

VOICE 4: how many are going to get it.

VOICE 1: I'm feeling fine, he's reported to have said whenever someone asked him how he was, which was almost always the first question anyone asked. Or: I'm feeling better, how are you? But he said other things, too.

VOICE 2: I'm playing leapfrog with myself, he is reported to have said, according to Victor.

VOICE 5: And: There must be a way to get something positive out of this situation, he's reported to have said to Kate.

VOICE 4: How American of him, said Paolo.

VOICE 5: Well, said Betsy, you know the old American adage: When you've got a lemon, make lemonade.

VOICE 3: The one thing I'm sure I couldn't take, Jan said he said to her, is becoming disfigured,

VOICE 1: but Stephen hastened to point out the disease doesn't take that form very often anymore,

VOICE 4: its profile is mutating,

VOICE 1: and, in conversation with Ellen, wheeled up words like

VOICE 4: blood-brain barrier;

VOICE 3: I never thought there was a barrier *there,* said Jan.

VOICE 5: But he mustn't know about Max, Ellen said, that would really depress him, please don't tell him,

VOICE 2: he'll have to know, Quentin said grimly, and he'll be furious not to have been told.

VOICE 5: But there's time for that, when they take Max off the respirator, said Ellen;

VOICE 2: but isn't it incredible, Frank said, Max was fine, not feeling ill at all, and then to wake up with a fever of a hundred and five, unable to breathe,

VOICE 4: but that's the way it often starts, with absolutely no warning, Stephen said, the disease has so many forms.

VOICE 1: And when, after another week had gone by, he asked Quentin where Max was, he didn't question Quentin's account of a spree in the Bahamas, but then the number of people who visited regularly was thinning out, partly because the old feuds that had been put aside through the first hospitalization and the return home had resurfaced, and the flickering enmity between Lewis and Frank exploded, even though Kate did her best to mediate between them, and also because he himself had done something to loosen the bonds of love that united the friends around him, by seeming to take them all for granted, as if it were perfectly normal for so many people to carve out so much time and attention for him, visit him every few days, talk about him incessantly on the phone with each other; but, according to Paolo, it wasn't that he was less grateful, it was just something he was getting used to, the visits. It had become, with time, a more ordinary kind of situation, a kind of ongoing party, first at the hospital and now since he was home, barely on his feet again,

VOICE 2: it being clear, said Robert, that I'm on the B list;

VOICE 5: but Kate said, that's absurd, there's no list;

VOICE 2: and Victor said, but there is, only it's not he, it's Quentin who's drawing it up. He wants to see us, we're helping him, we have to do it the way he wants, he fell down yesterday on the way to the bathroom, he mustn't be told about Max

VOICE 4: (but he already knew, according to Donny),

VOICE 2: it's getting worse.

SCENE FOURTEEN

VOICE 1: When I was home, he is reported to have said, I was afraid to sleep, as I was dropping off each night it felt like just that, as if I were falling down a black hole, to sleep felt like giving in to death, I slept every night with the light on; but here, in the hospital, I'm less afraid.

VOICE 2: And to Quentin he said, one morning, the fear rips through me, it tears me open;

VOICE 4: and, to Ira, it presses me together, squeezes me toward myself. Fear gives everything its hue, its high.

VOICE 2: I feel so, I don't know how to say it, exalted, he said to Quentin.

VOICE 1: Calamity is an amazing high, too. Sometimes I feel *so* well, so powerful, it's as if I could jump out of my skin. Am I going crazy, or what? Is it all this attention and coddling I'm getting from everybody, like a child's dream of being loved? Is it the drugs? I know it sounds crazy but sometimes I think this is a *fantastic* experience, he said shyly; but there was also the bad taste in the mouth, the pressure in the head and at the back of the neck, the red, bleeding gums, the painful, if pink-lobed, breathing, and his ivory pallor, color of white chocolate. Among those who wept when told over the phone that he was back in the hospital were Kate and Stephen

VOICE 2: (who'd been called by Quentin),

VOICE 1: and Ellen, Victor, Aileen, and Lewis

VOICE 5: (who were called by Kate),

VOICE 1: and Xavier and Ursula

VOICE 4: (who were called by Stephen).

VOICE 1: Among those who didn't weep were Hilda,

VOICE 3: who said that she'd just learned that her seventy-five-year-old aunt was dying of the disease, which she'd contracted from a transfusion given during her successful double bypass of five years ago,

VOICE 1: and Frank and Donny and Betsy, but this didn't mean,

VOICE 3: according to Tanya, that they weren't moved and appalled, and Quentin thought they might not be coming soon to the hospital but would send presents;

VOICE 1: the room, he was in a private room this time, was filling up with flowers, and plants, and books, and tapes. The high tide of barely suppressed acrimony of the last weeks at home subsided into the routines of hospital visiting, though more than a few resented Quentin's having charge of the visiting book

VOICE 4: (but it was Quentin who had the idea, Lewis pointed out);

VOICE 1: how, to insure a steady stream of visitors, preferably no more than two at a time (this, the rule in all hospitals, wasn't enforced here, at least on his floor; whether out of kindness or inefficiency, no one could decide), Quentin had to be called first, to get one's time slot, there was no more casual dropping by. And his mother could no longer be prevented from taking a plane and installing herself in a hotel near the hospital;

VOICE 2: but he seemed to mind her daily presence less than expected, Quentin said;

VOICE 5: said Ellen it's we who mind, do you suppose she'll stay long.

VOICE 4: It was easier to be generous with each other visiting him here in the hospital, as Donny pointed out, than at home, where one minded never being alone with him;

VOICE 5: coming here, in our twos and twos, there's no doubt about what our role is, how we should be, collective, funny, distracting, undemanding, light, it's important to be light, for in all this dread there is gaiety, too, as the poet said, said Kate.

VOICE 4: (His eyes, his glittering eyes, said Lewis.)

VOICE 2: His eyes looked dull, extinguished, Wesley said to Xavier,

VOICE 3: but Betsy said his face, not just his eyes, looked soulful, warm;

VOICE 5: whatever is there, said Kate, I've never been so aware of his eyes;

VOICE 4: and Stephen said, I'm afraid of what my eyes show, the way I watch him, with too much intensity,

VOICE 2: or a phony kind of casualness, said Victor.

VOICE 1: And, unlike at home, he was clean-shaven each morning, at whatever hour they visited him; his curly hair was always combed; but he complained that the nurses had changed since he was here the last time, and that he didn't like the change, he wanted everyone to be the same. The room was furnished now with some of his personal effects

VOICE 5: (odd word for one's things, said Ellen),

VOICE 3: and Tanya brought drawings and a letter from her nine-year-old dyslexic son, who was writing now, since she'd purchased a computer;

VOICE 4: and Donny brought champagne and some helium balloons, which were anchored to the foot of his bed;

VOICE 1: tell me about something that's going on, he said, waking up from a nap to find Donny and Kate at the side of his bed, beaming at him;

VOICE 4: tell me a story, he said wistfully, said Donny, who couldn't think of anything to say;

VOICE 5: *you're* the story, Kate said.

VOICE 1: And Xavier brought an eighteenth-century Guatemalan wooden statue of Saint Sebastian with upcast eyes and open mouth, and when Tanya said

VOICE 3: what's that, a tribute to eros past,

VOICE 4: Xavier said where I come from Sebastian is venerated as a protector against pestilence.

VOICE 3: Pestilence symbolized by arrows?

VOICE 4: Symbolized by arrows. All people remember is the body of a beautiful youth bound to a tree, pierced by arrows

VOICE 3: (of which he always seems oblivious, Tanya interjected),

VOICE 4: people forget that the story continues, Xavier continued, that when the Christian women came to bury the martyr they found him still alive and nursed him back to health.

VOICE 1: And he said, according to Stephen, I didn't know Saint Sebastian didn't die.

VOICE 5: It's undeniable, isn't it, said Kate on the phone to Stephen, the fascination of the dying. It makes me ashamed.

VOICE 1: We're learning how to die, said Hilda,

VOICE 3: I'm not ready to learn, said Aileen;

VOICE 1: and Lewis, who was coming straight from the other hospital, the hospital where Max was still being kept in ICU, met Tanya getting out of the elevator on the tenth floor, and as they walked together down the shiny corridor past the open doors,

VOICE 4: averting their eyes from the other patients sunk in their beds,

VOICE 3: with tubes in their noses,

VOICE 4: irradiated by the bluish light from the television sets,

VOICE 3: the thing I can't bear to think about, Tanya said to Lewis, is someone dying with the TV on.

SCENE FIFTEEN

VOICE 5: He has that strange, unnerving detachment now, said Ellen, that's what upsets me, even though it makes it easier to be with him.

VOICE 1: Sometimes he was querulous. I can't stand them coming in here taking my blood every morning, what are they doing with all that blood, he is reported to have said;

VOICE 3: but where was his anger, Jan wondered. Mostly he was lovely to be with, always saying how are *you,* how are you feeling.

VOICE 5: He's so sweet now, said Aileen.

VOICE 3: He's so nice, said Tanya.

VOICE 4: (Nice, nice, groaned Paolo.)

VOICE 1: At first he was very ill,

VOICE 4: but he was rallying, according to Stephen's best information, there was no fear of his not recovering this time,

VOICE 3: and the doctor spoke of his being discharged from the hospital in another ten days if all went well,

VOICE 5: and the mother was persuaded to fly back to Mississippi,

VOICE 2: and Quentin was readying the penthouse for his return.

VOICE 1: And he was still writing his diary, not showing it to anyone, though Tanya, first to arrive one late-winter morning, and finding him dozing, peeked, and was horrified, according to Greg, not by anything she read but by a progressive change in his handwriting: in the recent pages, it was becoming spidery, less legible, and some lines of script wandered and tilted about the page.

VOICE 5: I was thinking, Ursula said to Quentin, that the difference between a story and a painting or photograph is that in a story you can write, He's still alive. But in a painting or a photo you can't show "still." You can just show him being alive.

VOICE 4: He's still alive, Stephen said.

END OF PLAY

127

SUSAN SONTAG *is the author of two novels,* The Benefactor *and* Death Kit, *a volume of short stories,* I, etcetera, *and several collections of essays. Her most recent book is* AIDS and Its Metaphors. The Way We Live Now *was first published in the November 24, 1986 New Yorker, and then included in* The Best American Short Stories 1987.

Director EDWARD PARONE *conceived and produced the Mark Taper Forum's 1990 festival of thirteen plays from the 1950s and '60s. His arrangement of Susan Sontag's* The Way We Live Now *was first presented at the Itchey Foot, the Taper's literary cabaret in downtown Los Angeles, on February 19, 1989.*

from

Angels in America

BY TONY KUSHNER

CHARACTERS
    ROY COHN
    HENRY, his doctor

TIME Fall 1985.

PLACE Henry's office, New York City.

Editor's Note: Angels in America, *subtitled* "A Gay Fantasia on National Themes," *is an epic work in two parts. The story of Roy Cohn is just one of many threads in the play. This scene is taken from the first part, "Millennium Approaches."

HENRY: Nobody knows what causes it. And nobody knows how to cure it. The best theory is that we blame a retrovirus, the human immunodeficiency virus. The retro part means that it performs transcription, the process of reading its genetic material for the purpose of replication, in reverse. It has a special enzyme which makes its host cell read backwards—

ROY: Like Hebrew.

HENRY: Uh, right. Well, I mean, but basically it's a virus, just a terribly simple little protein package full of bad news. Which it releases in the form of strands of RNA. That's all; like every blessed thing in the animate universe it is hellbent on survival and proliferation. Its presence is made known to us by the useless antibodies which appear in reaction to its entrance into the bloodstream though a cut, or an orifice. The antibodies are powerless to protect the body against it. Why, we don't know. Unfortunately it matches best with the cells of the immune system; specifically, T4 helper lymphocytes, which it kills or uses as little RNA/DNA factories. And macrophages too—the large white blood cells. The bad news the virus contains gets replicated by the host cells at the expense of their own natural functioning and eventually at the expense of their survival. The body's immune system ceases to function. Sometimes the body even attacks itself. At any rate it's left open to a whole horror house of infections from microbes which it usually defends against.

Like Kaposi's sarcomas. These lesions. Or your throat problem. Or the glands.

We think it may also be able to slip past the blood-brain barrier into the brain. Which is of course very bad news.

And it's fatal in we don't know what percent of people with suppressed immune responses.

Pause.

ROY: This is very interesting, Mr. Wizard, but why the fuck are you telling me this?

Pause.

HENRY: Well, I have just removed one of three lesions which biopsy results will probably tell us is a Kaposi's sarcoma lesion. And you have a pronounced swelling of glands in your neck, groin, and armpits—lymphadenopathy is another sign. And you have oral candidiasis and maybe a little more fungus under the fingernails of two digits on your right hand. So that's why—
ROY: This disease . . .
HENRY: Syndrome.
ROY: Whatever. It afflicts mostly homosexuals and drug addicts.
HENRY: Mostly. Hemophiliacs are also at risk.
ROY: Homosexuals and drug addicts. So why are you implying—
HENRY: Roy—
ROY: I'm not a drug addict.
HENRY: Oh come on Roy.
ROY: What, what, come on Roy what? Do you think I'm a junkie, Henry, do you see tracks?
HENRY: This is absurd.
ROY: Say it.
HENRY: Say what?
ROY: Say, "Roy Cohn, you are a . . ."
HENRY: Roy.
ROY: "You are a . . . ." Go on. Not "Roy Cohn you are a drug fiend." "Roy Marcus Cohn, you are a . . . ." Go on, Henry, it starts with an H.
HENRY: Roy . . .
ROY: *With an H,* Henry, and it isn't "hemophiliac."
HENRY: What are you doing, Roy?
ROY: No, say it. Say: "Roy Cohn, you are a homosexual."

Pause.

ROY: And I will proceed systematically to destroy your reputation and your practice and your career in New York State, Henry. Which you know I can do.

Pause.

HENRY: Roy, you have been seeing me since 1958. Apart from the facelifts I have treated you for everything from syphilis—

ROY: From a whore in Dallas.

HENRY: From syphilis to venereal warts. In your rectum. Which you may have gotten from a whore in Dallas, but it wasn't a female whore.

Pause.

ROY: So say it.

HENRY: Roy Cohn, you are a . . . . You have had sex with men many many times, Roy, and one of them, or any number of them, has made you very sick. You have AIDS.

ROY: AIDS.

Your problem, Henry, is that you are hung up on words, on labels, that you believe they mean what they seem to mean. AIDS. Homosexual. Gay. Lesbian. You think these are names that tell you who someone sleeps with, but they don't tell you that.

HENRY: No?

ROY: No. Like all labels they tell you one thing and one thing only: where does an individual so identified fit in the food chain, in the pecking order? Not ideology, or sexual taste, but something much simpler: clout. Not who I fuck or who fucks me, but who will pick up the phone when I call, who owes me favors. This is what a label refers to. Now to someone who does not understand this, homosexual is what I am because I have sex with men. But really this is wrong. Homosexuals are not men who sleep with other men. Homosexuals are men who in fifteen years of trying cannot

133

get a pissant antidiscrimination bill through City Council. Homosexuals are men who know nobody and who nobody knows. Who have zero clout. Does this sound like me, Henry?

HENRY: No.

ROY: No. I have clout. A lot. I can pick up this phone, punch fifteen numbers, and you know who will be on the other end in under five minutes, Henry?

HENRY: The President.

ROY: Even better, Henry. His wife.

HENRY: I'm impressed.

ROY: I don't want you to be impressed. I want you to understand. This is not sophistry. And this is not hypocrisy. This is reality. I have sex with men. But unlike nearly every other man of whom this is true, I bring the guy I'm screwing to the White House and President Reagan smiles at us and shakes his hand. Because *what* I am is defined entirely by *who* I am. Roy Cohn is not a homosexual. Roy Cohn is a heterosexual man, Henry, who fucks around with guys.

HENRY: Okay, Roy.

ROY: And what is my diagnosis, Henry?

HENRY: You have AIDS, Roy.

ROY: No, Henry, no. AIDS is what homosexuals have. I have liver cancer.

Pause.

HENRY: Well, whatever the fuck you have, Roy, it's very serious, and I haven't got a damn thing for you. The NIH hospital in Bethesda has some experimental treatments with two-year waiting lists that not even I can get you onto. So get on the phone, Roy, and dial the fifteen numbers, and tell the First Lady you need in on an experimental treatment for liver cancer, because you can call it any damn thing you want, Roy, but what it boils down to is very bad news.

END OF SCENE

TONY KUSHNER *is a director and playwright whose plays include* A Bright Room Called Day *and a free adaptation of Corneille's* L'Illusion. *Productions of* Angels in America *are planned by San Francisco's Eureka Theatre, which commissioned the work, by the Mark Taper Forum in Los Angeles, and by New York Theatre Workshop.*

Jack

BY DAVID GREENSPAN

CHARACTERS

SPEAKER 1

SPEAKER 2

SPEAKER 3

CHARACTER 8

Darkness. Then dim light illuminates a circle of eight chairs located downstage, just left of center. The placement of the chairs is not so perfectly circular as it is pear shaped. The chair furthest upstage juts out most from what would be the circle. Seated in that chair is a man, Character 8. The remaining chairs are empty. Hold. Then light illuminates three females, Speaker 1, Speaker 2, and Speaker 3, standing upstage right, positioned above the floor of the stage. They are costumed and lit in a manner which exposes them only above their bosoms; their heads are capped in black from the hairline up—ideally, the image is one of floating busts. Before each, a music stand, on which is placed the text to which she (as needed) refers. With their lips pursed, gently but audibly exhaling, The Speakers open their texts. They then begin.

PART ONE

SPEAKER 1	SPEAKER 2	SPEAKER 3
And.		
And and		
	And now	
and		
and		
		Now as
	and	
as		
		and as it
it		
	it	
it began one		

day as
and
and

as
and as
and as it

began it
and

as it began

so it

began

it

it

it

it it

it began

one

day one.

day that it

or not

it

it never began but

but

But

always

always

was.

this-
this was-
was-
This was   was   was the-
   the beginning.
                  was beginning
Beginning.   no, wait;
Yes.   was   this was the not the-
Yes, yes.   no this was not the
                                   what(?)- the-

Beginning.

No

                                    so.
And as always it

                                                    never
                    Never(?)
it
                                                    never
it   never- it never began
                                                      but- but always
was
                    always
                                                    was his
                    his name
was and
                                                    and his name
was always.   always was   was Jack.
                                                    Jack.
                    Jack was his name.
His name   Name-
  Jack.
                    That's it.
                                                    That's right;
                                                    was Jack.
Got that?   Got that?
                    Got that!
His name was Jack.
                    And   And
He got   he got
  that   that   his name
  was Jack.   his was   what he
                      Jack   Jack
                      his name
                                                    Jack
                      got that it
                      was that
                      it got
                      what it
                      was what
                      it that

it was.

                    it was
                    it was
                    it was

You got?
It was   it was

          You get?

it was   it was.
it it
was   Was it?
  got?
Was got.

          What, that he-

                    Do you get what he
                      get what he got?

Did you
          Did-   Did

  get
  what he   Get what?
  got?   He got what   he get
                          what he
          Jack   got what he
That he   got   Jack that is
  got and   that   his name was
  yes and   Jack did   Jack as his name
                            Jack.
  he's   and
  dead   he's   And
  now.   dead   he's
             now   dead
                          now dead.
          (Dead now
          dead now
          dead now dead.)

This was the-
This is-
This was-

142

This was the-

    gone.
    Gone from   And he's gone.

Gone are we   here   We are here
  here to say   we're to say   to say
  he was   he's gone   he is gone.
  here   here   He was here
    from us

  in life.   in life a   in life
A life.   life.   a life now
    live no more.

    Jack's gone.

Jack is gone.

    Jack is.

And his life was
  here was

    His life
    was yes   Was his life
    Jack gone   not here?

Jack yes   as he begins we
  it began.
    Jack begins and
As it begins
  we
    Jack began
    and ending now
    he begins as we

Hold. Then with their lips pursed, gently but audibly exhaling, The Speakers turn to their next page.

PART TWO

    2

    And.
    And

1

And so Jack got ill he got sick and that that that's it plain and simple there's not much to say beyond that what can I what are you what are you going to say listen it's not so much a question of why he got sick or how he got sick I couldn't tell you what who's going to who knows how he got a million different opinions from this one from that one too much drinking from that one too much smoking from this one too much screwing around and around your head could spin with all the what do these people no I don't know what can I say for all I know they're all right for heaven's sake but who cares you think I care you think well Jack doesn't care anymore he's dead for heaven's sake he's buried or burned or I don't know I think he was cremated either way he doesn't care unless there's what life after listen I'm not going to get into that kind of no I'm not going to get started on that would be the end of who knows he got sick is what's important and the fact that now and this is important he didn't no he didn't tell any no he didn't tell a soul he didn't breathe a word of it to anyone but well there was one no one maybe two people he told for spite he told them over and over and over again how unfair and how goddamn unjust that he of all people should be struck down he said it was shit that life was shit that life was fucked over and over again he blamed it on this and that and this went on and on and on and no one knew why he left town that summer he went to California to a what some kind of natural healing with herbs and meditation he hated it so he settled in Los Angeles of all places Los Angeles as if there he would find health as if there he finally committed suicide after a year or so I think maybe less than a maybe a whole year I don't know.

Thank god by then he had seven tumors on the brain he had well over a hundred lesions and he was driving everybody crazy. He was driving everybody what do you think this experience made a better person out of him he was horrible yelling and screaming and blaming and

Hold. Then with their lips pursed, gently but audibly exhaling, The Speakers turn to their next page.

PART THREE

2

Now to speak of
to speak of

3

To speak of his mother is like
speaking of the dark past I remember
his mother was a fair-haired woman she was
in her youth a real beauty- that one was
a real beauty- who said that I can't
remember who said that it was it-
no, it wasn't . . . it was . . . it was . . .
it was what's her name from what's her name
who married- she married what's his name
in Israel- they had- they owned a restaurant in Haifa I never liked her
whatever her name- but she said
that Faith- that Jack's mother's name
is Faith was a real beauty she was a real
beauty in her youth a very pretty-
pretty girl she was but then-
well- for one thing she got ill she got
sick she got with lupus she got and she got-
she got heavy from the cortisone- she had to take
the cortisone. Plus she used to sit in bed in front of the television set
    watching *The Edge of Night* and *As the World Turns* with a half-gallon
    of ice cream on her lap from the- right from the carton she was a real
    chazzer that one,

1	2	3
	Yes, that one	yes.
Yes, but-	yes-	
but what could she do		
as she said herself		
her life was shit.		

                              her life didn't turn
                              out
Well, she said it was   well.
    shit. And

                                                    Her life really wasn't-

Shit; it was shit;
    and I'm quoting her
        directly.

2

Don't picture- you won't- you want to get a clear picture of this woman(?) don't picture her in color- in bright garish color, because I know we make it sound like a color picture- it's not- picture her in black and white and wearing I don't know what that shift she wore and her skin- her skin is puffy and her hands are swollen from the arthritis-

1

She had arthritis she had.

2

she couldn't open a can of soda if she tried but

1   2   3

                                                    But-

                          well

                                                    But but but
                                                    how she
                                                        beat him.
                          Jack
Let me- let me
    tell you I could

146

tell you
of her whacking
him with a
strap with

how she beat him
  is a real
  story let me-
I could
  tell you stories of
  how she could
  walloped him with
  anything she

How did she
  beat him I'd
  like to know
  how a woman and
  a big woman she
  wasn't let me tell
  you she

  could get her

a book with
her fist if she
felt so enraged to
pinch when

hands on him in
a moment's flurry
of fist and-

took anything she
could grab to
hit him across
the mouth along
his legs she'd
reach across
the dining-room
table and
just crack him.

And when she was
  too
  weak and tired to
  hit

too weak to smack.

Too sick to hit she'd
  just
  pinch him.

she'd pinch with all
her might she'd
  grab
his flesh between
  her
fingers and pinch
  hard.

And she had-
she-
she had long

She had long
  nails she

She had
  long very

nails she had
  frighteningly long
  nails.

She might scratch
  at him.

He was frightened
  of her I hardly
  remember- I
    hardly-
  remember his
    father.

I can't.

His-

No.
I don't.
Remember(?); no; I
  don't . . . his
    father . . .

---

had long nails
  that frightened him
  her nails.

She might-
  scratch him.

He was frightened
  of her but I

  really don't his
  father remember I

I- I really can't.

Who?

His
  father?
I-
no; I don't
  remember his
  father.

---

long nails she
had long nails
that frightened
  him.

She might . . . claw
  at him; did she
    sharpen
  those nails?

Of course he was she

  frightened him she
  frightened I-

I hardly I

I can't remember
  his father.

No.

His father?
I- no; I
  don't; no; I
  don't remember.
I- I- no;
  I don't remember
    his
    father.

Hold. Then with their lips pursed, gently but audibly exhaling, The Speakers turn to their next page.

PART FOUR

1

Jack had problems
  sleeping. He'd

wake up frightened
in the morning
  after a
nap in the
  afternoon or
during the night.

Wouldn't.

No sleep.

He'd take a walk.

He could walk then.

2

Now Jack had
  problems sleeping.

Frightened he'd wake
  up
in the dark.

During the night he'd
  constantly wake.

He couldn't.

So he'd walk.

 He'd walk to this

3

Jack
  had problems
    sleeping.

Long before he got
  sick
he had problems
  sleeping; he'd wake
    up

  frightened he'd
    wake
  in the dark he'd
  wake up.

Constantly wake up
  at night he couldn't
  wouldn't sleep.

Couldn't sleep.

Jack would walk.

park that he'd walk
to this park.

There was this park.

Jack thought of it as
his park.

And there
he'd walk.

There he would walk
around the park
and around and
around and
around the park
figure eight like on
the path that
wound
figure eight like round
the dark park Jack
would walk.

He'd walk
there.

And there
were others
there.

There were
others.

Other men were
there as well as
Jack was there with
other men walking
their figure eight
in the dark.

In the dark
were other
men.

Men would stand
under the trees.

Or sit cigarette lit
on the rail round
the moistened
grass.

Or pose lamp-lit
on the benches.

But but but-but-but-
    but-but most men
hushed men
passed each other on
    the path that
      wound
figure eight like round
the park they wound
figure eight like
    round.

          And and and Jack was

There was
  Jack.
                    Jack was
             There was   there.

2

Jack was then when he couldn't sleep he'd get dressed and go out to the park in the dark he would walk round the moist grass there the grass was moist grass there were the men on parade in the lamp-lit light the cigarette-lit light they'd circle figure eight like round the dark park in the dark like so many mice on a wheel like so many mice on a wheel like so many mice on a wheel like so many mice on a wheel like so many manymany manymany manymany men in the dark would would would stop to talk or stop to look or stop to touch- or not stop to look or talk or touch.

                  3

                  And

1

And

2

And Jack was there was Jack was always longing there for someone to take him for someone to call him for someone to call to his heart was

Hold. Then with their lips pursed, gently but audibly exhaling, The Speakers turn to their next page.

PART FIVE

1	2	3
		And.
And then one night Jack met John.		
	John.	
		John met Jack.
Jack met this John in the park they met in the park and went back to John's		
	One night John met Jack in- in the park they met and went back to Jack's	
place I think it	place I'm sure it was it	
was it . . . ?	maybe it was	No, it wasn't Jack's nor John's it was it Patrick's place a
Patrick's; yes.		friend of John or Jack I can't remember whose friend was Patrick was either John or- John or Jack's friend I think

                                        he was he
                                        out of town(?) and
                                        that's where they
Yes, that's right   went.
  they went to
    Patrick's
  place.   to Patrick's
                           place.
                                        Who
                                        ever which
Patrick's   ever one of them
  they went
  to Patrick's.   All right, fine,   was Patrick's friend
                         Patrick.   at the time was
                                           watching Patrick's
                                           place for Patrick
                                             and
                       That's where   took the other
Well that's   they went   there.
  where they   there together.
  went there.
                                        Together they spent
                                          the night there.

                       And they became
They became   lovers.
  lovers after that.   After that they
                                          became lovers.

                       Jack and John
                         became lovers.
Lovers, yes, but
  John was married
    to
  what was her   John was
  name, Sylvia?   married to   John was married
                         a woman named-   to a woman I
                         named . . .   think her name
                                            was Cynthia not

Yes it was
    her name was
    no, not Cynthia; it
    was Sylvia.
Sylvia.

It was maybe
    it wasn't- no,
    no; I think you're
    right it wasn't-
No; it wasn't Sylvia.
It- it wasn't Sylvia.

Sylvia it was her-
    was Cynthia.

Cynthia.

Right; it wasn't.

It was Alice.

Alice?

Alice!

Alice was her name.
Alice.
It was Alice.

That's right,
Alice.
Yes, yes, Alice.

Right
it was Alice.

Alice.

Alice.
Her name was Alice.

And she's dead
    now.

Now dead.
Alice is dead.

Yes, yes, she's dead.

But at the time
    alive.

At the time she was
    alive and married to
    John who was
        Jack's
        lover.

And Jack is dead.

That's right.

He's dead.

Jack's dead.

He is dead.

Ah well they-

They come they go.

They come they-
they come and they

yes they come and
    they go.

154

go.

                                                But at the time, she-

           Alice.

                                                she now gone
                                                    now dead-
                                                    she was married to

What did Alice die
   of?

                                                (I don't know) John
                                                    when she

                          She was hit by a
                            truck.

                                                  learned that- what?

                          She was-

No!

                          Yes; she was hit
                            by a truck.

                                                A truck? Oh god-
                                                but anyway when
                                                    she learned
                                                      that Jack was
                                                    John's lover

That they weren't
   just
   best friends they
   were lovers.
                          They were lovers and
                            she flipped
                            out.   she flipped out

Completely flipped   completely.
   and who could
      blame
      her I
      couldn't.   I'd never blame any
                            one for flipping
                            out.   I'd flip out myself
                                                if it happened to
                                              me.

And so she left.

She left.

Alice left John.

She packed her bags
and went back to
Rhode Island.

Alice had had it.

That's it.

She'd had it.

So Jack and John
were lovers.

Well, not exactly . . .
well, I suppose you
could
call them . . .

What?

lovers?

???

But then John met
Jennifer.

John met
Jennifer.

He then met
Jennifer who
would not stand for
what she called-
she-
she-
she called it
insanity.

And she wasn't
going to put up
with John seeing
Jack.

She would not
stand for this
kind of behavior.

So she told John
it was either
all or nothing.

She told John it
is either Jack
or her.

She said John it's
either him or me.
Me or him.

Who do you want
choose.

You have to

choose.

You'll have to make
a choice.

But John wouldn't
choose.

John couldn't make
a choice.

He couldn't-
wouldn't couldn't
wouldn't-
couldn't make a
decision.

And Jack was
unhappy and
Jennifer was
unhappy
and who knows
what
John felt.

John was-
I don't know what
John was.

John didn't know
what was going on.

No one knew what
was going on.

But finally Jennifer
said she had had
enough.

Jennifer said she'd
had it.

Enough already.

I've had it.

That's it.

I've had it.

So John left Jack for
Jennifer.

For his
peace of mind he
finally left Jack
after

two years and   After two years
                       together
                       and I-
and   I-
and   I think I-   And and
and   now I think
and so   I think it began; I
                       think this   this is-
                       is where it began.

                                         no- no; this is
                                         not when it
                                         started long before
                                         but no one knew it
                                            no
                                       one knew what was
                                       going on.

   it began.
It it   No. Christ!
it began.   No.
Jack began

                                     Began(?!) as if it
                                       could
                                       begin.

began to
                     I
   to get   think this is
it is where   when did Jack   Jack;
when   get sick?   no
                                     no.

   Jack got sick when-

                                     That's right
                                     blame it on John
                                       leaving Jack.

Who knows(?)
it might have had an
   effect.

             Well, for the

                                     No;

first time like-

For the first time
  Jack was sick.

                                                Jack
                                                  first got sick when

Jack was very ill

                                                who knows when.

                    Oh my god.

                                                Not that there
                                                weren't signs
                                                  before-
                                            long before
                                                there were
                                                signs before there
                                                were signs believe
                                                  me there
                                              were reasons for
                                              alarm and cause for
                                              concern, but like-

like
like
like
like
like
like
like
like-

                    Like one of the many
                    he was
                    is
                    just
                    one of the many to be
                      sure before
                    and many still to
                      come.

1

He got what he get what he Jack got what he never got enough he could never
get enough he'd never get enough I've had enough you selfish—leave me

159

alone for christ sake I'm a sick woman I can't take any more of this and I'll
beat the living shit out of you will you get out of the house- just get out of the
house before I break your legs so you can't walk anymore I can't take from
you will get out of this house until dinner until I call you go on get out and
play until I call you.

1   2   3

                    Go out and play until
                      I call you.
                    For fuck's sake.
                    Find some friends
                      and play.

                                            Make some friends
                                          for a change and
Make some friends   play.
  for christ sake
  will you go
  to the park and
    make
  some friends for
  christ
sake for christ
sake for fuck's
sake for-

Will you go out and
  play until I call
    you.

                    But.
Go.
                    Out.
                                          Until I call you.

*Hold. Light on The Speakers is dimmed as light on Character 8 inten-
sifies. Then with their lips pursed, gently but audibly exhaling, The
Speakers turn to their next page.*

PART SIX

CHARACTER 8

And I think my Aunt Rosie—that's my mother's aunt, Rosie, my great-aunt, was visiting us at the time from Chicago. And my mother was probably . . . had probably just gotten out of the hospital, because whenever she had a flareup, some relative would come out to look after us- or look after my mother- or whatever. And . . . yeah I'm probably six or seven.

So . . . now you know my father did everything; he did everything; everything; my father did everything for the beach. He packed . . . he'd pack up the ice chest . . . pack up the ice chest with sandwiches and sodas- things like that, you know- load the car with blankets, and sweaters, towels, beach chairs . . . the blanket, everything; and- oh and the umbrella- my mother- my mother would sit under this enormous beach umbrella- we had this beach umbrella because . . . well, I was going to say she was just- she just didn't- couldn't take the sun, and . . . so she'd just sit under this umbrella. Under the umbrella. She couldn't get out from under the umbrella. I mean as far as I know, so that was . . . you know, that's what she did.

So. Okay. So now . . . now I'm lost on the beach. And this is like- this is the time when Aunt Rosie is out from Chicago. And . . . oh- and Aunt Rosie, you know, Aunt Rosie, I mean was like four feet tall, and she had this orange hair- like from the beauty parlor, and she looked like . . . well, that's kind of what she looked like. And I'm lost because . . . well, I went along the . . . shore looking for shells; I used to collect shells- from the beach, and I've . . . gone, you know, too far I'm . . . lost; I'm . . . . . . well, I'd just gone too far. So . . . now I'm looking for the umbrella- for our umbrella. But it's hard, because . . . well, there are thousands of umbrellas. I mean everybody has an umbrella, you know- you can rent an umbrella- they have stands where- even if you don't have one you can rent one, and . . . anyway, that's just to say that there are thousands of umbrellas; and I can't locate— you see, every time I think I've located our umbrella, I run up to it and there are people I don't recognize. I mean, I don't know, you know, like when you think you've located your family and you run up to their their umbrella and it's not your family; it's people you don't know. So . . . and I was frightened that my parents are going to leave without me, and (I don't know why I thought that) but I was scared because . . . well, there are people on the beach, adults, you know, who obviously know that I'm lost and want to help me, but every time someone- I mean I was just scared that- I don't know that they'll arrest me or something, or that I'll get in trouble or something. You know, I'm just frightened. So if someone asked me if I was lost I'd just say no and try to look like, you know, I wasn't lost. I mean . . .

Anyway. So . . . anyway, suddenly I see my father. Well, actually it's my Aunt Rosie I see first because, you know, she had this orange hair that's very distinct. Distinctive. But I see my father next to her, and my father is walking towards me, and he has a big smile on his face, and I'm really happy- I must have been so relieved to see him; and maybe I start to cry or something like that. And he's calling out to me; he's calling my name. "Jack. Hey Jackie. Jack." My father. So I drop my shells; I had a plastic cup full of . . . ummm shells, and I run to him and I'm crying I'm pretty sure I'm crying at this point, and I throw my arms around his waist and I bury my face in his swimming trunks- which are wet and sandy- and wet. And my father is laughing. My father is . . . I don't know, embarrassed(?) because I'm crying—and he's laughing. I mean this is what it was always like; my mother would be screaming and yelling and throwing things around the apartment and

(*Hold. Turning sharply to the upstage right offstage*) What? (*Back to his audience*) Wait; wait a minute. (*Back to the offstage, very angry*) What?! No! No; we're not finished yet! We're not finished! All right, but we're not finished yet! (*Turns back to his audience, upset at being interrupted. Slight aggravated "Pheww"*) Don't put that on the tape. Don't leave that on the tape. You're not going to leave that on the tape(?). Yeah, don't leave that on the tape. All right, so where was . . . oh, right; she'd be screaming and yelling, right, and throwing things around the apartment and my father would be laughing at her- just laughing at her like . . . . Whatever. Something like that. And there's kind of a crowd of people gathered, and I'm crying, my father is laughing, and Aunt Rosie is telling everybody that I had gotten lost. "No, no; he just got lost." And- oh- and I can- I can hear my mother; my mother is calling to my father's- calling out my father's name. "Marty! Marty!!" And she's really yelling, and she's obviously very angry. She sounds very angry. So, you know. It wasn't . . . it . . . . No; it

162

JACK

Hold. Light on Character 8 is dimmed as light on The Speakers is intensified. Then with their lips pursed, gently but audibly exhaling, The Speakers turn to their next page.

PART SEVEN

1

2

3

And so Jack dead.

Ahhh.

Jack is gone his

Ahhh. Jack gone his

friends now his
friends have to-

Jack's friends had to
  call his mother his

friends called his
  mother

mother in where
I forget where
does his mother
live in-

Jack's friends made
  phone calls to his
  mother in she lives

in Atlanta- in
  Atlanta
she settled five, six
maybe six years ago
  in-

Where(?) for- no; are
  you kidding,
  Atlanta?

Yes
  in Atlanta she had
  a sister-

Hello, Faith; this is

someone

a sister or

someone.

someone who-

163

someone had to-
someone had to call
　his no his mother
　didn't even know
　　he
　was no she didn't
　　no
　he didn't tell her
　　he
　never no she didn't
　know he was

What?

　　　　She knew.
　　　　She knew.

He's dead my
　god.
　　　　　　　　　　　　God(?) what God(?)
　　　　　　　　　　　　　my-

　　　　Jackie my Jack is
　　　　　what
　　　　　happened to oh for
　　　　　　christ
　　　　　sake my baby they
　　　　　　killed my
　　　　　baby you son of a
　　　　　bitch what did you
　　　　　do to my baby is

Why does God
　punish me like
　this?
　　　　　　　　　　　　This is how she
　　　　　　　　　　　　　took the news that
　　　　　　　　　　　　　Jack was

　　　　dead.
　　　　　　　　　　　　now
　　　　Dead.
　　　　　　　　　　　　now Jack is dead
　　　　　　　　　　　　　yes
　　　　　　　　　　　　he's dead now but
　　　　　　　　　　　　happily died now in

164

                                                        peace does death
                                                            bring
                            Happily you   death brings
                                say to die?   happiness, rest,
                                                            who
Is there ever   Who knows?   can I say these
    peace in   What peace?   things(?) no.
    death who   Is there any who
    can say   can tell?
    what you will
death is death.

                                                        Me I say I
                                                            know only nothing
                                                                to
                                                            speak of what but I
                                                            know what I know
                                                            nothing of what
                                                                beyond
                                                            I know not; death
                                                                not
                                                            known.

                            Who can speak of
                                Jack but Jack who
                                knows(?) what do I
                                no nothing know
                                of death.   Of death?
                                                   Who knows?

Nothing no I
    know no no
    nothing.   No no nothing
                                known.
                            I know only what I
                                know what.   No thing is known of
                                                           death nothing
Nothing is-   is.

165

what's known?

                 And.
                 And
                 and so and

And

                                       And and so as

as

as

                 as spoken before.

                                     and spoken since
spoken a   again.
gain nothing only
and

                                     And

                 Nothing.
and

                 Nothing.

                                     No no no no nothing.

                                     Nothing. Only
nothing.
Nothing.

                                     and.

                                     And

Hold. Light on the chairs fades to black. Hold. Then with their lips pursed, gently but audibly exhaling, The Speakers turn to their next page. Hold. Light on The Speakers fades to black.

END OF PLAY

DAVID GREENSPAN *is an playwright/director/actor whose works include* Principia, The HOME Show Pieces *and* 2 Samuel 11, Etc. Jack *was first staged by the author on May 27, 1987 at New York's HOME for Contemporary Theatre and Art, where he is playwright in residence.*

from

Laughing Wild

by Christopher Durang

CHARACTER

MAN

TIME 1987.

PLACE New York City.

Editor's Note: "Seeking Wild," the man's monologue presented here, is the middle section of the play Laughing Wild. *It is preceded by a monologue in which a woman tells about—among other things—hitting a man over the head in the tuna-fish section of the supermarket; it is followed by a series of nightmares the man and woman share.*

A space in which a talk is about to be given, i.e., a lecture hall, a stage, or a room. There is a dark curtain midstage. In front of the curtain stage right is a chair next to a table. On the table is a water pitcher and a glass. Stage left is a columnlike stand (a pedestal), on which there are three crystals: a large, jagged, clear crystal; a chunk of amethyst (which is purple); a piece of citrine (amber-colored).

Hanging on the curtain (upstage center) and dominating the stage is a very large hand-painted canvas poster of an Egyptian Eye. The poster may be patterned after the Eye of Ra (or "Horus card") found in the book The Way of Cartouche. *It is a large eye, with a primitive, bold look to it. Beneath the eye there is a small line (where "circles under your eyes" would be on a person) underneath which "hangs" a stylized, primitive design, possibly forming little icicles or teardrops.*

After a few beats, a Man *enters. The* Man *is dressed well, maybe even a little trendy. He is dressed up to give a talk, to share his new thoughts. He carries with him a few file cards that he has made notes on. He smiles at the audience briefly, checks his first note card quickly before beginning, and then speaks with earnestness and purpose.*

MAN: I used to be a very negative person. But then I took this personality workshop that totally turned my life around. Now when something bad or negative happens, I can see the positive. Now when I have a really bad day, or when someone I thought was a really good friend betrays me, or maybe when I've been hit by one of those damn people riding bicycles the opposite way on a one-way street, so, of course, one hadn't looked in that direction and there they are bearing down on you, about to kill or maim you — anyway, I look at any of these things and I say to myself: this glass is not half full, it's half empty.

171

No—I said it backwards, force of habit. This glass is not half empty, it is half *full*.

Of course, if they hit you with the stupid bicycle your glass will not be half full or half empty, it will be shattered to pieces, and you'll be dead or in the hospital.

But really I'm trying to be positive, that's what I'm doing with my life these days. (*Reads from a note card*) I was tired of not being joyful and happy, I was sick of my personality, and I had to change it.

(*Off the card; back to speaking extemporaneously*) Half full, *not* half empty. I had to say to myself: you do not have cancer—at least not today. You are not blind. You are not one of the starving children in India or China or in Africa. Look at the sunset, look at the sunrise, why don't you enjoy them, for God's sake? And now I do. (*Almost as a sidetrack to himself*) Except if it's cloudy, of course, and you can't see the sun. Or if it's cold. Or if it's too hot.

(*Hearing his negativity above*) I probably need to take a few more personality workshops to complete the process. It's still not quite within my grasp, this being-positive business.

(*Reads from cards again*) But I'm making great strides. My friends don't recognize me. (*Smiles*)

(*Off the cards again*) And it is hard for me to be positive because I'm very sensitive to the vibrations of people around me, or maybe I'm just paranoid. But in any case, I used to find it difficult to go out of the house sometimes because of coming into contact with other people.

You've probably experienced something similar—you know, the tough on the subway who keeps staring at you and you're the only two people in the car and he keeps staring and after a while you think, does he want to kill me? Or just intimidate me? Which is annoying enough.

Or the people in movie theaters who talk endlessly during the opening credits so you can just *tell* they're going to talk through the entire movie and that it will be utterly useless to ask them not to talk.

And even if you do ask them not to talk and they ungraciously acquiesce, they're going to send out vibrations that they hate you all during the entire film, and then it will be impossible to concentrate.

You can move, but the person next to you in the new location will probably, you know, rattle candy wrappers endlessly all through the movie. Basically I don't go to the movies anymore. What's the point?

But even if you can skip going to the movies, you pretty much have to go to the supermarket.

(*Steps closer to the audience*) I was in the supermarket the other day about to buy some tuna fish when I sensed this very disturbed presence right behind me. There was something about her focus that made it very clear to me that she was a disturbed person. So I thought—well, you should never look at a crazy person directly, so I thought, I'll just keep looking at these tuna-fish cans, pretending to be engrossed in whether they're in oil or in water, and the person will then go away. But instead *wham!* she brings her fist down on my head and screams: "Would you move, asshole!"

Pause.

Now why did she do that? She hadn't even said, "Would you please move" at some initial point, so I would've known what her problem was. Admittedly I don't always tell people what I want either—like the people in the movie theaters who keep talking, you know, I just give up and resent them—but on the other hand, I don't take my fist and go wham! on their heads!

I mean, analyzing it, looking at it in a positive light, this woman probably had some really horrible life story that, you know, kind of explained how she got to this point in time, hitting me in the supermarket. And perhaps if her life—*since birth*—had been explained to me, I could probably have made some sense out of her action and how she got there. But even with that knowledge— which I didn't have—it was *my* head she was hitting, and it's just so unfair.

It makes me want to never leave my apartment *ever ever again.*

Suddenly he closes his eyes and moves his arms in a circular motion around himself, round and round, soothingly.

I am the predominant source of energy in my life. I let go of the pain from the past. I let go of the pain from the present. In the places in my body where pain lived previously, now there is light and love and joy.

He opens his eyes again and looks at the audience peacefully and happily.

That was an affirmation.

Now the theory of affirmations is that by saying something positive about yourself in the present tense—as if the positive thing is already happening—you draw in positive energies to you. For instance, who do you think will have the easier life? Someone who goes around saying inside their head, "Everyone hates me, they try to avoid me, my job stinks, my life is miserable." Or the person who says, "Everyone likes me exactly as I am, every time I turn around people offer me friendship and money, my life is delightful and effortless."

Pause.

Obviously, the second person will be much happier.

There's an additional theory that by thinking negatively, you actually cause, and are thus responsible for, the bad things that happen to you. Thus I need to look at whether I maybe *caused* the woman in the tuna-fish aisle to hit me on the head. Or, since that sounds rather blaming, I need to look at the incident and see how else I could have behaved so she might *not* have hit me on the head.

When I sensed her presence, rather than doing nothing and pretending I didn't *notice* that she seemed odd, maybe I could have said, "Is something the matter?" Then maybe she would have said, "Yes, you're in my way," and I would have moved. Or, if

174

when I said, "Is something the matter?" she stayed hostile and said, "Why???" defensively or something, if I stayed honest and said . . . "Well, you seem odd," or, "I sense you're distressed," she might have felt that I was "responding" to her as another human being, and that might have relaxed her, and *then* she might have told me what was the matter.

So you see, I shouldn't feel like a victim. We have power.

(Reads from his note cards) We can change our own thoughts, from negative to positive. *(Off the cards again, explaining)* Say I feel bad; I can *choose* to feel good.

How do I feel right now? *(Thinks)* I feel fine. Everything's fine. Of course, that's just on the surface, underneath there's always this gnawing residue of anxiety. But is feeling anxious just part of the human condition? Or do I feel more anxious than one should normally due to some psychological maladjustment or something? Maybe I wasn't breast-fed enough as an infant. Actually I don't even know if I was breast-fed at all. *(Thinks with concern about his lack of knowledge concerning this)* Oh well, enough about breast-feeding.

(A surge of positive energy) Let me try to *change* how I feel. Let me try to feel happy for a moment.

He closes his eyes, puts his fingers to his forehead and "flicks away" negative energy; waits for happiness.

No, I was just thinking about Chernobyl. That's like a scream from the universe warning us, but we're not paying attention. I can't believe they don't know what to do with nuclear waste, and then they keep building these things. I'm sorry, I was trying to feel happy. Let me try again.

He closes his eyes, tries again.

Sorry, I was just thinking of something else, something I read in the newspaper about this fourteen-year-old boy in Montana who shot his geometry teacher — *to death* because the teacher was flunking him. Now that's crazy enough, but it seems that this particular teacher didn't come to school that day, and so this fourteen-year-old boy shot the substitute teacher instead. Shot her dead. I don't know how to cope with that.

I mean, positive thinking aside, how do you protect yourself from these sorts of things?

He suddenly wants some water, goes up to the table and pours himself some while he's on this tangent of upset and negativity.

And there's acid rain and something wrong with the ozone layer, and the secretary of education doesn't want schools to educate students about the dangers of nuclear proliferation, but instead to focus on how terrible the communists are. And the secretary of the environment isn't in favor of protecting the environment, doesn't see a problem. The appointments to these offices in the Reagan administration seem like a sick joke . . . like naming Typhoid Mary the secretary of health and welfare. God, it's discouraging.

Drinks water.

And think about God. You know, it was nice to believe in God, and an afterlife, and I'm sometimes envious of the people who seem comfortable because they still have this belief. But I remember when everybody won Tonys for *Dreamgirls*, and they all got up there thanking God for letting them win this award, and I was thinking to myself: God is silent on the Holocaust, but he involves himself in the Tony awards? It doesn't seem very likely.

Feels a need for affirmation; does the circular arm motions again.

I am the predominant source of my life. I release anger from my solar plexus. It is replaced by serenity and white light and joy and . . . serenity. Everything in my life works. Except the plumbing and career and relationships.

176

Laughs at his joke, then talks sincerely.

I'm sorry, I was planning on being positive out here, and it's just not happening. But I guess whatever happens is okay. Is that right?

This personality workshop I took taught me that I judge things too much, that some things just "are," you don't have to label them. And also that you shouldn't judge feelings.

This workshop also said to forgive yourself for what you haven't achieved. For instance, I had wanted to be a university professor, maybe in New England somewhere—summers off, tutorials, sherry. I'm very verbal, and that would have been a good thing to do with it.

Instead I work for a magazine, not a bad job, but not great—it's sort of a cross between . . . *TV Guide* and pornography. Well, that's too strong—but I do have to interview people who are on television series, and if they're at all attractive, they have them photographed with their blouses undone or with their shirts off. Sometimes I have nightmares about the upper bodies of Barbara Bach and Lorenzo Lamas. People whose first and last names begin with the same letter. Lorenzo Lamas. Erik Estrada. Suzanne Somers. Cher.

Time for another affirmation.

Everything unfolds in my life exactly as it should, including my career. Abundance is my natural state of being, and I accept it now. I let go of anger and resentment. *(A sudden addition to the affirmation)* I love the woman in the tuna-fish aisle. I accept her exactly as she is. I accept myself exactly as I am. I approve of my body. *(Makes equivocal face)* I approve of *other* people's bodies.

You know, I don't like meeting people who are too attractive, and not just TV stars at my job, but anyone who's good-looking or charismatic. I hate being attracted to people, it's exhausting. It stirs up longing.

Of course, one can just do one's best to have sex with the

person, and that assuages some of the longing. But the problem is, that sexual longing has no real assuagement ever, it's like longing for the moon; you can never have the moon no matter what you do, and if you were foolish enough to take a spaceship up there—and if the people running NASA didn't see to it that you were killed—you would just find that the moon was this big chunk of nothing that had nothing to do with what you were longing for at all. Oh, Olga, let's go to Moscow, and all that. There is no Moscow, there is no moon, there is no assuagement of longing.

Affirmation.

I let go of my need for longing. I let go of sexual interest. I become like Buddha, and want nothing. (*Abruptly stops, to audience*) Do these affirmations sound right to you? They sound off to me. And I've certainly never successfully acted them out. 'Cause as soon as sexual attraction kicks in, the Zen in one's nature flies out the window. You meet someone, sometimes they really are terrific, other times they're just awful but nonetheless you find yourself attracted to them anyway, knowing you're an utter fool and will be very sorry later on. And then the pursuit begins. All those opening weeks of interested conversation, with the eyes more lively than usual, and each party finding the other's comments and insights more than usually charming and delightful. And then if you've been in therapy like me, there are the flirtatious exchanges of childhood traumas—all of my family were borderline schizophrenic, they beat me, they had terrible taste in furniture—and after a while one's mind starts to reverberate with, when will I have an orgasm with this person?

If there is a God, his design about sex is certainly humiliating. It's humiliating to want things. And sex itself people say is beautiful—but is it? Maybe you think it is. Terrible viscous discharges erupting in various openings may strike you as the equivalent of the Sistine Chapel ceiling, for all I know. It doesn't strike me that way.

He stops. He realizes how extreme and cranklike his comments have begun to sound. He smiles at the audience, wanting to reestablish his rapport and his reasonability with them.

But I am being negative again. And clearly sex isn't just disgusting. I know that, and you know that. And when I'm lucky enough to go off with someone to his or her apartment, I certainly anticipate a pleasant time.

Now he stops dead. He had no intention of going into this area of his life with this audience, and he's suddenly uncertain how he even got into it. Or, more to the point, how he can get out of it. He thinks, can't come up with any way to camouflage or take back what he's just said. For better or for worse, he decides just to speak honestly.

As the "his or her" comment suggests, I am attracted to women and to men. Though more frequently to other guys, which I find rather embarrassing to admit to publicly. Why do I bring it *up* publicly then, you may well ask? Well . . . I don't know. Why not? All my relatives are dead, and those that aren't I'm willing not to talk to. And things like the recent Supreme Court ruling that sex between consenting adult homosexuals *not* be included in what's considered the rights of privacy—this makes me think it's now important to be open about this. Look, I've even brought pictures of myself in bed with people! *(Pats his inside jacket pocket)* At intermission the ushers will let you look at them! . . . Although I suppose the Meese Commission will run in here and try to take them away from you and then force you to buy milk at a 7-Eleven store. God, I took some Valium before I came out here, but it hasn't calmed me down a bit.

Anyway, I didn't mean to get into this . . . *(Puts his note cards away in his jacket)* but I find the Supreme Court's ruling on this issue deeply disturbing. I mean, so much of the evil that men do to one another has at its core the inability of people to *empathize* with another person's position. Say when you're seven, you find yourself slightly more drawn to Johnny than you are to Jane. This is not a conscious decision on your part, it just happens, it's an instinct like . . . liking the color blue.

Now in less tolerant times, you were put to death for this attraction. As time went on, this punishment was sometimes reduced to mere castration, or just imprisonment. Until recently this attraction was considered so horrific that society pretty much expected you to lie to yourself about your sexual and emotional feelings, and if you couldn't do that, certainly expected you to *shut up* about it and go live your life bottled up and terrified; and if you would be so kind as to never have any physical closeness with anyone *ever*, when you were buried you could know that society would feel you had handled your disgraceful situation with tact and willpower. That was one *cheery* option—nothing, and then the grave.

Or, you might make a false marriage with some woman who wouldn't know what was going on with you, and you could *both* be miserable and unfulfilled. That was *another* respectable option. Or you might kill yourself. There's not a lot of empathy evident in the people who prefer these options.

He takes out his note cards again, starts to look at them, but then his mind isn't ready to leave this topic yet.

I mean, *I* certainly realize how insane it would be to ask a heterosexual to deny his or her natural sexual feelings and perform homosexual acts that went against *their* nature. If I can have that empathy, why can't others have the same empathy in reverse? I want some empathy here! *(Goes into an affirmation)* I am the predominant source of . . . well, fuck that.

Throws his note cards over his shoulder, drives on ahead.

And then, of course, there are all the religious teachings about homosexuality. The Book of Leviticus, for instance, says that homosexuals should basically be put to death. It also tells you how to sacrifice rams and bullocks and instructs you not to sit in a chair sat in by any woman who's had her period in the last seven days or something. To me, this is not a book to look to for much modern wisdom.

If the audience laughs, he might smile with them.

People's concepts of God are so odd. For instance, take the Christians—"take them, please"—who seem to believe that God is so disgusted by the sexual activities of homosexuals that he created AIDS to punish them, apparently waiting until 1978 or so to do this, even though homosexual acts have been going on for considerably longer than that, at least since . . . 1956.

I mean, what do they think? God sits around in a lounge chair chatting with Gabriel, planning the fall foliage in Vermont—"I think a lot of orange this year"—when suddenly he says: "Boy oh boy, do I find homosexuals disgusting. I'm going to give them a really horrifying disease!"

And Gabriel says: "Oh yes?"

(As God) Yes! And drug addicts and . . . and . . . hemophiliacs!

Gabriel looks fairly appalled.

(As Gabriel) But why hemophiliacs?

(God) Oh, no reason. I want the disease to go through the bloodstream and even though I'm all-powerful and can do everything 'cause I'm God, I'm too tired today to figure out how to connect the disease to the bloodstream and *not* affect hemophiliacs. Besides, the suffering will be good for them.

(Gabriel) Really? In what way?

(God) Oh, I don't know. I'll explain it at the end of the world.

(Gabriel) I see. Tell me, what about the children of drug addicts? Will they get the disease through their mother's wombs?

(God) Oh, I hadn't thought about that. Well—why not? Serve the hophead mothers right. Boy oh boy, do I hate women drug addicts!

(*Gabriel*) Yes, but why punish their babies?

(*God*) And I hate homosexuals!

(*Gabriel*) Yes, yes, we got you hate homosexuals . . .

(*God*) Except for Noël Coward; he was droll.

(*Gabriel*) Yes, he was droll.

(*God*) And I hate Haitians. Anything beginning with the letter H.

(*Gabriel*) Yes, but isn't it unfair to infect innocent babies in the womb with this dreadful disease?

(*God*) Look, homosexuals and drug addicts are very, very bad people; and if babies get it, well, don't forget I'm God, so you better just presume I have some secret reason why it's good they get it too.

(*Gabriel*) Yes, but what *is* this secret reason?

(*God*) Stop asking so many questions.

(*Gabriel*) Yes, but . . .

(*God*) There you go again, trying to horn in on the Tree of Knowledge just like Adam and Eve did. Boy oh boy, does that make me wrathful. Okay, Gabriel, you asked for it: I hereby sentence you to become man; I give you suffering and death; I give you psychological pain; I give you AIDS, your immune system will shut down totally, you'll die from brain tumors and diarrhea and horrible random infections. I give you bone cancer, lymph cancer, breast cancer—lots of cancer.

(*Still as God; a good idea, whimsical*) Oh! . . . And I hereby revoke penicillin. Anyone out there who has ever been exposed to syphilis will suffer and die just like they used to—as a side issue, I love to connect sex and death, I don't know why I invented sex to begin with, it's a revolting idea, but as long as I have, I want it done *properly*, in the *missionary* position, with *one* person for life, or I want those who disobey me to die a horrible death from AIDS and syphilis and God knows what else. Is that clear???

(*Breaks character and talks to the audience as himself again*) Now surely that God can't exist—I mean, surely the Christ who said, "Blessed are the merciful" could hardly have come from such a raging, spiteful God.

Pause, his agitation not quite gone yet. He turns around and stares upstage at the banner for a moment. Turns back to the audience.

What *is* that???

Looks again. Then back.

You know, I don't want to take *away* faith in God from anyone who has it; it's just that I don't follow it. And it's not as if living without a belief in God is so pleasant. In moments of deep despair you have absolutely nothing to fall back on. You just stay in the deep despair for a while, and then if you're lucky, you go to sleep.

But I find more and more that I'm starting to long for some sense of value in things. My mind wanders to reincarnation and karma and karmic paths and so on; in some ways I am turning into Shirley MacLaine. Now one does laugh at her, but I'm starting to really identify with the desire to find some meaning out there.

Because I'm really tired of where I've been. I've been . . . a pretty good "ad-hoc existentialist" for about twenty years. I've gotten up every morning, and I've carried on with my life, acting decent and getting things done, while all the time believing none of it mattered. And I'm really sick of it. I'm *starved* for some meaning. For some belief in something. I'm tired of being an existentialist. It's hard to be joyful when you're an existentialist. Albert Camus was not a laugh riot.

I even went to the Harmonic Convergence ceremony in Central Park this summer. Do you know what I'm referring to? It's this strange, New Age-connected belief, prophesied in several ancient cultures—the Mayan, the Aztec, and the Hopi Indians—that August sixteenth and seventeenth of 1987 represent a window in time in which the planets line up in some special way or other, and that, supposedly, there is an opportunity for mankind to make a spiritual shift away from pollution and destruction of the planet back to being "in alignment" with mother earth, and so on.

The newspapers made fun of the event, and people at the magazine where I work thought I was nuts, but I found I really wanted to believe in this Harmonic Convergence. And even if it was a lot of nonsense, I *liked* the idea of people getting up in the morning all over the world to greet the sunrise and to, if nothing else, sort of hope for a better way of living. I mean, it beats a punch in the eye, doesn't it?

So a couple of friends and I—I'm starting to have more friends who think this way—set our alarms for four in the morning to head up to Eighty-third and Central Park West, which had been designated as a sacred site. *(Realizing that sounds a bit funny)* Or at least as a place where people were going to gather.

We went over to Sixth Avenue for a taxi and saw all these people getting out of cabs who looked like they were leaving clubs together, going home to have sex, or take cocaine or . . . otherwise give *New York* magazine topics to write on. I guess people still go to clubs. I don't really know anyone who does.

Anyway, predictably we got an absolutely *terrifying* taxi driver. He'd race up to every red light at sixty miles an hour, never slowing down at all just in case the light turned green, which it sometimes did, but you had to worry about the people coming in the other direction who might be trying to run their lights. Anyway, it was harrowing. I kept saying to myself, "All is well in my universe, everyone is calm, no one rushes," but it didn't make him slow down. Finally I had to say, slow down, goddamn it, only I didn't say goddamn it, and he didn't slow down, and eventually we killed two people and a dog. Well, just kidding. But it was a disorienting beginning to the Harmonic Convergence.

Well, in any case, at the sacred site itself, it was very crowded, and there was incense and so on, and wind chimes, and we all sat in a circle. And in the center of the circle there were five women and one man who were blowing on conch shells; and one of the women explained to the crowd that we were all there to align the "horizontal plane" of our present existence with the "vertical plane" of mother earth and the planets or . . . something like that . . . but she seemed a very *warm* woman—she reminded me of someone I know and like named Martha Rhodes. And then the woman said we should all join in and make sounds like the conch shell if we wanted to, and eventually most of the crowd sort of hit this one sustained note that in these circles is described as "toning."

He takes a moment to breathe and then lets out a low, sustained note, kind of like chanting "Om." It's just a held note.

Ahhhhhhhhhhhhhhhhhhhhhhhhhhhhhhhhhhhhhhmmmmmm-mmmmmmmmmmmmm.

I liked doing that. I'm not comfortable meditating yet, but this I could do, and it was nice to be connected to the crowd that way.

And then the sun came up, but the "sacred site chosen" had all these *trees* around it so you couldn't actually *see* the sun. I had almost gone to my friend's roof and part of me wished I were there instead. And then this sort of . . . loopy woman who'd been dancing around the periphery of the circle saying kind of corny things like, "I dance for mother moon and sister star," and stuff like that, and whom I almost admired for having the guts to say things like that, and yet I also thought her sensibility was kind of . . . icky . . . anyway, she got up and invited everyone who wanted to get up and share their hopes and dreams and prayers for the future. And I realized I didn't want to hear *everyone* in the crowd verbalize their hopes, we'd be stuck for *hours*, listening to a lot of gobbledygook.

And then, of course, the first person to get up to share with the group was one of those mental patients who wander the streets of New York—she looked *demented*, and she was yellow from nicotine, and she talked on and on. And what she said wasn't wrong, exactly—something about why don't people say "I love you" rather than "I hate you"?—but it was upsetting that she was crazy. She reminded me of the woman in the tuna-fish aisle, but much more clearly crazy. The woman in the tuna-fish aisle could pass for normal on a good day, but this woman really couldn't.

And then the "icky woman" gave the "demented woman" a great big hug in order to *shut her up*, and then some teenager got up to recite a song—not sing it, *recite* it. I don't remember what song it was. Maybe "Blowin' in the Wind." (*Jokes*) Or "Bali Ha'i." Anyway, it was turning into a nightmare. I didn't want anyone else to speak, I just wanted instant transformation of the planet, and I didn't want to take potluck of listening to any strangers in the crowd say how we should go about it, I didn't trust that they'd know, I just *wanted the transformation*. I didn't want to have to deal with *people* about it. And the Harmonic Convergence is about people coming together, and here I was disliking everyone. So I wasn't being very transformed. And my back was sore from sitting—I need to exercise, but I guess I never will—so I asked my friends if we could *please* leave the group and go out into an open area of the park so that we could actually see the sun.

And we did that, and the Great Lawn was very pretty, but I was irritated that we hadn't been there for the actual sunrise.

Well, you can see I was quite resistant, and I did feel bad I was judging everyone there, but then it doesn't really work to pretend you're not feeling something you're feeling. But when you're judging people, you certainly don't feel a sense of unity, do you?

Maybe I shouldn't be so judgmental of people. And it was moving that everyone went there and showed up. I liked that part. And I liked the toning. But otherwise, I felt . . . very separate.

He looks thoughtful and a little sad at this. He stays in the moment for a bit, and then goes into another affirmation, moving his arms in that circular motion again.

I am *not* separate. I am one with the universe. We are all one. We are all part of the same divine energy. (*His tone becomes slightly tongue-in-cheek*) There are spirit guides above, waiting to guide us. They speak to us through Shirley MacLaine; they knew enough not to choose Shelley Winters. These spirit guides help us. They drive Shirley's car, they make airline reservations for her, they're just great. Bali Ha'i will call you, any night, any day. And they call the wind Maria. (*Pronounced "Ma-rye-a"*) Kumbaya, kumbayae. (*Rhymes with day*)

Well, now I've depressed myself. But I really am much more

positive than I ever used to be, and I think these affirmations are a good thing. It's just that . . . sometimes the bottom drops out for me. And then I need to go sleep for a while and see if tomorrow feels better.

(*Looks around at banner again*) I wish I knew what that was. It's a great big eye, I see that. I don't know what those things dripping off it are. It looks Egyptian. Or Columbus Avenue. I shouldn't make fun of it. Maybe it is a guide. (*Makes something up*) It's an "all-seeing eye" that represents inner knowingness, all the wisdom we know from the collective unconscious but, alas, have forgotten.

He looks over to the crystals and crosses to them.

What about crystals? Do you think crystals work? *What works*, do you think?

He stares at the crystals, wondering what works.

Let me try to feel happy again.

Puts his fingers to his forehead, "flicks" away negativity; pause.

Let me hold a crystal to my head and try to feel happy.

Holds the clear crystal to his head; pause; puts the crystal down again.

Let me give up on feeling happy for now and just concentrate on breathing.

He inhales audibly, but stops and comes closer to the audience, a little disappointed.

I don't feel I've helped you very much. But I want you to remember what I said about affirmations. We *can* change our thoughts. And even when we can't, just kinda . . . try to . . .

187

silence your mind, and then just breathe. As the last thing between us, let's just breathe, all right?

He breathes in an exaggerated way, so the audience can get in synch with him. On inhalation he moves his arms up from his diaphragm to his chin; on exhalation, his arms relax downward, the palms open in the "receiving" mode. He keeps his eyes closed.

In, out. In, out. In, out. God, life's monotonous, isn't it? No, I keep judging things, I'm going to stop doing that. I'm going to stop talking. Just breathe.

He returns to his exaggerated breathing again, this time without words. Inhale—arms up to chin; exhale—arms down to the side. He keeps his eyes closed, except on his second full breath, when he opens them to check how the audience is doing, breathing with him. On his third breath, he closes his eyes again, and the lights fade.

END OF SCENE

CHRISTOPHER DURANG's *plays* include Sister Mary Ignatius Explains It All for You, Beyond Therapy *and* The Marriage of Bette and Boo. Laughing Wild *was first presented at Playwrights Horizons in New York City on October 23, 1987. Durang himself played the Man in this production.*

Andre's Mother

BY TERRENCE MCNALLY

Four people—Cal, Arthur, Penny and Andre's Mother—enter. They are nicely dressed and carry white helium-filled balloons on a string.

CAL: You know what's really terrible? I can't think of anything terrific to say. Good-bye. I love you. I'll miss you. And I'm supposed to be so great with words!

PENNY: What's that over there?

ARTHUR: Ask your brother.

CAL: It's a theatre. An outdoor theatre. They do plays there in the summer. Shakespeare's plays. *(To Andre's Mother)* God, how much he wanted to play Hamlet again. He would have gone to Timbuktu to have another go at that part. The summer he did it in Boston, he was so happy!

PENNY: Cal, I don't think she . . . ! It's not the time. Later.

ARTHUR: Your son was a . . . the Jews have a word for it . . .

PENNY *(Quietly appalled)*: Oh my God!

ARTHUR: Mensch, I believe it is, and I think I'm using it right. It means warm, solid, the real thing. Correct me if I'm wrong.

PENNY: Fine, Dad, fine. Just quit while you're ahead.

ARTHUR: I won't say he was like a son to me. Even my son isn't always like a son to me. I mean . . . ! In my clumsy way, I'm trying to say how much I liked Andre. And how much he helped me to know my own boy. Cal was always two handsful but Andre and I could talk about anything under the sun. My wife was very fond of him, too.

PENNY: Cal, I don't understand about the balloons.

CAL: They represent the soul. When you let go, it means you're letting his soul ascend to Heaven. That you're willing to let go. Breaking the last earthly ties.

PENNY: Does the Pope know about this?

ARTHUR: Penny!

191

PENNY: Andre loved my sense of humor. Listen, you can hear him laughing. (*She lets go of her white balloon*) So long, you glorious, wonderful, I-know-what-Cal-means-about-words . . . *man*! God forgive me for wishing you were straight every time I laid eyes on you. But if any man was going to have you, I'm glad it was my brother! Look how fast it went up. I bet that means something. Something terrific.

Arthur lets his balloon go.

ARTHUR: Good-bye. God speed.

PENNY: Cal?

CAL: I'm not ready yet.

PENNY: Okay. We'll be over there. Come on, Pop, you can buy your little girl a Good Humor.

ARTHUR: They still make Good Humor?

PENNY: Only now they're called Dove Bars and they cost twelve dollars.

Penny takes Arthur off. Cal and Andre's Mother stand with their balloons.

CAL: I wish I knew what you were thinking. I think it would help me. You know almost nothing about me and I only know what Andre told me about you. I'd always had it in my mind that one day we would be friends, you and me. But if you didn't know about Andre and me . . . . If this hadn't happened, I wonder if he would have ever told you. When he was so sick, if I asked him once I asked him a thousand times, tell her. She's your mother. She won't mind. But he was so afraid of hurting you and of your disapproval. I don't know which was worse.

   (*No response. He sighs*) God, how many of us live in this city because we don't want to hurt our mothers and live in mortal terror of their disapproval. We lose ourselves here. Our lives aren't furtive, just our feelings toward people like you are! A city of fugitives from our parents' scorn or heartbreak. Sometimes he'd seem a little down and I'd say, "What's the matter, babe?" and this funny sweet, sad smile would cross his face and he'd say, "Just a little homesick, Cal, just a little bit." I always accused him of being a country boy just playing at being a hotshot, sophisticated New Yorker.

(*He sighs*) It's bullshit. It's all bullshit.

(*Still no response*) Do you remember the comic strip *Little Lulu*? Her mother had no name, she was so remote, so formidable to all the children. She was just Lulu's mother. "Hello, Lulu's Mother," Lulu's friends would say. She was almost anonymous in her remoteness. You remind me of her. Andre's mother. Let me answer the questions you can't ask and then I'll leave you alone and you won't ever have to see me again. Andre died of AIDS. I don't know how he got it. I tested negative. He died bravely. You would have been proud of him. The only thing that frightened him was you. I'll have everything that was his sent to you. I'll pay for it. There isn't much. You should have come up the summer he played Hamlet. He was magnificent. Yes, I'm bittter. I'm bitter I've lost him. I'm bitter what's happening. I'm bitter even now, after all this, I can't reach you. I'm beginning to feel your disapproval and it's making me ill.

(*He looks at his balloon*) Sorry, old friend. I blew it.

(*He lets go of the balloon*) Good night, sweet prince, and flights of angels sing thee to thy rest!

(*Beat*) Good-bye, Andre's mother.

He goes. Andre's Mother stands alone holding her white balloon. Her lips tremble. She looks on the verge of breaking down. She is about to let go of the balloon when she pull it down to her. She looks at it awhile before she gently kisses it. She lets go of the balloon. She follows it with her eyes as it rises and rises. The lights are beginning to fade. Andre's Mother's eyes are still on the balloon. The lights fade.

THE END

TERRENCE MCNALLY's *plays include* Bad Habits, Frankie and Johnny in the Clair de Lune *and* The Lisbon Traviata. Andre's Mother *was originally part of an evening of vignettes and songs entitled* Urban Blight, *first seen at Manhattan Theatre Club on May 18, 1988. McNally subsequently expanded* Andre's Mother *into a teleplay for Amer*-ican Playhouse, *first aired in March 1990.*

from

The Baltimore Waltz

BY PAULA VOGEL

Ron Vawter: . . . I always saw myself as a surrogate who, in the absence of anyone else, would stand in for him.

—Breaking the Rules, *David Savran*

Editor's Note: The Baltimore Waltz *is essentially Anna's fantasy, her response to her brother's illness. She imagines that she is the one who is stricken, and she and Carl travel through a Hollywood version of Europe—an escape that confronts them with intimations of death at every turn. They are accompanied on their trip by Carl's stuffed rabbit.*

To the memory of Carl—because I cannot sew

ANNA AND THE THIRD MAN *(Simultaneously)*: Wann geht der nächste Zug nach Hamburg?

German band music swells as Anna and Carl sit in their railroad compartment, side by side. Anna, pale, holds the rabbit in her lap.

CARL: Ah, Saxony, Bavaria, the Black Forest, the Rhineland . . . I love them all. I think perhaps now would be a good time to show the slides . . .

ANNA: I'm so sorry. I hate it when people do that to me. They usually wait until right after dinner, so you're slightly glazed and passive, but before they give you some really fabulous dessert so that you're stuck there, looking at out-of-focus slides of India or Scotland . . .

CARL: Nonsense. People like to see slides of other people's trips. We'll only show a few, just to give a taste of the German countryside . . .

ANNA: Carl took over two hours' worth of slides . . .

CARL: If you'll just dim the lights, please.

The Third Man wheels in the projector and operates it throughout the travelogue.

CARL: These aren't in any particular order. This is just a light pastiche of impressions of the cognoscenti who travel far from the maddening crowd; who disdain tour-bus guides that lead you to Maria von Trapp's house and assure you that Germany is the land where *Amadeus* was filmed on location. Well. Bonn's as good a place to start as anywhere. This is the view from our snug little

199

hotel we stayed in. The gateway to the Rhine Valley, a city that has seen two thousand years of travelers. The birthplace of Beethoven, and the resting place of Schumann.

Slide: the view of downtown Baltimore from the Ramada Inn near Johns Hopkins Hospital, overlooking the industrial harbor.

ANNA: Looks a lot like Baltimore to me.

CARL: My sister jests. As you can see in the slide, one night we splurged and stayed in a rather dear inn near the Drachenfels Mountains, where Lord Byron sported among the romantic ruins of castles.

Slide: a closeup of the balcony railing looking into the Ramada Inn hotel room.

ANNA: *(Deadpan)*: This is the room I slept in while I stayed with my brother Carl.

CARL: I might mention in passing my appreciation for the baroque Jesu Church in Köln, for those who like the baroque. Anna prefers the bizarre, don't you dear?

Slide: gutted ruins of inner-city Baltimore near the Jones-Fall Expressway; rubble and obvious urban blight. Black children playing who look impassively at the camera.

CARL: Alas, poor Köln. Practically wiped out by airplane raids during World War II, and yet, out of this destruction, the cathedral of Köln managed to survive: one of the most beautiful Gothic churches in the world, with a superb altar painted by the master artist of Köln, Stefan Lochner.

Slide: an impoverished storefront church, a black evangelical sect in Baltimore.

CARL: Let's see: what do we have next?

Slide: a Sabrett's hotdog cart in front of Johns Hopkins Hospital with its blue-and-orange umbrella.

CARL: Oh, yes. Let's talk about the food. Anna had an *idée fixe* about the food; whereas I snapped mementos of the gardens, the fountains, the regal pines of the Black Forest, Anna insisted on taking photos of everything she ate.

ANNA: I can remember things I feel.

CARL: Well, then, let's talk about the food. Germany has a more robust gustatory outlook than the delicate palate of France. The Germans positively celebrate the pig from snout to tail in the local specialties. From the Bavarian *Spanferkel,* the roasted suckling pig of that region, to the hundreds of sausages and *Leberwurst.* Although she became more and more adventurous, I could not convince Anna to sample the *Sulperknochen,* which is a Rheingau concoction of ears, snout, tail and feet.

ANNA: Ugh.

Slide: closeup of vendor placing a hot dog on a bun and lathering it with mustard; there are canned sodas in wide variety.

CARL: Everything is garnished with potatoes, *Bratkartoffeln,* sauerkraut, and the *Rotkraut,* the sweet and sour red cabbage with apples and raisins. And of course, everything is washed down with beer *von Fass* (on tap)—the *dunkels,* the dark malt, or the *helles*—the cold, lighter brew.

Slide: Anna sips a Bud Light.

ANNA: It was delicious.

CARL: Enough of food. May we talk about culture, sister, dear? Next slide, please.

Slide: Johns Hopkins University.

CARL: Ah, Heidelberg. Dueling scars and castles. The gem of the

Neckar River, the town, castle and wooded hills soaring above the sparkling waters. The castle, a spectacular ruin which serves as the locale for open-air concerts and fireworks—

Slide: the Admissions Office Building at Johns Hopkins.

CARL: —and by a quaint cable car, you can reach the peak at Königstuhl, two thousand feet high, with its breathtaking view of Neckar Valley—

Slide: the Bromo Seltzer tower in Baltimore. Slide: the interstate highways viewed from the tower.

CARL: One of the things I must mention is rather a common impression for Americans traveling throughout Germany. Every cobblestoned street, every alleyway, was so pristine and clean—

Slide: the row houses on Monument Street. Slide: a corridor of Hopkins Hospital, outside the basement laboratories. Slide: a hospital aide washing the floor.

CARL: Wasn't it, Anna?
ANNA (*Deadpan*): Yes. Sterile.

Slide: a small park in Baltimore—perhaps near Fells Point.

CARL: Even the Black Forest looked swept. The dark evergreens east of the Rhine broken by green valleys, meadows, farmhouses with steep, thatched roofs. I felt so well there, walking in Freudenstadt, shown here, which has more than a hundred miles of very lovingly tended paths. We splurged once again and stayed at the Waldhorn Post here—outside of Freudenstadt and Wilbad—

Slide: a postcard of a Baltimore hotel's reception room as a promotion for conferences.

CARL: —the hotel dates back to 1145 and boasts tennis courts, indoor saunas and this lovely restaurant furnished with period pieces; the chef there is renowned for his game dishes.

Slide: Anna in front of a vending machine dispensing wrapped sandwiches in the Hopkins Hospital cafeteria.

ANNA: I wasn't too hungry.
CARL: I was ravenous.

Slide: Busch Gardens in Williamsburg, Virginia. A promotional shot, showing "old country" costumed maidens, amusement rides, all the kitsch of the tourist spot.

CARL: We did stop and visit the camps at Dachau. Only the Germans would whitewash their death camps for tourists; it looked like a summer camp for Hitler Youth. It was oppressive.

Slide: Route 95 outside the Harbor Tunnel; the large toll signs are visible.

CARL: Let's see: the Romantic Road . . . Die Romantische Strasse . . . a trek through picture-book Bavaria and the Allgau Alps— Füssen to Würzburg.
ANNA: Honey—perhaps they've seen enough. It's hard to sit through this many—
CARL: Wait—just one more. They've got to see Neuschwanstein, built by mad King Ludwig II. It's so rococo it's Las Vegas.

Slide: Disneyland.

CARL: I believe that Ludwig was reincarnated in the twentieth century as Liberace. Wait a moment—that's not the castle.
ANNA: Yes, it is.
CARL *(Upset)*: It looks like—how did that get in here?

ANNA: I don't know which castle you're referring to, but it's definitely a castle—

Slide: closeup of Disneyland, with a large Mickey Mouse in the picture.

CARL: That's not funny, Anna! Are you making fun of me?
ANNA: Don't get upset—

Slide: Donald Duck has joined Mickey Mouse with tourists.

CARL: I went to Europe. I walked through Bavaria and the Black Forest. I combed through Neuschwanstein! I did these things, and I will remember the beauty of it all my life! I don't appreciate your mockery!
ANNA: It's just a little—
CARL: You went through Germany on your back; all you'll remember are hotel ceilings. You can show them your Germany—

Carl rushes off, angry.

ANNA: Sometimes my brother gets upset for no apparent reason. Some wires cross in his brain and he—I'm sorry. Lights, please.

The Third Man wheels the projector offstage.

ANNA: I would like to show you my impressions of Germany. They were something like this—

END OF SCENE

PAULA VOGEL's *plays include* Desdemona, The Oldest Profession *and* And Baby Makes Seven. The Baltimore Waltz *was written at the MacDowell Colony in the summer of 1989, and has had readings at Brown University, where Vogel teaches playwriting, and at the Los Angeles Theatre Center.*

Zero Positive

BY HARRY KONDOLEON

I remember the Roman Emperor, one of the cruellest of them,
Who used to visit for pleasure his poor prisoners cramped in dungeons,
So then they would beg him for death, and then he would say:
Oh no, oh no, we are not yet friends enough.
He meant they were not yet friends enough for him to give them death.
So I fancy my Muse says, when I wish to die:
Oh no, Oh no, we are not yet friends enough,

And Virtue also says:
We are not yet friends enough.

—from "Exeat," *Stevie Smith*

CHARACTERS

HIMMER

JACOB BLANK

SAMANTHA

PRENTICE

PATRICK

DEBBIE FINE

TIME August 1987.

PLACE New York City.

It is a dusty old Upper West Side apartment, lots of old furniture high in quality, covered with china relics, paintings on the walls of country landscapes dark with the shellac of decades. It is a deathly apartment, heavy with drapes on all walls, rugs, slipcovers, throw pillows thrown too often, vases, figurines. Toy trains have the run of the place; tracks run into other rooms. Trains are atop tables; they have shelves to themselves; they run. The paintings are hung with decorative rope from the molding near the ceiling.

It is lunchtime. It is always lunchtime. Himmer is preparing lunch to be served in the living room on a low coffee table. Himmer's father, Jacob Blank, is wearing makeshift mourning clothes: black trousers, black house slippers, an old navy blue shirt buttoned up to the neck and a black thin cardigan or mismatched thin suit jacket. He is tinkering with a caboose now, later adjusting wires, adjusting tracks, inserting smoke pellets in the engine: he is absorbed by the world of trains. Himmer is barefoot, old white Brooks Brothers shirt bedeviled with bleach burns, blue jeans eaten by wear.

The air conditioner is on and it hums its ominous background music. Himmer goes in and out of the room. He gets china from the cupboards, inspecting the plates like a shopper. This is his father's apartment.

HIMMER: You won't be talking all afternoon like a singing magpie, will you, and interrupt our conversations with interesting contributions or one-liners, even bits of jingles you recall for products long fallen out of use? No, no, I didn't think so: silent again today. I'll count on you to join us for a sandwich or two though, shouldn't I? You like Samantha, don't you? She's coming alone. Daddy, say something, please. I'm as upset as you are you know. I wish you'd talk to me.

JACOB BLANK (*Crusty*): Don't call me Daddy.

HIMMER (*His minor relief shows through his attitude*): What shall I call you then? Tell me. (*After a pause, clattering coffee cups he tries to match but they must belong to a great-grandmother or something, they are so old and fragile and so few saucers have matching mates*) I'll call you Father if you like but I prefer Daddy. Would you rather have Dad? Damn! Doesn't even one piece of china match here? It's like a Chinese puzzle setting lunch for three in this place. Maybe I'll just put mine on a paper napkin. These are Grandma's, aren't they? Was she into throwing dishes? Ahh, well, that's all that's available, disappearing patterns, chips and chips.

The buzzer on the intercom alarms. Himmer speaks into it.

HIMMER: Ralph, send her up. (*To his father*) Now, you like Samantha a lot, so you join us for a little conversation, okay, Dad? You know she's supersensitive and she's going to think you don't like her or something if you just sit there like a big boogieman. Wouldn't you be more comfortable in some brighter clothes? No? How about if I lower the air conditioner a little, the sound drives me nuts and it's colder than hell in here.

JACOB BLANK: No.

HIMMER: Oh we make a great team.

A knock at the door, a soft knock, not aggressive.

HIMMER: Be nice, talk.

As Himmer answers the door, Jacob Blank, train car in hand, head bowed down over it, exits to the bedrooms. Samantha enters. She is attractive, perhaps black or Oriental or Hispanic. Her dress is summery, it must be very hot outside. Himmer and Samantha are great friends, it's obvious. We can hear them talk in the hall as they enter the room.

SAMANTHA: No, I had to take the subway. The bus crawls.

HIMMER: You look great like this. This kind of look really shows off your good looks.

SAMANTHA: And if you get into a cab there's no luxury involved, you're booted around like a dog to the kennel. Where's your father?

HIMMER: Oh, the incredible disappearing man? Dad! Oh, he's just impossible.

SAMANTHA: Is he still not talking?

HIMMER: What do you think? Sit down. What's in the bag?

SAMANTHA: Grapes.

HIMMER: Not from Chile I hope. It is Chile, isn't it, that we're supposed to not eat grapes from? After those contra hearings I'm not so sure it's American food we shouldn't be eating. They must not teach what democracy is very clearly in the schools because everyone seems to love fascism. I don't care how appealing the man is, he advocates fascist ideals. My mother was a typical American and her only criticism of him was his teeth were bad. The moral order of our country is periodontal.

SAMANTHA: They're seedless. Wash them. Himmer, I got the test results.

Himmer exits to wash the grapes. Samantha looks around the room, inspects the toy trains. Himmer enters with the grapes now in a bowl.

HIMMER: Impressed with Santa's workshop? Pour some iced tea. What's new?

SAMANTHA: What's new. Johnny again.

HIMMER: Oh God.

SAMANTHA: Don't start.

HIMMER: Sex with Johnny: a book without end. What chapter have we gone back to?

SAMANTHA: If you ever tell anyone any of this I will personally come over and kill you.

HIMMER: Thanks for telling me, I'll throw away my cyanide capsules and depend on you. These sandwiches are delicious: I'm such a

211

good cook. Tell me something boring. Between my mother's death, my father's weirdness and all my creepy relatives descending upon me like the acid dream of an I-don't-know-what, I'm ready myself, as they say, for the box.

SAMANTHA (*French pronunciation of the first phrase*): Oo-la-la, shut up already, I just walked in. Did you hear what I said when you went in the kitchen?

HIMMER: When are we going to have a smart President, that's what I'd like to know. You wouldn't mind so much that they're stupid but they're deceitful too—what a combination: they're stupid *and* they *lie*.

SAMANTHA: *Shut up.*

HIMMER: Look, if you were locked up all week with your father who won't talk you'd be a babbling brook too. Tell me something interesting.

The intercom buzzer again.

HIMMER: Oh God, who's that? If it's my stupid Aunt Mary I'm just going to tell her I'm not here. (*Into the intercom*) Who? Oh. Okay, send'm up. (*To Samantha*) It's Prentice. That's weird.

SAMANTHA: He's not still mad at me from your birthday when I said he looked tired, is he?

HIMMER: I don't know, ask him.

SAMANTHA: I'm sorry, that's just petty. In France that's not an insult if you tell someone they look tired.

HIMMER: Well, apparently in the United States of New York it is. I don't care, everyone looks tired to me too.

SAMANTHA: If someone tells me I look fat I don't get mad. I know I'm fat. They're just saying what they see.

HIMMER: You are not fat. (*She is not but it doesn't matter if she is*)

SAMANTHA: I'm not going to worry about it. I've got enough problems.

Knock at the door. Himmer goes to answer it. Prentice enters. Crisply attired, pronounced good manners, on, *measured.*

PRENTICE: Hi, I was visiting my parents and dropping a stack of books off at Nita's who it turns out wasn't in—Samantha, I didn't know you were here. Nice to see you. I came by to say hello to your father, see how he was doing. My parents send their condolences.

SAMANTHA: You look great, what nice trousers.

PRENTICE: Oh, these are old. What a pretty dress.

Jacob Blank enters.

HIMMER: Oh, Dad, terrific, look who dropped by to see you and say hello.

PRENTICE: Mr. Blank, I just came from my parents and they wanted me to express for them how much they felt for you in your loss.

SAMANTHA: Hi, Mr. Blank, how'ya doin'?

Jacob Blank exits.

HIMMER: Well, there you got a good sample.

PRENTICE: It's grief, he's in grief.

SAMANTHA: Poor thing.

HIMMER: He's very weird. I don't think I took that into account. You know how when you're growing up you only think you're weird, you don't think how weird your parents are too but they're weird, you know what I mean. Have you eaten?

PRENTICE: I'm not hungry.

HIMMER: You'll join us.

SAMANTHA: So, what's new?

PRENTICE: Nothing.

HIMMER: Samantha's seeing another married man.

SAMANTHA: Himmer, that really makes me mad when you just blurt out my private life like that.

PRENTICE: You look beautiful. I haven't seen you in a long time but you look beautiful.

SAMANTHA: No, I look terrible. You look good. Very relax— you look great. Look, Himmer told me it upset you that I said you looked tired and I'm sorry.

213

PRENTICE: Oh, God, forget about it. Himmer, you have a big mouth, I made you swear not to repeat that. I wasn't mad.

SAMANTHA: And you know you really didn't look tired, you looked . . . fatigued.

PRENTICE: Let's forget about it.

SAMANTHA: Yes, let's forget about it.

HIMMER: Tell about your married man.

SAMANTHA: Oh, you're an idiot, Himmer. I'm not going to march through the streets telling every private detail of my life just because you want me to. *(To Prentice)* You remember that handsome man I was with New Year's?

HIMMER: It turned out he was married.

PRENTICE: Johnny.

SAMANTHA: That's right, Johnny.

HIMMER: Tell it all, start in the middle.

SAMANTHA: I'm not going to tell anything.

HIMMER: Well, make something up then, I'm going in the kitchen to toss the salad.

SAMANTHA: Not too oily as usual.

HIMMER: How about just vinegar?

PRENTICE: But not too vinegary.

HIMMER: I know, I'll just toss it through with tap water. *(He exits)*

SAMANTHA *(Calling after Himmer)*: No salt. *(To Prentice)* I'm salt free these days.

PRENTICE: Me too.

SAMANTHA: Anyway, apropos of my Johnny story I'm really too sick to tell it, sick of it, I mean. It's all very familiar material.

PRENTICE: It's the same thing with me and Rick, when that thing lived I was too sick of it to even see it. It didn't even really exist until it was over.

SAMANTHA: Right. Anyway . . . *(All of a sudden she is overcome with emotion, crying like someone choking up food, immediately covering her face and turning her shoulders away; it looks like she will become ill)* Of course it's all very tiresome to listen to unless it's happening to you then every cliché has a vividness that's overwhelming to the

214

point of asphyxiation. You think if you love someone and they love you it can overcome all those simple idiotic obstacles constructed by people who simply cannot abide even one grain of happiness in this miserable world! Well, anyway the details are too saturated with vinegar and oil to go over. And salt, too. You don't smoke anymore, do you?

PRENTICE: No.

SAMANTHA: No, me neither. But I'd like one now. You know, I've often thought perhaps one is better off a mummy in a crypt. Have you been to the Metropolitan lately? They have lovely mummy crypts painted orange and blue. Museums are nice.

PRENTICE: I like them too.

Himmer enters with platter of salad.

HIMMER: Here it is all undressed. What Sturm und Drang have I missed? Oh, I see, roadblock ahead, broken heart. Maybe you both want alcohol instead of tea. I don't know what he's got here. Vermouth? He's really very sweet though, don't you think so? Growing up I never appreciated having a poet for a father. I just thought it meant a good-for-nothing. Oh look, old champagne! But it's hot. I'll put it in the freezer. (*He exits running*)

PRENTICE (*Sipping what he's holding*): So everything just goes on, right? What can you do? And summer just keeps doing its thing, sun and fun. It's the most evil season, I've always thought so, the way it insists upon itself until it finally just burns out.

Himmer enters.

HIMMER: Don't let me forget that in the freezer. What was I saying? Oh yes, can't you picture my father and me traveling around like Deborah Kerr and that character Nono, giving readings for pennies, dependent on the rudeness of strangers?

PRENTICE: You'd give up your job at *Life*?

HIMMER: That's a job? Please, it's embarrassing that job and I work for a big homophobe, one of the biggest. I should fix a plate for my father and bring it in to him. He'll pretend he's not interested in it but then when I go back in later the plate will be empty.

SAMANTHA (*Offering a sandwich from her plate*): Here, I didn't touch that.

PRENTICE: He's going to eat all that?

HIMMER: He might. (*He exits*)

PRENTICE: So, after I threw Rick out or he ran away—whosever translation you've read—I thought, okay, now, I'm a sane person, I'll live without hope, expectations, happiness, joy, ecstasy.

SAMANTHA: Like a mummy.

PRENTICE: Right, like a mummy, more bandage than wound.

SAMANTHA: And you say, oh my work will sustain me.

PRENTICE: And it does.

SAMANTHA: For a while.

PRENTICE: For a while.

SAMANTHA: If you're lucky.

PRENTICE: Right. And if your work isn't too jerky, too conspicuously jerky to yourself, then you can get something out of it.

SAMANTHA: Yes.

PRENTICE: And kindness. Kindness can have a kind of beauty, being kind to people and things. It has a return. You feel better for it.

SAMANTHA: Yes, all this is true.

PRENTICE: But of course, then, a snowfield enters you, a plain flat snowfield, midwestern, trackless, it goes on for days, it's your state and you move around on it, bluish, frosty, this is where I've arrived, you tell yourself, what a long way I've come since Miss Tulip said I was the sunniest boy in the third grade.

Himmer enters.

HIMMER: He's not talking. What are you talking about?

PRENTICE: Rick.

HIMMER: I think I've changed my mind about Rick. At first I thought if someone you live with throws your radios and other appliances out the windows and scars up the tables with matches and knife marks and then adds to this, hitting, drunken absences, name-calling, infidelity, meanness and borrowing money, then maybe you are better off without this person, better off alone or with someone else, whatever.

SAMANTHA: But now you think . . .

HIMMER: But now I think . . . . Don't forget to remind me about the champagne in the—

PRENTICE: You just put it in. What do you now think?

HIMMER: I now think you cannot win. You just can't win, there's no winning.

SAMANTHA: That's a generalization.

PRENTICE: And a banal sentiment. But true.

SAMANTHA: But true, absolutely true.

HIMMER: I mean you can *appear* to win. Mind you, my father had that horror-show marriage with my mother who he couldn't run fast enough away from and she couldn't kill herself slow enough for human science—it took twenty-five years from when I started counting, who knows when she started. But then other women came along loaded to the gills with cash—all Pisceans—and a bulb has never been turned on as thoroughly! My father on poetic tiptoe ran from bed to bed: penniless-and-for-the-most-part-unheralded poet, faithful slave to love, art, letters or whatever little gremlin in the archaic pantheon represents the composite sum of such worthy pastimes.

SAMANTHA: So he won.

PRENTICE: But he didn't love any of those women.

HIMMER: He loved my mother.

SAMANTHA (*With the sense of doom that realizing the truth gives you*): Who he ran from.

HIMMER: Now you're getting it, you're advancing a reading level. The happy answers have been removed from the deck; the only thing wild about the wild card is how wildly disappointed you'll be when you get it.

SAMANTHA: Give me some salad.

217

PRENTICE: That sort of sour prognosis is too easy to give and ulti-
mately not even particularly accurate or helpful, in fact it rings at
its worst of—of—of stupidity!

HIMMER: Okay, you're saying you're happier now?

PRENTICE: No!

HIMMER: Okay, I'll talk about me instead. I'm alone, I'm unhappy. I
used to have desires, dreams, the usual things, they got so banged
up and hard to look at I took them out one afternoon and shot
them.

PRENTICE: And you're happy now?

HIMMER: Of course not! And you know I'm not! And I don't even have
that "free" feeling you expect to get at the least when you've
burned your last fire ladder. Oh but they say the songs are always
sweetest sung from the burning building.

PRENTICE: Let's change the subject.

HIMMER: What was the funeral like? Glad you asked—you only
stopped in for a minute—and I don't blame you, if I didn't have to I
wouldn't have gone at all—it was a zoo, my friends, a living zoo.
You know, when a person has been impossible to reach by telephone, an enormous number of people want to see what the
corpse looks like!

PRENTICE: Samantha, tell me about your work.

SAMANTHA: A lot of people sobbing about various injustices. I'm
thinking of quitting.

HIMMER: Anyway, there's some furniture in my mother's hovel in
Stockbridge—actually it's a very sweet little house and if it didn't
make me think of crying the minute I'd walk in I'd move there and
just lock the door—anyway, the furniture is lovely really: tiger
maple with funny brass knobs shaped like antelope heads—and
we're sitting in front of the open coffin—why it's open I haven't a
clue—ritual and religion having more weird gyrations than a fan
dancer. Anyway, there we're sitting and my Aunt Mary who
belongs in name-a-women's-prison . . .

PRENTICE: Is she still restless?

HIMMER: Oh, you remember her? Her hair's purple. Anyway, two
inches from the open coffin she starts asking my father for this

tiger-maple furniture, not for herself, mind you, but for one of her half-dozen illegitimate children.

PRENTICE: Oh, I heard this.

HIMMER: And my father says, "Oh, Himmer's had his eye on that furniture for a long time."

PRENTICE: That's not so bad.

HIMMER: Can you imagine? It makes it seem I've rented a car and driven however many hours it is to the Berkshires to kill my own mother for a chifforobe, two night tables and a headboard! So I told my father to shut up. I shouted at him to shut up. No one heard me, I mean the place is like a surprise party with everyone waving and greeting everyone they haven't seen in a lifetime—it's a scene.

SAMANTHA (*Concurring*): It's a scene.

HIMMER: Anyway, I told him to shut up and he did. He hasn't said more than really a few words.

PRENTICE: He couldn't possibly be mad at that, it's too little.

HIMMER: You're right, it's not enough to be mad like that. Oh, he's probably not even mad, he's just in grief, right?

SAMANTHA AND PRENTICE: Right.

HIMMER: Let's talk about something else.

Jacob Blank enters.

HIMMER: Dad, hi. How was lunch? I put green pepper and scallion in there and lots of black pepper, the way you like it. Would you like a cookie, they're from the bakery. They're your favorite kind . . . with the pignoli nuts.

Jacob Blank, having gotten two train cars, exits back to his room.

SAMANTHA: He's spooky.

PRENTICE: Himmer, you need a vacation.

HIMMER: And you know whose fault it is? Bonnie. Oh yes it is! I wouldn't give two hoots about a lot of broken-down furniture stuck up in Massachusetts if Bonnie the psychopath hadn't talked me into buying a lot of deco shit I can't look at. Well, that's nothing, she talked me into marrying her, didn't she?

PRENTICE: Don't think about her.

HIMMER: I mean I told her point-blank, "I'm queer, dear," but no, that was okay. And in the back of my mind I thought, oh, I'll have a child, that'll be nice, a nice little girl or boy to take on this long walk through harsh weather.

PRENTICE: Don't think about her.

HIMMER: It's just as well we had no children—less attachments to her, to anyone.

SAMANTHA: She was certifiable.

HIMMER: Oh, you say that about any female friends I have, you're a misogynist.

SAMANTHA: I'm not, you are. That's why they're all crazy, they are certifiable.

HIMMER: Uh-huh, I'm a misogynist—that's such a cliché. Because I have women friends you find crazy—you're just jealous.

SAMANTHA: Yeah, I'm jealous of—let's see what have we got—the liar—

HIMMER: She doesn't lie.

SAMANTHA: —the liar, the tit-slasher, the—

PRENTICE: Who's the tit-slasher?

HIMMER: Zara Bannon when she had that weird brief affair with Lorraine Coke. You remember.

SAMANTHA: Shall I go on?

HIMMER: No, it's a bore, shut up.

SAMANTHA: As my grandmother used to say in another language and I loosely translate, all the insane people are not in the insane asylum.

HIMMER: And Esther is not a liar. You're a woman-hater.

SAMANTHA (*Leaning over to hit his shoulder*): Stop saying that or I'll hit you!

The buzzer rings.

HIMMER: Who's that?

220

PRENTICE: Oh, I know who it is. I left a note with Nita's doorman I'd be here if she came back in five minutes. She needs these books I borrowed. She's going to Cyprus and Tunis.

HIMMER: Why didn't you leave them with her doorman?

PRENTICE: She says he steals books.

The buzzer again.

SAMANTHA: I don't want to see her. I'll explain later. *(Clearly)* I don't want to see her.

HIMMER *(Grabbing the books Prentice carried in)*: I'll go down and say you left, P., and that my father's stark raving mad up here and I've got my hands full.

Himmer exits. The buzzer rings again while Samantha and Prentice sit still. Jacob Blank enters. Suddenly he seems much more normal and sits with them for a friendly chat.

JACOB BLANK: Hello.

PRENTICE: Hi, Mr. Blank.

JACOB BLANK: I'm fine, thanks. You know they say someone close to me passed away recently so I'm not myself entirely. I'm in mourning.

PRENTICE: Of course. You look fine, you look healthy.

JACOB BLANK: I'm left with a little child to raise and it's a burden really, maybe more than I can handle. And little boys are more wild than little girls.

SAMANTHA *(After a long pause)*: What little boy?

JACOB BLANK: Himmer.

PRENTICE *(After another long pause)*: Your trains are so nice, I love them, I'll bet they're really valuable antiques and fun to play with.

JACOB BLANK *(Simply)*: They don't interest me. *(After his own pause)* Both of you are very young and have your whole life ahead of you so anything having to do with a really deep, punishing loss really no one could expect you to comprehend. You remember my wife Lolly, Samantha?

221

SAMANTHA (*Cautiously*): No, well, I met a woman here once, a lady friend of yours, I think her name was Francine.

JACOB BLANK: Francine? Who's Francine? (*He laughs good-naturedly*) Francine's nobody, Francine's nobody at all. Oh my goodness! Francine, that's funny.

Jacob Blank stands, still laughing, staggers, lets out a moan, half falls over a table. The delicate table falls over. Prentice and Samantha, utterly startled, catch him.

JACOB BLANK: Help me, help me, help me to lie down.

They help him to the couch. Prentice immediately restores the table, making adjustments so everything is ordered again: disorder is too terrible for him, he is frightened.

JACOB BLANK: Get her, would you, get her, please.

PRENTICE: *Who?*

JACOB BLANK: She's in the other room, get her. She's in the bedroom, get her. Lolly. Get her. GET HER!

SAMANTHA (*Shocked by his shouting she half-shouts at Prentice*): Go check!

Prentice exits running to the bedroom.

SAMANTHA (*To Jacob Blank*): He's checking, he's gone to check.

Prentice enters.

PRENTICE: There's no one in there.

SAMANTHA (*As if translating*): There's no one in there.

Jacob Blank lets out a cry like an animal being suffocated. He is prone on the couch, face up with his arms over his face.

PRENTICE (*Covering his ears—this sound must have some private awful association for him*): Don't cry! (*Realizing that what he has just said is far too sharp*) Please don't cry, please.

SAMANTHA (*Panicked for lack of resources*): Maybe I should get Himmer. What is he doing down there!

JACOB BLANK (*Sitting up suddenly*): Children, come here, don't be put off by me, I need your help, *sincerely*. Come closer. (*Trying to make light of it*) I said something to her, I don't know, something offensive. When you get older you'll learn how silly adults can be and say things to each other they don't mean. Tell her that, tell her I didn't mean it, will you?

PRENTICE AND SAMANTHA (*Coincidentally at the same time*): Yes.

JACOB BLANK: Tell her I love her. That's all. Tell that to her. Pick some flowers and give them to her when you say it. (*He takes out his wallet from his back pocket and removes several dollars and hands them to Prentice and Samantha*) Here. Take it, in case the gardens are closed you can go to the florist. The sun's come out, I'm feeling a lot more optimistic and then we're going to have some clams and oysters later with beer, would you like that?

SAMANTHA (*She has stopped listening, her own longing has come in*): Yes.

JACOB BLANK: And we'll have a little dance. My mother puts up a little tent near the water with candles stuck on the rocks when it gets dark. You can stay up very late. Pack a change of clothes.

Jacob Blank exits to the bedroom. Prentice and Samantha sit still, lost in their own unhappy thoughts. Himmer, practically racing from one end of the room to the other, enters from the outside hall and exits to the bedroom.

HIMMER (*As he dashes through*): Oooo I have to pee so bad I could die!

Prentice and Samantha see him come and go and realize what he's said but it doesn't much change their mood.

SAMANTHA (*After a moment*): I guess I should break up with him. But there's nothing to break up, we're not really together. He's just the

Married Man, that's all, the man who's married and not to me. Like a song. Piaf. Holiday. Garland. I mean even if he won't leave his wife for me, won't marry me, won't ever let me have my fantasy of haute bourgeoise, I still want to have sex with Johnny. That's that.

PRENTICE (*Brushing something slowly off his knee, looking down, answering a question only he's hearing*): Yeah.

Himmer enters pulling up his fly.

HIMMER: Man alive, can that character talk, Nita, she wouldn't let me go. And I still don't know why she's going to Tunis. You know who she reminds me of, Prentice? That woman Daria Klein I went to Hawaii with. She liked to talk too. (*Eating cookies*) And she's put on weight. Jesus Christ, she's gotten so heavy. What on earth would she be eating all day to keep up that weight?

SAMANTHA: She's unhappy.

HIMMER: No doubt. Cookie?

SAMANTHA: No thanks.

HIMMER: Cookie?

PRENTICE: No thanks.

HIMMER: Is she divorced again? Second time, right?

PRENTICE: I don't know.

HIMMER: She's your friend. At one point she just started kissing me. I said Nita, have a good trip. Has there been a peep out of my dad?

SAMANTHA AND PRENTICE: Yes.

HIMMER: Oh yeah, what'd he say?

PRENTICE (*Suddenly it doesn't even seem true*): It seems he's gone into some time warp where he's still married to your mother or maybe they're just dating. Anyway, he was calling for her. He hasn't seen her in twenty years so I guess the funeral really threw him, right?

Prentice and Samantha, out of nervous release, start to laugh. Himmer joins them in laughter.

HIMMER: Well, that's a turn of the screw, isn't it? Really snapped his twig, heh? Split his gourd, went round the bend.

They are all laughing in spite of themselves and then they come to a gradual silence in which we can again concentrate on the sound the air conditioner makes.

HIMMER: This happened once before. Oh well, it's not very funny, it's not funny at all. I guess I should go in and check on him. (*After a little pause*) I don't feel like it. Oh well. Have you noticed how many times I say oh well these days? That's all I say: oh well.

SAMANTHA: I don't want to be on the side of chaos.

HIMMER: What? (*Slight pause*) Why didn't you want to speak to Nita?

SAMANTHA: We were on that panel together "The Scourge of the Cities." I scored some easy points off of her and I'm ashamed of it.

PRENTICE: I go a lot to places of worship lately, I light a candle, whatever. I just go in for a prayer. I've been to most denominations now. I feel I've only scratched a fraction of the work there is to do praying. The task of it puts most else I have to do on the back burner.

HIMMER: I was going through some of my mother's old things she had in boxes from years ago and I found all these old little plays. I'm quite taken with them. I'm guessing she wrote them in college or after she dropped out and ran off with my father—Jacob Blank, then boy wonder of verse. (*Handing a wilted old manuscript to Prentice*) Take a look at this.

PRENTICE (*After turning a page, reading the title*): *The Ruins of Athens.*

HIMMER: There are others but that's the one I liked the best. They're all vaguely or mostly grecophile, taking place at some twilight time before the eyes of the gods. You know, a lot of chest-beating, invocations and dainty interludes between fauns and toga-wearers. No butt-fucking though. I thought of calling up Patrick and finding out what he thought of all of it. He's in the theatre and all or sort of—anyway, get his opinion. What do you think?

SAMANTHA: And do what with it?

225

HIMMER: I don't know. Something.

PRENTICE: He died. Her husband.

SAMANTHA: Her first husband. Nita's.

PRENTICE: They'd divorced already. But the other one is sick with you-know-what.

HIMMER: I bumped into Allan Sodas who said no one should go to Rio. He said they steal your wallet from your trousers when you go swimming and that the police work in cahoots with the thieves and that things are so bad there are giant signs everywhere that say check your valuables.

SAMANTHA: Who's going to Rio?

HIMMER: No one.

SAMANTHA: Why bring it up then?

HIMMER: Because, why not, what else is there to say, what else should I be saying? If there's no action to take at least I don't fake it. I think everyone's faking it, don't you? I'm sitting here and I'm doing nothing, I'm talking about nothing, I'm wasting your time you're wasting my time, but on some level we've all become terribly suspicious of action, of any action to take to effect a change, especially for the better. After all these centuries we still all fundamentally believe in the fate machine. We don't have to move, we don't even have to get up, the fate machine will do it all. That's why we can sit here like this.

PRENTICE: I still miss Rick. I still haven't found anyone I like as much. I could call up and say so but it just wouldn't work out. It's not meant to be. (*Slight pause*) Blah blah blah. (*Slight pause, resuming a more normal tone of voice*) I've spoken to my parents about the whole thing, the whole relationship, they were very understanding, very sympathetic.

SAMANTHA: I don't want to be on the side of chaos.

After a slight pause—they are as still as Beckett's characters caught in urns, almost without movement—Himmer reaches for an envelope on the end table nearest him.

HIMMER: I have a photo of Bonnie pregnant. She found a Swedish boy just out of high school who subsequently has had a nervous breakdown and gone back to Sweden. Here.

PRENTICE *(Looking at the photo)*: She's nude. *(Pause)* Here.

SAMANTHA *(Passive)*: She sent you this of herself? She looks like one of those women who say they've been with the devil. *(Putting the photo down on the table)* Look at her eyes.

HIMMER: There's no devil.

SAMANTHA: No?

A train whistle blows. It is the whistle from one of the engines on the tracks in the room. The toy engine lights up and toots twice in a row quietly and little, toot-toot. If they hear it, it's only in the back of their minds. After a slight pause Samantha speaks again but no one moves.

SAMANTHA: Maybe one of us should go in and check up on your father. Prentice, I need to talk to Himmer for a minute alone.

HIMMER: Prentice doesn't have to leave the room. I tell him everything anyway.

SAMANTHA: Yes, I know that. Well, I've spoken to my friend Cecile.

HIMMER: Oh.

SAMANTHA: Yes.

HIMMER *(To Prentice)*: Cecile was going to do our tests. She's a doctor.

PRENTICE: I'm against those tests. I wouldn't get it.

HIMMER: I guess I am too, but I don't know. What did she say? I'm not sure I want to know.

PRENTICE: I'll leave.

HIMMER: No, stay.

SAMANTHA: I took it too.

PRENTICE: You did, what for?

HIMMER: What was it, what did she say?

SAMANTHA: They were positive.

HIMMER: Both?

SAMANTHA: Yep.

HIMMER: Both positive. But it doesn't mean anything.

PRENTICE: It doesn't mean anything.

HIMMER: What did she say?

SAMANTHA: Seropositive, what else is there to say?

HIMMER: Zero positive? The zero for the infinite nothingness and the plus sign like a cross on a grave.

SAMANTHA: The word is sero not zero.

PRENTICE: It doesn't mean anything.

HIMMER: It's a death sentence.

The train whistles again. They turn to look at it but don't do anything about it.

HIMMER: I wanted to be reminded of something what was it? Something before. *(He starts to laugh)* I don't know why I'm laughing. *(He is laughing)* There's nothing funny. You know what my problem is? I drop people and I pick them up. That's the opposite of what most people do. I'm talking nonsense.

SAMANTHA: You asked to be reminded of the champagne.

HIMMER: The what? I have no feelings left, there's a fancy word for that, isn't there? You too, Samantha? How queer.

PRENTICE: It doesn't mean a thing.

HIMMER *(Sharply, very loud)*: Stop saying that!

Prentice buries his face in his hands crying. He deliberately knocks over the small table that he had restored before. Himmer now speaks calmly.

HIMMER: Toot-toot, the train is pulling out, see you at the next station. I need to hear some music. What shall we listen to, something beautiful and self-pitying.

Himmer presses a button on the stereo, which is encased in an old-fashioned console. It lights up green and red and instantly emits the most loud music. Thumping, ancient or up-to-the-minute, it is alarming, cathartic. Prentice and Samantha are on the couch crying in an embrace. Himmer begins to dance, aware of the Dionysian payoff of dancing at the news of your own death. The trains light up and begin to revolve around their tracks as Jacob Blank enters. There are little

*model houses, post offices and banks built to scale around the trains;
they are tin and lit from within. I'm particularly interested in these
little houses making an effect.*

*Jacob Blank, having heard the music and seeing his son, whom he
doesn't recognize, dances. He believes this is the little beachside dance
his mother is hosting. Himmer is maybe turning in a circle upstage.
Fadeout; last to fade are the tiny buildings.*

ACT ONE, SCENE 2: LUST FOR LIFE

*Slight pause, no change in the set or in Himmer's clothing is necessary
except to restore whatever Prentice pushed over near the end of Scene 1.
I want to avoid that disconcerting flurry of stagehands between scenes
that destroys spells. It is a week later. Himmer is sitting on the couch.
He is having lunch with his friend Patrick. The air conditioner is still
on. Patrick is an actor, good-looking but banal, one of a million. As he
will go mad in this scene, it is important he start with a place to build,
gradually becoming furious, making little peaks and valleys of emotional outburst before falling off the top.*

HIMMER: More salad, Patrick?

PATRICK: It's delicious! Oh, I've dirtied another plate.

HIMMER: That's okay, there are lots.

PATRICK: Which is my glass? I'm drinking out of every glass.

HIMMER: It doesn't matter, they're all yours. I'm just chewing gum,
I'm not hungry. Tell me about your new film.

PATRICK: I'm not in it, I'm just up for it.

HIMMER: You're up for it. That means you're auditioning and hope to
get it, right?

PATRICK: I'm perfect for it, but you know the casting people are very
narrow. Very narrow. So, how are you doin'?

HIMMER: I'm not very well.

PATRICK: You're sick?

HIMMER: No, I'm not sick.

Patrick is suddenly singing, lots of energy, musical-comedy style. The song wavers between furiously happy and stagy shyness. Who is he singing to? His eyes are focused on everything and nothing.

PATRICK:

Hey! Aren't you the one I've been looking for?
Hey girl! I think it's you, yeah.
Woke up in the morning
Had no warning
Took a shower
Picked a flower
Said howdy-do to the people I met
My life I figured was all set.

Walked on, yeah, I walked on
What was I looking for?
What was I looking for?
Hey, nothing! Nothing till I found you.
You girl, yeah you girl.
Popped into my life!
Took me by surprise!
Just about my size—
Took you for my wife!
Took a second to realize, girl
You're the one I'd been looking for
Without knowing what I'd been looking for.

Oh, now I feel twice as good
Kinda knew I would
Drifting around like wood
You threw me in the fire
Hmmm, that warm desire
Now when I take a shower
Or I pick a flower
Hmmm, it's for you girl
Hmmm, I think it's you girl.

HIMMER *(After a slight pause)*: My goodness, what's that?

PATRICK: It's my song. What do you think, fantastic, right? My voice teacher can't believe how far along I've come. I'm one of those people who never thought they could sing who really can. It's important to have an audition song at your fingertips you can just leap up and do whenever you have an opportunity. *(Singing suddenly again, peppy)* Took me by surprise! *(Winking)* Just about my size! *(Stopping)* What do you think?

HIMMER: Well, it's very moon and spoon.

PATRICK *(Happily, uncomprehending)*: Yeah, it is, right. I wrote it myself. I figured I didn't want to screw around with copyright and all, you know, if something takes off.

HIMMER: How are your children?

PATRICK: Why did you ask me that?

HIMMER: I wondered how they were.

PATRICK: They're fine. It's a very small part, but that's all I go up for these days is very small parts. I'm between age groups. I'm too old to play a teenager and too young to play an old man. And in TV, film and theatre they're very narrow. They admit it, they say they're very narrow. I go to an audition and I'm brilliant, I mean it, *drop-dead brilliant*. I know it, it's not an opinion. My cues are superb. I'm incapable of uttering a false word. I'm tops in emotional guns! A relative of Stella Adler told me she'd never seen physical work like mine. I'm a natural that way. My childhood was very athletic. I fence. I dive. I ski. I can climb ropes. I can shoot a pistol. I can do modern dance. I have an appreciation for the ballet. *Why won't my career take off?!*

HIMMER: Patrick, I really don't know the answer to that question. Would you like a cookie? Actually one of the reasons I thought it might be fun to have lunch together today was that I accidentally unearthed these little slivers of plays I guess my mother wrote at school and then forgot about and you're the only person I know in theatre and all so I thought I might show one to you and get your opinion, find out if it's possible to maybe put it on somewhere in some way.

PATRICK: Your mom just passed away, right?

HIMMER: That's right, recently.

PATRICK: And here I am going on about my career. I must make you sick to your stomach.

HIMMER: Not at all, I'm interested in all that stuff, it's like a foreign country to me. You know in my job all I do is paste pieces of paper together.

PATRICK: Oh, I know what you do, you're great! I just have to get a foothold, you know, just a foothold! They have you hanging on by your teeth, from a ledge, for years. What do they want, blood? My balls? What do they want? Do you know?!

HIMMER: No, no, I don't know.

PATRICK: No. How was the funeral? Was there a funeral?

HIMMER: Oh, yeah, it was okay, nothing special.

PATRICK: Right. I've got a good face, the camera likes my face, *a lot.* There was this book written by a big wheel in Hollywood, he said there was a day you could throw a stick and hit ten Robert Redfords on the beach in Malibu. Ten of them, a hundred, and then *Butch Cassidy* came out and he's on the cover of *Life*—your magazine.

HIMMER: It's not my magazine, I just—

PATRICK: One hundred Robert Redfords standing around Malibu, you just had to throw a stick! And I haven't even been to Malibu.

HIMMER: It's nothing.

PATRICK: I haven't been anywhere! And why because every nickel goes to my two children and don't get me wrong—I love my boy and girl—I mean two girls—I love them, but the truth is I don't even know them. I had my divorce in the maternity ward. I wouldn't recognize them if the two of them flew into the room this second!

HIMMER: Patrick, I seem to have a little headache, maybe it would be better if we another time—

PATRICK (*Suddenly this is an audition for him, this event, imbued with all life-and-death terror*): No, no! No! Show me your mother's thing. Where is it, her play, what's it called?

HIMMER (*Handing it to him with reservations*): Here. That's the best of the bunch.

232

PATRICK: *The Ruins of Athens.* That's not a good title. It's not commercial. I have to be straight with you, Himmy, the first thing you'll have to do is come up with something else. I work with these people so I know. I walk up and down Times Square all day so I know. The titles defy your eyes. *My Pussy Is on Fire*—that's new, a huge hit. Maybe I should do porn. I've got the body. I have an excellent body and a nice penis. I can keep an erection for hours. I shock my girlfriends. And I don't have to come until I'm told to, I just say tell me when you want me to come and then I come. I swim. I box. I do sit-ups while I'm waiting for my tub to fill. *(Frightened suddenly by the trains, which are still)* What are all these toys in here?

HIMMER: They're my father's.

PATRICK: Is he senile? That's my big fear.

HIMMER: He has sort of lost his mind a bit. He's sort of skipped to another place in time, with my mother apparently. But that's so long ago I don't remember them together. Although he thinks I'm a little boy. It's weird, everything juggled up. I find him more lovable now, though, more tender. I never cared for his poems. I'm reading them all again. I like them.

PATRICK: I can do backflips, cartwheels, somersaults.

Suddenly Patrick's attempting one or more of these feats; if he can do them, fine, if not, the attempt will do. Either way he may collapse with exhaustion and/or frustration.

HIMMER: Patrick! Patrick, take it easy. What are you doing. Take it easy now.

PATRICK *(Out of breath)*: I used to walk on a rope. I was so balanced. Help me, help me somehow.

HIMMER: How can I help you, Patrick, I called you up for your help.

PATRICK: That's right, that's right, and I can give it to you. You want to put your mom's play on, that makes sense. You miss her, you were very close.

HIMMER: Actually no, she lived alone in the woods and drank a lot.

PATRICK: That's my big fear.

Patrick quickly drinks—downs—whatever is left in the glasses on the table—iced tea, water, vermouth, whatever is there, like a man in the desert at a mirage.

HIMMER: She lived with two gay guys who got depressed and drowned themselves.

PATRICK: She liked gay guys, then why didn't she like you?

HIMMER: She did like me, a lot, she just drank and we lost touch with each other. Why do you say that?

PATRICK: Nothing. I came from a strict family. A strict religious household where nothing was permitted, nothing. We had to sit still and wait, for everything. I'm tired of waiting! I don't want to wait anymore! What am I waiting for! I went up for *The Big Knife*—I'm perfect for it—I could've written the part! I get the call, you're not right for it. *(Between his teeth)* I'm telling you if there's a human being right for it I'm right for it! I'd kill the fuckin' bastards if I could just see them! *(He twirls around in place in one frantic sweep to see no one is around him, and then suddenly speaks more calmly)* I'm up for *The Screens*. That's hardly ever done. Lots of Algerians. Jean Genet, you know. What do you think? Do you think I have a chance at it?

HIMMER: Patrick, you should go home now. I recently got some very bad news and I misjudged my ability to have company, okay?

PATRICK *(Distracted, talking to no one)*: No, no, let me stay just a little bit longer. Please, I'll stay. You're upset about your mom. How did her friends drown themselves, the two fellows?

HIMMER *(Uncomfortable cooperating)*: In a pond.

PATRICK *(Logical)*: Now, what we have to do is think of the name of this gal I know who just came into a large fortune from some brouhaha with her family's estate. She's a millionairess, a frustrated something-or-other, art lover, just have to think of her name and then you call her. She'll go for it, yeah. She'll put on your mom's show. When I think of her name I'll tell you.

HIMMER: Patrick, I really have to go to sleep now. I want to take a nap.

PATRICK *(Deaf)*: I come from a strict household religious.

234

HIMMER: Strict what? What religion? Catholic? Protestant? Jewish? Buddhist? Strict what?

PATRICK: Strict nothing. You don't understand. My father disapproves of me and I take money from him to feed my children. I take money from an old man! I'm a failure!

HIMMER: No, you're not.

PATRICK (*Picking up a penknife from a table*): What's this?

HIMMER: A penknife. It was my mother's, in with her things.

Patrick uses the penknife to point, to become deliberately pedantic and lend, he thinks, some dignity to the points he makes.

PATRICK: They are the devils. The evil devils. I swear on your mother's grave, devils walk the earth and they pray to their greedy god called Personal Gain and everything is sacrificed to its big fat mouth. Now, I'm an actor so I don't know your career but you can make an analogy to your experience at *Life,* everything is cutthroat, I know that, I'm not getting special bad treatment. But there are certain arenas where one is led to suspect beauty of spirit will rule the day and if not why then do the devils that tread there pick such a puny arena to pitch their tents? *What a bright nice fire!* I'll say when I watch them burn. And I will. I'll come back from the dead if I have to and chew on the devils' throats . . . I cannot get a job, I cannot get a job.

HIMMER: Patrick.

The shock of hearing his own name jolts to mind the name Patrick has been trying to remember. With every utterance of her name he jabs the penknife into his left wrist, up and down quickly and violently as if to accomplish a task and switching hands quickly to accomplish the right wrist with one quick stroke before dropping the implement and staring wildly up, crying out horrified as if an entirely different soul committed the violence, crying and shaking.

PATRICK: Deborah Fine! Deborah Fine! Deborah Fine!

235

HIMMER: What are you doing!

Blood pouring out of Patrick's wrists gets all over Himmer's white shirt. Patrick staggers about hysterical, going into shock.

PATRICK: Call Deborah Fine. Call Deborah Fine.
HIMMER *(Running out of the room)*: I'm calling an ambulance.
PATRICK *(Before collapsing to the floor)*: Someone call Deborah Fine. Call Debbie Fine. One good nude scene and I could make it. Make a name for myself. One. Nude. Scene.

Fadeout.

ACT ONE, SCENE 3: THE TOPLESS NURSE

Pause only to clear off the actor. It is lunchtime again, another day, it is noon always. Brighter lights for this scene. No one is on stage as the lights go up. The intercom buzzes, once, pause, twice, pause, three times and Jacob Blank enters. The buzzer matches the jazz in his head. He is in a good mood, into cool—unheard by us—jazz.

JACOB BLANK *(Snapping his fingers)*: Yeah! Do it! Hot! Blow that horn, brother! Yeah! Hot! Hot! *(He practically sings his line into the little old-fashioned mouthpiece of the intercom, which hangs on a hook on the wall)* Yes, tell me what you want. All right. Righty-o. *(He goes back to bopping around his living room, grooving to the jazz)* Yeah! Do it! Yeah! All right, that's it, that's it, blow that horn, I'm with ya! That's right, make it cool now, make it cool.

A knock at the door.

JACOB BLANK *(Practically singing)*: It's not locked, come in, come in.

Enter Debbie Fine. She's nice, pretty, unthreatening although dressed up in some extreme fashion interpretation of what seems like a forties

236

women's military outfit. It even has a hat like a military cap, pointed, tilted to one side. She has high heels on. I don't really care how old she is, between twenty-five and fifty-five, she is always someone's girl, not quite an adult or her own person. I like her. She has rouge on her cheeks, her hair curled, nails polished, and yet no chic, no place in time.

DEBBIE FINE: Hi, I'm Debbie Fine. Is Himmer here?

JACOB BLANK: Hi. Are you my nurse?

DEBBIE FINE: No, I don't think so. Are you expecting a nurse?

JACOB BLANK (*After a moment's thought*): I don't know. Some people think I need one.

DEBBIE FINE: Now why is that? May I sit down?

JACOB BLANK: Please suit yourself. Why I don't know except some think I've snapped my twig.

He bursts out laughing. She joins in.

DEBBIE FINE: People say that about me, too.

JACOB BLANK: Really? Interesting. (*Holding up the empty delicate plate*) Cookie?

DEBBIE FINE: Pardon?

JACOB BLANK: Would you care for a cookie?

DEBBIE FINE: There seem to be none left.

JACOB BLANK: Let's each have an imaginary one, they're so much better.

DEBBIE FINE (*Taking one*): Yes, you're right. Wonderful, did you bake them yourself?

JACOB BLANK (*Simply*): No, they're store bought.

They chew the crunchy imaginary cookies.

JACOB BLANK (*Nicely*): What are you doing here?

DEBBIE FINE: I've come to see your son, I was invited.

JACOB BLANK: Why would you want to see him when you can see me?

DEBBIE FINE: We had an appointment.

JACOB BLANK: He's too young for you.

DEBBIE FINE: You think so?

JACOB BLANK: Most definitely but I assure you that's no slur on your attractiveness; clearly you're at your peak of sexual attractiveness.

DEBBIE FINE: Oh? Yes?

JACOB BLANK: I'm an expert on that sort of thing. I'm a poet, you see, and consequently have a lot of time on my hands to contemplate that sort of thing. If you're around long enough I'll whip up a poem about you.

DEBBIE FINE: That would be nice.

JACOB BLANK: You're sure you're not my nurse?

DEBBIE FINE: I could be.

JACOB BLANK: That's the spirit! Things have been in a bit of a havoc around here. There've been some tragedies in the family and I'm trapped here with Himmer's grandfather, taking care of an old fellow. I see him when I look in the mirror, it's quite horrifying actually to encounter someone old in the hall when you least expect to see'm. I just have to keep an open mind about it. How old are you, about sixteen?

DEBBIE FINE (*Meaning a lot older than that!*): A little bit older than that!

JACOB BLANK: Good, because I don't want to get into any trouble with the law.

DEBBIE FINE (*Delicately*): Have you often been in trouble with the law?

JACOB BLANK: No, but I have to be careful. (*Confidentially*) I like the ladies and I like'm young! (*He cracks himself up*) There! I've spilled my beans! (*Moving close to her, practically snuggling up to her*) Now, you've got to tell me more about yourself, what nursing school are you graduating from?

DEBBIE FINE (*Searching*): Well, it's up in the air, right now.

JACOB BLANK: Do before you go on let me show you my book. Where is it now?! (*He finds it tucked away under piles of other old things. It is an old, slim, small navy blue volume with gold print on the cover. The pages are yellowing and when you open the book bits of crumbled paper fall out. He's proud of it although he tries to cover that and show some modicum of modesty)* Here it is! It was just published. *(Pages crumble)* They use such cheap paper! See, there's my name, Jacob Blank, *Poems* by Jacob Blank. Do you think I should've come up with more of a title? Here's one I almost called the book: "Sorrows Are for Everyone." What do you think?

DEBBIE FINE: What a lovely book, I'm so impressed.

JACOB BLANK *(Seductive, boyish)*: Well, I showed it to you to impress you. I have a promising career ahead of me. There's no telling where I'll stop.

DEBBIE FINE: No.

JACOB BLANK: You're awfully nice! Polite, civilized, pretty, alert, have you always wanted to be a nurse? Some doctor's going to snatch you up! What are we doing here together? I could fall in love with you, I'm three-quarters in love with you now.

DEBBIE FINE: Oh, I don't know about that. I like all these trains, they're darling.

JACOB BLANK *(Nonchalant)*: They belong to the little boy who lives here.

DEBBIE FINE: Do you know how to work them?

JACOB BLANK: Oh, no! I'm not mechanical. I'm poetical. *(He laughs)*

DEBBIE FINE: Well, I would love to see them go, it's like Christmas.

JACOB BLANK: Well, then, I'm sure if we both concentrated together we could figure it out. After all, they're made for little tykes, aren't they. Okay, what's this switch? Maybe this button does something. Holy God, this looks complicated.

DEBBIE FINE: This is the transformer. We control the trains from here.

JACOB BLANK: All right, if you say so. My, you're pretty! Keep smiling, I'm nuts about your smile. *(Out of the corner of his mouth)* Slap me when I get out of line, I tend to get a little fresh around lunchtime.

DEBBIE FINE: I think I've got it. First we've got to plug it in. Oh, look, the houses light up! And there's little people going in and out of the bank and post office. This is charming.

JACOB BLANK: I'm a little more charmed by adult games myself.

DEBBIE FINE: Now, you said you'd be a gentleman.

JACOB BLANK: I said that?

The trains are on, or at least one small set is revolving, hopefully without mishap, in a circle on the tracks. It would be nice if Debbie Fine could somehow get in the middle of the circle, especially if the track is elevated. She is fascinated by the trains and likes being a giantess in comparison to them. Jacob Blank wanders to the couch or some chair so she must shout to be heard.

DEBBIE FINE: This is wonderful! I'm so happy observing this little kingdom!

JACOB BLANK (*Spoiled*): You'll have to speak up if you expect me to hear you over that racket!

DEBBIE FINE (*Shouting but not unpleasantly, she's so happy*): I'm not a nurse! My father is a very rich mean man who thinks he's God and he doesn't want to see me happy so I sold all my stocks in his company and have several million dollars to show for it. Many millions. (*She toots the train whistle twice and laughs*) This is marvelous!

Jacob Blank pulls the plug on the trains and it all stops, lights out in the houses too.

JACOB BLANK: I pulled the plug! I pulled the plug!

DEBBIE FINE: That's not very nice.

JACOB BLANK (*Embarrassed confession*): I can't stand to have divided attention.

DEBBIE FINE: Were you listening to what I was saying?

JACOB BLANK: Yes but I've been leading you on unfairly. My heart is not my own to give.

DEBBIE FINE: No?

JACOB BLANK: I've given it away already.

DEBBIE FINE: To whom?

JACOB BLANK: A girl named Lolly. (*Shrugging*) I love her. She's tops. Do you hate me now?

240

DEBBIE FINE: No, we can be friends.

JACOB BLANK: I suppose, but the whole issue of desire will always come into it.

DEBBIE FINE: Well, you can make an effort to control yourself.

JACOB BLANK: I could, but it all seems so counterproductive. Your pop, he's a meany?

DEBBIE FINE: He's the meanest man in the whole world.

JACOB BLANK: That's mean! Lolly is so sweet. Well, she's not so sweet really but that's what I like about her, she's sassy and tastes like licorice. Wanna see what she did? It flipped me out. *(He gets this thin, yellowed, 8½" by 11" manuscript we've seen before, bound with clips, limp from time)* Here, you say you go in for artistic things, take a look at this.

DEBBIE FINE: *The Ruins of Athens.* What's it about?

JACOB BLANK: Very heady stuff. Way beyond her years she's writing. I'm telling her to leave school. Academic circles are very tight. Well, I'm sure you know. You probably got pressured into nursing when you might've made a perfectly decent doctor.

DEBBIE FINE: Oh, I could never have become a doctor, my grades weren't good enough.

JACOB BLANK: No? Well then maybe your father isn't such a bad character, pushing you into nursing, at least you're useful.

DEBBIE FINE *(Giving up and not unconfused)*: That's true.

JACOB BLANK: Now, I have a big favor to ask you but I'm a little embarrassed to ask it.

DEBBIE FINE: Go ahead.

JACOB BLANK: It's improper.

DEBBIE FINE: I'll brace myself.

JACOB BLANK: You'd best. A while ago, when I was in grade school, Charlie Runner passed around a hot-book. You know what a hot-book is, don't you?

DEBBIE FINE *(After a slight pause to dismiss the idea he means a stolen book)*: Pornography?

JACOB BLANK: Okay, yeah, and it was about this nurse, this beautiful nurse who worked in an amazing hospital who arrived one day to discover the top of her uniform was missing but because it was a particularly busy day with a lot of emergencies to attend to, the nurse was forced more or less to make a quick decision whether she will perform her duties that day topless.

DEBBIE FINE: I see.

JACOB BLANK: So, she does, and henceforth is known in the hospital—and not unkindly—as the Topless Nurse.

DEBBIE FINE: This is a whole novel?

JACOB BLANK: Oh yes, it's rather detailed, following her through her day, running from emergency to emergency, her breasts bouncing slightly as she comes into each room.

DEBBIE FINE: I see.

JACOB BLANK: She deserved a medal for what she did for those patients.

DEBBIE FINE: I'm sure of it.

JACOB BLANK: So I've always remembered the Topless Nurse, for a long time I dreamt of her, wished to have her next to me, imagined kissing her lips, touching her . . . toplessness.

DEBBIE FINE: And you've never found her?

JACOB BLANK: No. I imagine she's a fictitious character. But I wondered if you perhaps wouldn't be completely adverse to maybe removing your top, if you wouldn't mind so much.

DEBBIE FINE: I really don't think so.

JACOB BLANK: No?

DEBBIE FINE: No.

JACOB BLANK: Oh, that's too bad.

DEBBIE FINE: My father isn't the only mean man; he works for a foundation that is filled with mean men, mean men and women, all mean. They get together every once in a while in a walnut-lined room and decide what to do with other people's lives, as meanly as possible.

JACOB BLANK: I know these people.

DEBBIE FINE: I want to escape them. I know I can't slay them, their replacements wait at every exit and they smell so much you have to hold your nose when you go up next to them, that's their decay.

JACOB BLANK: Yes.

DEBBIE FINE: And though they think God loves them, God does not love them, God is embarrassed for them, God can't look away quick enough and think of something else. And if they got some inkling as to the way God felt, they'd drop their posts and cover up their heads with their hands, instead of holding up placards that say bad things about people or holding up their hands to vote against people or using their mouths to see people suffer.

JACOB BLANK: You're a very smart woman with good looks.

DEBBIE FINE: Am I? And you know something else, I've got a lot of ready money.

JACOB BLANK: A lot?

DEBBIE FINE: Um-hm.

JACOB BLANK: Well, that makes you just about a perfect catch for someone.

DEBBIE FINE: But I can't find anyone.

JACOB BLANK: It's a pity I'm taken.

DEBBIE FINE: A pity but maybe you can give me some advice.

JACOB BLANK: What kind of advice?

DEBBIE FINE: Advice. General advice.

JACOB BLANK: That would be a favor, wouldn't it?

DEBBIE FINE: It could be.

JACOB BLANK: So if I did you a favor maybe you could do me a favor too.

DEBBIE FINE: It's possible.

JACOB BLANK: And then we could have some champagne. I don't know how it got there but there's some champagne in the refrigerator.

DEBBIE FINE: We could.

JACOB BLANK: What do you want to know?

DEBBIE FINE: What to do with my life.

JACOB BLANK: You mean your money, that's easy. There's a little boy who runs around this apartment. He says he has to go to the hospital. You should give your money there.

The pace slows down, slower and slower to the fadeout.

243

DEBBIE FINE: Is that a place the Topless Nurse could work?

She has begun to slowly remove her jacketlike top. They talk slow.

JACOB BLANK: She might. In an emergency.

DEBBIE FINE: What might qualify as an emergency?

JACOB BLANK: Life-and-death cases, things like that.

DEBBIE FINE: And there's some solace in having seen her, the Topless Nurse?

JACOB BLANK: A lot of solace, people respect her.

DEBBIE FINE: She never appears in the same place twice I'm told.

JACOB BLANK: She's like a deity, people feel redeemed for having stood in her presence.

With her back to the audience, Debbie Fine is facing Jacob Blank, unhooking her bra slowly as the lights fade, Jacob Blank agape.

DEBBIE FINE: Some say the Topless Nurse is just a mythological figure and they don't believe in her, they say she doesn't exist.

JACOB BLANK: They're so wrong.

ACT TWO, SCENE I: CURTAIN RAISER

All that remains of the set is the drapes covering the three walls. All else is removed, including the Persian rugs that covered the now visible marbleized linoleum floor. This is a room in a hospital, a biggish room intended eventually as a sitting room or solarium. Because we are to presume a muralist has been painting on the walls under the curtains, messy paint cans sit about with their brushes and rags. Stools of varying size and a stepladder are there too. Light from above, probably we are to think the ceiling is glass. Lights fade up on the unoccupied stage. Enter Samantha and Prentice. Samantha is wearing a hospital smock and a light cotton robe, open. She's barefoot. Having come off the street, Prentice is wearing perhaps the thinnest khaki raincoat, grays and beige, black shoes.

SAMANTHA: This is it?

PRENTICE: Well, I don't think it's finished. It's going to be a kind of solarium, a sitting room.

SAMANTHA: Sunset for the twilight set.

PRENTICE: You're barefoot!

SAMANTHA: So what?

PRENTICE: I don't think you should be walking around barefoot. Don't you have slippers?

SAMANTHA: Sure I have slippers, somewhere, but I don't feel like wearing them.

PRENTICE: You have to wear something on your feet, the floor is cold.

SAMANTHA: I'm fine.

PRENTICE (*Taking off his own shoes, he's wearing socks*): Here, take these, put mine on. Samantha, really, put them on, the floor is too cold to walk barefoot.

SAMANTHA: Oh, all right. (*She slips on the black shoes and clunks around*) Now I look really adorable. Let's peek under the curtains. When are they supposed to be through?

They peek under the heavy cover-up curtain against the walls. We can't see what they see.

PRENTICE: I don't know.

SAMANTHA: Pretty lurid.

PRENTICE: What's new with your doctor?

SAMANTHA: Cecile, nothing, you know we've been friends since elementary school but I think this whole epidemic is over her head. I mean she's working and working doing tests till her head's unscrewing and I'm a willing enough guinea pig but you sense everyone's faithlessness in their own attempts and then you find your stiff upper lip hanging over your knee.

PRENTICE: I've been doing a lot of research myself, reading every-thing available, I have theories of my own.

SAMANTHA: Have you read "How to Embrace the Incurable"? That's my favorite.

PRENTICE: I saw that.

SAMANTHA: Ghastly! Actually that was the least offensive. Some just come right out and make an argument for internment camps, quarantines, divestment of property, the stripping of insurance, of all but minimal care, a thin blanket and some spittle. A woman in the *New York Times* compared the United States to India.

PRENTICE: I read that.

SAMANTHA: In the United States when you are out of the game you are out of the game.

PRENTICE: Where's Himmer?

SAMANTHA: He'll be here. I'm hungry. I wonder if they prepare last-supper requests.

PRENTICE: Oh Samantha, come on already.

SAMANTHA: No, I mean it, shouldn't they take requests for last suppers?

PRENTICE: I imagine anyone sick enough to be approaching a last supper would have lost their appetite by then.

SAMANTHA: Oh, yeah. I guess you're right.

PRENTICE: Except, when I was little, I remember there was a whole slew of black-and-white pictures on the four-thirty movie, I think it was Prison Week or Death Row Week or something and several of the movies had last-supper scenes.

SAMANTHA: Well, you see.

PRENTICE: I got very involved in the idea of what I would eat and I drew up this whole long elaborate menu for my mother to follow and when I handed it to her and told her what it was for, she said, "Fine, I'll file it away."

SAMANTHA: I'm going to ask Cecile.

PRENTICE: Maybe you shouldn't be out of bed.

SAMANTHA: Sure, I can, I can do what I like, Himmy and I have the run of the place since they think we got that Deborah Fine lady to donate her dollars. Are you seeing anyone new?

PRENTICE: No.

SAMANTHA: No, why not?

PRENTICE: What would be the point?

SAMANTHA: Oh, come on, leave those lines for me. There'd be lots of

point. I should set you up with William at my old office. He's a doll
and he's very involved in the politics of this whole epidemic. He'd
love you.

PRENTICE: I don't think so.

SAMANTHA: You meet this guy, he's the type that could run for
President and win, and I know what I'm talking about.

PRENTICE: No, the whole romance angle of life has been drained out
of everyday experience. Everyone meets everyone else and sus-
pects they're meeting their executioner, it makes the most casual
overtures seem extinctionary . . . no, that's not a word . . .
extinctive, that's a word. Anyway, the days of introduction and
casual handshakes must be held for a while, it seems, at arm's
distance. I have a candy bar in my pocket.

SAMANTHA (*With exaggerated greed*): Give it to me!

*Enter Patrick. His wrists are bandaged but it's not so easy to see that.
He wears a long-sleeved shirt, casual clothes, maybe his hair is brushed
differently. He's much calmer now.*

PATRICK: Hi, is Himmer here?

PRENTICE: Hi, Patrick, do you know Samantha?

PATRICK: Yeah, we met before.

SAMANTHA: Yeah, where, I remember. Someone's party. I know, you
were in A *Summer Thing!* The pool attendant in A *Summer Thing!* I
can't believe I remember that, I never remember things like that.

PATRICK: I look different now.

PRENTICE (*Generous*): Better.

SAMANTHA: The movie had very good things in it. (*Holding up the
candy bar she hasn't unwrapped yet*) Want half?

PATRICK: Sure.

*Samantha cuts the candy bar in half, hands it to Patrick. They stand
there and eat it.*

SAMANTHA: It's good.

PATRICK: Chewy.

SAMANTHA *(To Prentice)*: You're sure you don't want any?

PRENTICE: No, thanks.

SAMANTHA: Chewy.

PATRICK: Well, see you later. *(He exits)*

SAMANTHA: Did you see his bandages?

PRENTICE: Hmm, poor thing.

SAMANTHA: How did he get here, don't they lock the door behind you or in front of you or something?

PRENTICE: I guess he got a pass.

SAMANTHA: He's more attractive than I thought. Less banal.

PRENTICE: I've always thought he was cute.

SAMANTHA: But less banal now. Maybe that cliché that misfortune puts interesting lines on people's faces is true in some cases. Much cuter. *(Chewing)* So it turns out one of my married men spent some of his time off with other married men. So I die, I tell myself, so what, everyone's scheduled to die.

PRENTICE: Don't make light of it, please.

SAMANTHA: No, I'm serious. *(Slight pause)* They put so much salt in candy bars.

Enter Himmer. He is in a hospital smock and robe and beach thongs.

HIMMER *(Good mood)*: Hi. Oh, the walls are still covered up. Did you peek? *(Peeking)* Almost done it looks, no? I'm so excited!

SAMANTHA: It looks like fire, like it's on fire.

HIMMER: No, it's a sunset. It'll be beautiful. Look, it had to be something that would pass as a reasonable mural after we were done with it too. *(Confident)* It'll work out fine. When the artist is through, they'll just have to get rid of these curtains and *(Vaguely gesturing to where the audience is)* set up chairs there for the audience. I'm so excited! Everything is going so well.

PRENTICE *(Hopefully)*: Good news from your doctor?

HIMMER: Oh, no! I'm not even thinking about that anymore: good news/bad news, it's become a ferocious bore. No, I got these hilarious Tom Collins glasses at the hospital flea market. *(He takes the tall stenciled glasses from a bag)*

SAMANTHA: Let me see.

PRENTICE: They let you traipse through their flea market dressed like that?

HIMMER: I went with Debbie. Anyway, I thought it would be a gas if during the hemlock-drinking scene we all used these Tom Collins glasses, wouldn't that be funny?

PRENTICE: No.

HIMMER: It would, kill-joy. I got all these chores done today, made copies of the script, picked up the hemlock—

PRENTICE: Hold on, back up. You don't mean hemlock literally?

HIMMER: No, of course not, I wouldn't have any idea where to get hemlock. I have some other kind of over-the-counter poison that'll work just as well.

PRENTICE: Are you saying you're going to pass out poison in these Tom Collins glasses and we're expected to drink it?

HIMMER: I don't expect anyone who doesn't want to drink it to drink it. I just know I intend to drink it. To the last drop.

PRENTICE: Have you flipped out?

HIMMER: Yes, I have. Funny you should ask, yes, yes, yes. What a drag it was clinging to whatever little shred of sanity's the minimum daily requirement to pass as sane. If it had some payoff—a good job, high salary, marriage, children, vivid love affairs, new clothes, travel, cars, what have you—it would all seem worth it. And it does, I suppose, for a while. Anyway, I never had much investment in that world, I was only pretending, playacting. "Oh hello, Mrs. Brown, how is your cow? Healthy, I'm so glad. Is that your barn on fire? No? Oh well, see you later."

SAMANTHA: It's enough I've consented to run around in a toga for a half hour.

HIMMER: Fine. I must say, Samantha, I'm surprised at you, I mean do you really give a shit, I mean really? All I can say is when I get to the climax and reach for my hemlock substitute in my Tom Collins glass it's going to taste like a Coca-Cola after running all day in the Sahara.

PRENTICE: Have I missed something here? You both are in good health, right?

HIMMER: Okay, so?

PRENTICE: I think it's repulsive—truly repulsive—that you're standing here talking about suicide—if that's what you're even talking
about—it's so kooky I'm not even sure—when this building alone
is packed with suffering and ailing people who you could probably
help in some way.

HIMMER: Oh, I've been visiting the sick. Ever since I got here. Let's
see, I've been to the room of the I-can't-wait-until-tomorrows.
What big eyes they've got! That's a symptom. "I-can't-wait-until-
tomorrow," they sing when you press them with a tongue depres-
sor. Then there's the room of the immortal soul. How dank it is!
Centuries it's been sealed up, waiting for a miracle drug to set it
free.

SAMANTHA: Prentice, we've donated ourselves to experimentation,
that's some small effort, don't be too critical.

HIMMER: The drug I'm taking makes me vomit. And we're putting on
my mother's entertainment gratis, I won't feel guilty for doing
myself in in lieu of a curtain call.

PRENTICE: Anyone's life can end in a minute—you didn't know that
before? You shouldn't have gotten that test, neither of you. You
know I'm probably zero positive too. Two years ago I slept with
Vaughn Bertish and he's dead now.

HIMMER: Well, you have your opportunity too to drink up at curtain
time.

SAMANTHA: I'm not drinking poison.

HIMMER: Don't, more for me that way. I'll have a whole pitcher. I
could skip with joy I feel so free. When my father flipped out I
grew so envious. The whole list of responsibilities that burden
each day with suffocating banality doubled for me—I had this
cut-free adult on my hands living in his head like a teenager. Not
so strange he should have refallen in love with my dead mother.
She was an old teenager in a state of arrested development too,
pickling her teenagerness in solitude, or whatever it is she did all
those years tucked away in the woods. I'm very sentimental about
my mother's play; I think, well, here's this little piece of art
written by this nineteen-year-old girl and I read it over and over

and I think oh, I'm really seeing into this thing. She'd probably just read Plato or Feydeau or someone and has the essence of playacting which must be wish fulfillment, no? I mean that's the whole story of life, isn't it, just getting whatever it is you want, plain and simple. And when getting what you want is no longer tenable/possible/imaginable then life as even a premise to proceed becomes funhouse-ridiculous only without the fun.

SAMANTHA: You're babbling.

PRENTICE: By that analysis, I have more reason than anyone to sip hemlock. I wake up, I go out, I do whatever dull routine my exhausted senses can execute, I make small talk, I hang up telephones, I come home. A large expanse of homelessness sits at home waiting for me, it's always at home. I'm homesick in and out of home.

SAMANTHA: I wake up. I do my thing. I meet the people who meet me. What a tired little lot it is! The exciting people, yes, they must be hidden, secluded in some soundproof room and just when you need them most they'll be ushered on, all crisp and ready to fulfill your needs, to be there for you. You give up on that eventually, and take up reading, but books are too hard, too similar, you see through the optimistic little plots: ruthless fiend schemes her way to riches, all happiness floods her apartment. She drowns there in an excruciating shudder of satisfaction.

HIMMER: I read that book.

Enter Debbie Fine.

HIMMER: Hi, Debbie!

DEBBIE FINE: Hi. Hi, everyone.

HIMMER: Debbie, did you find anything else at the flea market?

DEBBIE FINE: Oh I did, I had great luck. Look at this. (*Picking up out of a bag a bolt of cream-colored gauzy fabric*) I found the perfect fabric for the togas.

HIMMER: Terrific. That is perfect. Prentice, isn't that perfect?

SAMANTHA: It better not be transparent, I'm not walking around naked.

251

DEBBIE FINE: Have you peeked, under the curtains?

SAMANTHA: Nice.

DEBBIE FINE: I was so nervous, interviewing all the painters, they all seemed equally equipped. I just hired the nicest.

HIMMER: That's what I would do, all talent being relative, and all art boiled down to the ability to portray a sunset or not.

SAMANTHA: Debbie, did you know Himmer's planning on serving poison highballs in *The Ruins of Athens* and we're all welcome to drink up and die?

DEBBIE FINE: Yes, I heard that.

SAMANTHA: Well, are you going to drink it?

DEBBIE FINE (*Pleasantly*): No, I don't think so. I like my life. I never used to but then I think you really have to have had a crummy life and have it improve to feel your life is going well.

PRENTICE: What was crummy about your life?

DEBBIE FINE: Nothing. But that was what was crummy about it. I'd say "Daddy, oh Daddy, that's the car I've had my eye on," and in the morning I'd be in the driver's seat. I'd say "Oh Daddy, my car displeases me, it's not the auto I want to sit in," and then by afternoon I'm in something bigger. Every hour's a fantasy when you've an accommodating daddy. But Daddy, in the final analysis, was rather disapproving. When I used words like oppression aggression repression Daddy would make loud squealing remarks about ingratitude and the various nuances of the word *allowance*. And then, as these stories go, I had to finally admit my life was indeed quite crummy.

SAMANTHA: And you're happy now?

DEBBIE FINE (*After the second to feel it*): Yes! Yes I am! And it's a delight to realize it so entirely.

SAMANTHA: Even though you're going out with a married man?

PRENTICE: He's not married.

SAMANTHA: He thinks he's married, he thinks he's cheating on Himmer's mother who he thinks is alive.

DEBBIE FINE: That's true. But he loves me and I love him. I'm happy.

SAMANTHA: And happiness is love, you believe that?

DEBBIE FINE: Sure, why not? Don't I look happy? Before Mr. Blank I had other boyfriends and they were not entirely without qualities. We did things together, looked at movies, ran around tracks, ate unusual flavors and discussed fluctuations of all kinds. Several, who couldn't even be described as mercenary, proposed, and I had to consider what kind of happiness would be mine feeling wishy-washy about a fellow who when he paints a picture of harmonial bliss all I can think of is how cheap and crooked the frame is hanging on a wall I occasionally imagine is blocking my way.

SAMANTHA: Trippy description.

HIMMER: I have no more room in my head for love hopes. They were nice while they lasted but—no, that's not true—they were horrible while they lasted, waking me up in the middle of the night, cross-eyed and painting a happy face to go out in the streets.

SAMANTHA (*To Debbie Fine, testing her happiness, she seems so unaffected by negative input*): Doesn't he depress you, put any nick at all in your happiness?

DEBBIE FINE (*Brightly*): No, everyone's happiness is absolute to themselves. I suppose it is a little disheartening, knowing that when you're in your own prison—cold, rat-infested and smelly as it might be—no one is thinking of you. It's true, they may write to you, send you tins of cookies, light candles and pay priests five dollars to mention your name in their prayers but finally and essentially your unhappiness is your own.

SAMANTHA: I used to date a man, an eye doctor as a matter of fact, who had not an apartment but a house in the East 60s, enormous art collection, African sculpture, New Guinea masks, Klee, Calder, Kandinsky, Cornell, et al, derailed parlor cars parked for kicks in the bedroom upholstered in Fortuny, and not a nitwit or a bore, he could discuss you-name-it with noteworthy aplomb, all this, a social conscience, a not-bad face, and a decent sense of humor.

DEBBIE FINE: So why didn't you marry him?

SAMANTHA: I wasn't interested.

PRENTICE: Why not?

SAMANTHA: I don't know.

PRENTICE: It happened to me too. I kept wishing for one kind of

253

person to spend my life with and further than that, one kind of life to lead in general. I pictured the apartment and though it had no African sculpture or Kandinsky, it was nice, there was a green couch with maroon pillows you could sit on, interesting lamps and an excellent stereo system. When I introduced myself to the six or seven people I could've found some measure of happiness with they revolted me. It was as if getting my way or nearly was the opposite of what I wanted. I wanted everything to be a mess. A mess that would create such a frenzied hullabaloo around me of sharp words, thrown objects and ugly accusations that I would not, though I might try, hear the needling scratch of existence's speedy automatic play toward my terminus.

The lights blink.

SAMANTHA: What's that? Don't tell me there's going to be a blackout, not in a hospital.
PRENTICE: No, they have their own generators.
HIMMER: That's right, anything to keep everyone on as long as possible.

Enter Jacob Blank, same dark outfit but with a boutonniere now, perhaps a dark beret. He's holding bags from the deli, a long baguette sticks out of the bag, he has a bottle of red wine and a bunch of flowers wrapped in florist's paper. He's in good spirits.

JACOB BLANK: Darling, am I terribly late?
DEBBIE FINE: Just on time.

Debbie Fine and Jacob Blank kiss.

JACOB BLANK: The liquor store had me quite baffled with crazy made-up dates on all the bottles, I got this one anyway, the gentleman assured me it's excellent and, quite frankly, for what I paid for it, it must be. I have extra cups, would the little children like some wine?

SAMANTHA: This little child would.

HIMMER: Dad, we're not children, we're adults.

JACOB BLANK: Why must he persist in calling me Dad, it embarrasses me. It doesn't put you off now does it, Deborah?

DEBBIE FINE: No, no, not at all, I'm very fond of Himmer.

HIMMER: Well, at least you give me the courtesy of saying my name right. One of the brainy on-the-verge-of-a-breakthrough doctors here calls me Himmler.

PRENTICE: Well, you advocate euthanasia, don't you?

HIMMER: Only for those so inclined.

JACOB BLANK (*Unloading his bags*): Your favorite, darling, Westphalia ham.

DEBBIE FINE: You're too dear, I'm mad for Westphalia ham.

JACOB BLANK: Cornichon?

PRENTICE: I'll have one.

JACOB BLANK: Cherries, brownies, lemonade for those too drunk to drink. Oh darling, don't sit on the ground in your lovely dress.

DEBBIE FINE (*Spreading her shoulder scarf on the floor*): Oh, my scarf will make a better picnic table than garment. Come sit by me.

PRENTICE: What pretty flowers!

DEBBIE FINE: You don't have any hot mustard, do you?

JACOB BLANK: For you? Hot mustard galore.

DEBBIE FINE: Here's a pre-mustard kiss.

JACOB BLANK: Hotter for the promise of kisses to come.

Jacob Blank and Debbie Fine laugh and eat.

SAMANTHA: I'll have a brownie. Where are the brownies?

DEBBIE FINE: Here.

PRENTICE: This bread is superb.

SAMANTHA: Give me some. (*Eating*) Carbohydrates are the single most reassuring thing.

PRENTICE: Have some berries.

DEBBIE FINE: Darling, let me feed you, you're eating too fast.

JACOB BLANK: I'm too eager to get back to the kissing part.

PRENTICE: Pass the pickles.

HIMMER: Well, it seems no matter how dark high noon is, it's always time for lunch when the bell rings.

JACOB BLANK: What bell?

HIMMER: Good question, what bell, the bell of appetite, the bell of dinner, the bell of anticipation, the Belle of Amherst, the bell of antiquity, the bell-bottom.

JACOB BLANK (*Eating, to Debbie Fine*): I don't feel children mix well with adults in social functions. Are you set on having children?

DEBBIE FINE: We'll see, we don't have to think about it now.

JACOB BLANK: You're perfect.

HIMMER: I spoke to Doctor Anger. He wanted me to go on at length about my childhood. He had his heart set on understanding all my bad attitudes and bad fortune in terms of my upbringing. I have total recall of any given situation from the past so I let his little ears fasten to my rather lengthy list of what by now must be to all twentieth-century psychologists a rather commonplace harangue of baffled infanthood, estranged toddler days, wounding adolescence, and stultifying adulthood. In short, it would take a traveler looking long and far to find a soul not rich with the soil of complaint.

JACOB BLANK: My childhood was only good, glorious I'd go as far to say. I found two pearls on the open clam of my arrival: I called them my parents. They called me their prize. I was encouraged to write poetry and so I did on a daily basis until discovering I was an addict and had to have the kiss of a beautiful woman on my lips constantly; consequently, my mouth full most of the time, my metaphor suffered. Marriage I decided would be the correct girdle for my excesses but how was I to know love could hit the same place twice? I'm only glad there've been no offspring to attach me irrevocably to my wiles. Babies seem to be Cupid's little party favors—there are times one looks down at the favor and thinks was the party really worth it?

HIMMER: But you are attached irrevocably to me—you're my father!

JACOB BLANK: You're an impertinent rascal. If you've misplaced your natural parents and need temporary shelter, we're happy to lend you a piece of bread and a sip of lemonade but please understand, if you understand nothing else, I am responsible for no one, I am as lost and alone in the world as the next guy unless of course one lends oneself to another in the greedy charity work of love—as I've been able to do now, I suppose because I'm blessed, twice. My advice—when you're old enough, find yourself a mate. Brownie, please.

HIMMER: Don't you remember Francine? She was the most recent of the dozen or so women you proposed to!

JACOB BLANK *(Half to Debbie Fine)*: I've never heard that name before, it sounds like a horse one would lose a bet on, Francine.

HIMMER: She bet on you, it seems a bit of a gyp you can't even remember who she is.

JACOB BLANK: All this talk of childhood and romances from the past is futile in the extreme. Let's live in the present, fleeting though it be; and wearing as it may be to be reminded, it's all we've got.

HIMMER: Coming from you that's priceless!

JACOB BLANK: Thank you.

Enter Patrick, as before.

HIMMER: Hi, Patrick.

SAMANTHA: Hi, Patrick.

PRENTICE: Hi, Patrick.

DEBBIE FINE: Hi, Patrick.

JACOB BLANK: Hi, Patrick.

PATRICK *(A little stunned)*: Hi.

JACOB BLANK: Patrick, why are you so popular? Sit down and have a sandwich.

PATRICK: I didn't know I was, thanks.

HIMMER: Patrick, you just tried to kill yourself—

PRENTICE: Himmer—

HIMMER: Well, he did. I don't see why we should act like it's a big secret.

PATRICK: Yes, I did try, it's no secret.

HIMMER: There, you see. Now, I've been talking to Doctor Anger about my idea to drink poison at the end of *The Ruins of Athens* and

257

he thinks it's insane. He says I'm falling prey to despair and that by Tuesday happy news may spring forth making of all despairs of the past idle powerless memories.

PATRICK: I see Doctor Anger.

HIMMER: You see Doctor Anger too?

PATRICK: Yes, I like him. I see him. I sang him my original song and he liked it. He recommended I write other songs. I wrote one about him. I'll sing it to you. *(He sings the ballad calmly)*

Hey Doctor Anger
You told me to write your song
So I wrote it
I wrote the song on Doctor Anger
Wake up and sing it
It doesn't rhyme, no only sporadic
There it goes the words democratic:

"No expectations" it said on the bottle
Take two said the doc, take two and don't call me.
"No expectations" swallow the dosage
Swallow the dosage and don't call me.
Oh Doctor Anger your prescription is bitter.
"Take two and don't call me."
Oh Doctor Anger, what's there to look forward to?
"Take two more, take four."
Oh Doctor Anger, don't want to overdose
Feel so bitter already, dear doctor, .
Your prescription may kill me.

Oh Doctor Doctor what floor did you move to?
I hear them page you on the loudspeaker.
The connection grows weaker and weaker.
Have you cured me Doctor Anger?
When do I start my long languor?
In the halls I hear them sing
"Doctor Anger, plain and mild
Lets his patients all run wild."

Doctor Doctor rest assured
I'll never sue
Oh Doctor the truth I tell you
I'm glad I knew you.

JACOB BLANK (*After a small pause*): Well, that's a baffling little number.

HIMMER: Oh, he does that sort of thing. Have a seat, Patrick.

PATRICK: I'll stand.

HIMMER: By the way, here's your script.

PATRICK: Do I get to come on first?

HIMMER: What?

PATRICK: Do I get to come on first, come on and talk for a while, I like that. What do I play?

HIMMER: Well, a soldier of some kind. Is that okay?

PATRICK: I can play a soldier. Do I talk about Vietnam or Central America or World War Two, or Korea, or Grenada?

HIMMER: I don't think so, it's not that sort of thing. It takes place in Ancient Greece.

PATRICK: It's a costume play.

HIMMER: If all goes well, yes. And at the climax there'll be a big Kool-Aid pitcher of end-it-all-now beverage and anyone so inclined is welcome to partake, it's entirely optional though more controversial than I'd have first imagined.

PATRICK: Oh, I won't do that.

HIMMER: That's fine with me but if you don't mind my asking, why? A short while ago you were rather set against a future of low prospects.

PATRICK: I acted rashly.

SAMANTHA: But now you have something to look forward to.

PATRICK: No.

PRENTICE: You have people who depend on you.

PATRICK: No.

DEBBIE FINE: You would miss certain things too much.

PATRICK: I don't know.

PRENTICE: Like your children, right? You have children.

PATRICK: Yes, I'd miss them.

259

SAMANTHA: And you'd miss spontaneous things like coming upon a small dance hall at the edge of a city near a harbor and dancing there late as the waiters stack the chairs.

PATRICK: Yes, I could.

DEBBIE FINE: Or the lovely smell of leaves burning. It's autumn, you're walking alone to collect your thoughts, you come upon the burning pile raked by someone who lives nearby and kisses you softly when you get there.

PATRICK: Yes, why not.

JACOB BLANK: Sure, I get it, name something nice. Pizza.

PRENTICE: Elegant gloves.

SAMANTHA: Music.

DEBBIE FINE: Chrysanthemums.

JACOB BLANK: Adulation. Pizza. Pizza with everything.

DEBBIE FINE: Lilies of the valley.

JACOB BLANK: I'll buy you some, darling, I'll spread them on our bed.

HIMMER: You're indecent, keep your sex life to yourself and private. Deborah, control him.

DEBBIE FINE: He loves me.

PRENTICE: You're just jealous, Himmer, because you've killed in the crib all your budding romances.

HIMMER: Oh please stop—you're at your worst when you get on your moral high horse. And enough of all these flowers—flowers are no more than, at their best, bright little sex organs hoodwinking insects into their sticky business and passing themselves off then hypocritically at holidays as fit subjects for centerpieces.

PATRICK (*Quietly*): I like holly. The red berries against the pointy green leaves. But holly's not a flower. I just want a big part. I just don't want to come on with very little to say and then go off, I've done that. I want to make a difference. I want to know when I go off it makes sense that I came on in the first place. I don't want to just hold a spear and say here comes the king.

HIMMER: There's no line like that but, Patrick, soldier characters hold spears, that's what they do, there's no getting around it. We can't very well cast you as the goddess can we? I mean the ability to hold a spear or not is destiny, isn't it?

PATRICK (*Sad, resolute, calm*): I want to come on first. I want to talk. I don't care if I'm not the goddess but I want to say something worth listening to. (*He exits*)

HIMMER: Well, good gracious, next we're going to have union problems.

JACOB BLANK: Now, we mustn't blow this whole thing out of proportion. After all, Lolly's more or less abandoned *The Ruins of Athens* apparently for greener pastures so if it's artistic license we're barking for we should consider the bone ours.

HIMMER: Right, well put, here's your copy.

JACOB BLANK: My dear boy, I hardly need it. I know *The Ruins of Athens* like I know the streets of Brooklyn: inside out.

HIMMER: Well, here, you may need it as a place mat or something at your next picnic.

The lights blink.

JACOB BLANK: Oh my goodness, it's going to rain. We better pack up and get going.

HIMMER: Rain? We're indoors, that was electrical lights.

JACOB BLANK: You don't want to wet your dress, hurry up, Deborah.

PRENTICE AND SAMANTHA: Let me help.

They clean up the picnic.

JACOB BLANK: It's chillier suddenly too. It's treacherous how the weather can change so suddenly. The last thing I want to do is catch a cold! Hurry now, Deborah. Let's use the picnic cloth as an umbrella. (*He flaps her scarf over their two heads*)

DEBBIE FINE: What a hurry—see you soon, bye-bye now.

Jacob Blank and Debbie Fine exit running together as if from a downpour.

SAMANTHA: A picnic was a pleasant surprise.

PRENTICE: I enjoyed it. I was hungry.

HIMMER: I was thirsty. I'm still thirsty. The truth is I'm not so sure I'd like to slurp down my final brew. I keep thinking what if there really is a soul, some filament only vacationing in you for a time, wouldn't it be a terrible pity then to find out you'd muffed its smooth flight with your unhappy intervention? What if impatience really is somehow punished after life as it is so often punished in life, wouldn't that be awful?

PRENTICE: It would be awful.

SAMANTHA: There is no god. There is no heaven. There is no soul, no afterlife, no nothing. When I was little I memorized the peregrinations of Christ, I was fascinated by the concept of holiness. My parents screaming made a tent over my head of complaints with the world. I interviewed Christ. I said, Christ, do you have any patience left?

HIMMER: No, none.

SAMANTHA: I said, Christ, have you any investments left in heaven?

PRENTICE: No, none.

SAMANTHA: I said, can you speak highly, oh good Christ, of the awful awful people who so trashily invoke your name to barbecue others to make their Sundays that much more festive?

HIMMER AND PRENTICE: No, not at all.

SAMANTHA: And then Christ called me on the telephone. I was thirteen. He said, we're relocating, discontinue correspondence until further notice, utilities shut off until further notice, stop wondering until further notice.

The lights blink.

HIMMER: Well, I suppose we should get out of here before the whole place blows up.

PRENTICE: You yelled at me before.

HIMMER: No I didn't.

PRENTICE: Yes, you said I was on a moral high horse.

HIMMER: I'm sorry.

PRENTICE: Yes, you have to say you're sorry to me.

HIMMER: I'm sorry.

PRENTICE: And I'm sorry for anything I said to you bitter or envious or angry. But because we may not be here tomorrow—no, let me finish—we may not be here tomorrow and I want to say I'm sorry to everyone before it's too late.

SAMANTHA: I'm sorry too.

PRENTICE: You have no reason to say you're sorry to me.

SAMANTHA: Yes, I said you looked tired and I'm sorry I said it because you're not tired at all, you're the least tired person I know.

PRENTICE: Thank you.

SAMANTHA: You're welcome.

HIMMER: What cute socks, who are those by?

PRENTICE: Cacherel.

The lights blink.

HIMMER: Let's go before it rains.

SAMANTHA: I think I felt a drop.

PRENTICE: Me too, let's hurry before we get soaked.

The lights blink again, it's lightning.

HIMMER: Let's promise to always have some love for each other even after we're gone.

Lightning and thunder now too and then the sound of a sudden downpour of rain. Himmer, Samantha and Prentice run out holding hands as if from a great downpour. The curtains covering the walls are taken down or, perhaps better yet, taken up.

ACT TWO, SCENE 2: DENOUEMENT

The rain has cleared up, it is dawn after a dark night of rain, rosy golden light on the ruins of Athens: the mural is exposed. The walls are

263

painted as what must loosely be the Acropolis in disarray from the war.
The perspective is that of one standing in the center of the ruins. Some
columns are still standing here and there; others, knocked over, lean up
against one another. The light, as painted on these walls, is dawn but
sunset too; they are indistinguishable or rather, here, intermingled:
sunrise here, sunset there, but with no particular orb anywhere to settle
on. With the light of early morning fading up, birds sing, cicadas too.

Enter Patrick dressed as a soldier. He's impressive with helmet,
breastplate, short pleated metallic skirt, gladiator sandals and spear.
Laurel leaf is woven about his helmet. He is solemn, he addresses the
defeated.

PATRICK:

I am the herald, sad messenger of the gods too weary to make of my
    job lightness,
I arrive at dawn with heavy news of a world crashing down.
I stand before it, the ruins of Athens.
Woe to all things.
Woe to us witnesses as the sun rises.
We witness the waste of all things' power.
Woe to me, sad herald, witness to the pestilence of the city —
A city that during holy season could not be polluted by public
    executions
Lies now an open grave.
Every misery that can befall a city falls here.
It is a deep and narrow grave:
Scorching in heat, freezing by night.
Hunger and thirst.
The corpses of those who died
Lie with those that follow.
Fleet and army perished, few return home.
O Muse, help me to finish.
The words stick in my mouth, sad soldiers.
Messengers of the gods, take back your prophecies.
They say the war is over
But in the vanquished city

Defeat and ruin battle still for title
As morning makes its mark
Upon the dug-deep scars of Fate.

*The goddess appears; it is Samantha attired in white toga gown, gold
decorations, gold sandals, gold snakes around her arms, branches in
her hair; she looks gorgeous. Awed, Patrick, the messenger, falls to his
knee to honor her. Her tone is worthy of a goddess—imperious,
important, trying to cover she is in love with her messenger.*

SAMANTHA:
 Good messenger, good servant,
 It is I, Goddess of Battles All Lost,
 Distant cousin of wars won without valor.
 I cast my wretched eyes upon a city ripe with shame.
 It is harvest here for Hades and the death wheel
 Stalls its engine in the blood-filled avenues.
PATRICK: Hail, Goddess!
SAMANTHA:
 Hail.
 I answer your lone prayer
 Although the air is heavy with requests,
 Because you have been a faithful servant
   during this long ordeal
     where funeral garlands have gone from hand to hand
     never wilting for lack of use,
 Because my mob of worshippers
   lie now in quarries captive of the Spartans,
   cursing my deafness, calling me Ineptitude,
   never knowing my true name—
 A city survives its own defeat
   as a face that sits for a death mask
   is survived by a more patient self,
   clay and dust.
 I answer your call
   although the city is alive in death

265

with screams for salvation barely audible
as the walls are torn down to
the merry whistle of the flute.
Death's caprice is playing there;
empires dissolve in song.
I answer your call
though slow starvation, sunk fleets
and slaughtered heroes take up all our time.
I answer your call, good herald
sweet in loyalty and durable for wear,
as fair in face as the soldiers of Parnassus.
I answer your call, if you must know,
because I want you!
Be mine,
Come to where I sit in the cloudy heavens
Where I keep counsel with the weather.
Come be my husband,
Give up political partisanship
And the incompetence of government
Where all ships sink at last.
Sooner than later
All souls evaporate to god.
Come sooner, marry me
Sweet bad news bearer.
A lyre sits in heaven.
We can play it there.
Say you love me.
I am a goddess
And I think you should.
PATRICK: O hail, good Goddess.
SAMANTHA:
   Hail, hail—
   Answer the question—
   What do you think?
PATRICK:
   Goddess of Battles All Lost

I bow before you
A servant of the state,
Survivor in this time
Wealthy only in calamity.
We the hordes weep only that death
Not pause too long in striking.
My brothers suffer the most prodigious miseries
   and daily seek solace
   from any hand
   dismembered by necessity
   from the dismembered State
   and the ancient godless Church
   that has chased all gods
   from its crumbling pews.
For anyone who has not learned the lesson of pity
Sings in the chorus of the tin clang.
And by all that is holy
It is known in life
That Death without the clarification
Of the mystery of Life
Is a death eternal
And it is eternal death
In life we live in terror of
And not understanding what we must know
We watch our terror grow and grow.

SAMANTHA:

All too true,
But do not try my patience,
I bid you by all that is Dionysian
To hold off your long speeches
And answer my short question:
Do
   you
      want
         to
            marry

267

me?!

PATRICK: But good Goddess—

SAMANTHA: Better than you know—

PATRICK:

You are Goddess
And I mere mortal.

SAMANTHA:

True again but as I've already hinted
I like you
And am willing to overlook your
Drawbacks.

PATRICK:

Could such a union indeed take place?

SAMANTHA: I say it could.

PATRICK:

The gods in envy would not intercede?

SAMANTHA:

Let them try, there'll be hell to pay.
So, what do you say?

PATRICK:

Dear Goddess,
I find your face a comely grace,
I find it joy to gaze on,
I find a double joy imagining
Your robes about your feet,
A body I guess to be godly lies
Under there.

SAMANTHA: You're right.

PATRICK:

I bid you,
Come from your airy station
And kiss my mortal lips.

SAMANTHA:

I can't,
You've got to come here.

PATRICK: And die first?

SAMANTHA: You won't be sorry.

PATRICK:

I don't know—
How?

SAMANTHA:

I've an elixir, you drink it.
When you wake
As naked lovers
We meet again.

PATRICK:

Dread Goddess, tell me
Is eternity very dark?

SAMANTHA:

Hesitate and lose me forever!
I've been on the shelf too long.
Now, prove your seriousness
And blow me a kiss.
That's better.
Now, go perform your final libations,
Prayers, toilette or whatever you men do
And I will send you the elixir presently.
Go now! Here comes another victim,
A foolish servant girl, how I envy her sprightly walk.
In this time of ceaseless woe
It is the fool who happy here and there does go.
Go now, go!

Debbie Fine enters as the foolish servant girl, wearing a shorter version of the cream-colored toga, decorated with pretty but faded flowers. She holds a small basket made of dark twigs; it is filled with these faded flowers as well as bones and skulls. She is quite silly and empty-headed, this girl. Patrick exits. She sings to herself, la la la la.

SAMANTHA:

Oh, Foolish Servant Girl,
Hello, over here.

269

Oh, Foolish Servant Girl,
This way, that's right,
Hello.
DEBBIE FINE: Oh, hi, who are you?
SAMANTHA:
Never mind who I am,
I have a little chore
I'd like you to perform.
DEBBIE FINE:
Oh, no, I'm much too busy.
SAMANTHA:
Busy doing what may I ask,
Collecting dead flowers from the funeral processions?
You should be ashamed, little girl,
Give up your hobby, it's morbid.
DEBBIE FINE:
Oh no, Mysterious Lady, it's not flowers I collect
But bones.
You see, here is a head
And here a hand
And here, eventually, a foot.
Before long I should put my brother back together
Bone for bone.
I should breathe life into him then
And we should sit to supper
In our mother's house
And pray to God for thanks.
SAMANTHA:
Poor girl.
She has had her divorce with reason.
What alimony of fancy is compensation there
I've often wondered.
One walks alone so much in life
Perhaps it is best at times to walk
With one's pockets filled with the change of mind.
I'll ask her. Girl, girl, are you a mad girl?

DEBBIE FINE: No, I'm not angry.

SAMANTHA: No, no, girl, are you truly mad?

DEBBIE FINE:

No, I said no, but I could get pretty mad
If you keep asking me!

SAMANTHA:

I must quote this to the Sophists, they won't believe it.
Girl, I understand you are looking for bones for your brother's
tomb.

DEBBIE FINE: Not his tomb, his home.

SAMANTHA:

I assure when you reach the former you will have reached the
latter.
Let me be of assistance, Good Innocent, come closer,
Do you see this precious vial,
Can you guess its contents?
It is an elixir.

DEBBIE FINE:

An elixir.
What's an elixir?

SAMANTHA:

Well, it's going to help you put your brother back together
If you can follow some simple directions.
A herald prays now at the Temple of Hope Abandoned.
Go there to him with this and entreat him to drink it.
Give him this message:
If you really want me
You will drink this.
Can you remember that?

DEBBIE FINE:

If you really drink this you will want me.

SAMANTHA:

That's close enough.
Then, once he has consumed the potion
Your wait will be brief.
At your feet you will find all the bones needed to complete your

little project.
Agreed, simple.
Now, take this glass and don't spill it.
I'm due on other plateaus.
So tarry not.

Himmer and Prentice in thigh-length togas and sandals enter laughing.

SAMANTHA:

Two fellows come this way
Who do seem gay
And happiness of any kind today
I cannot, until my own arrives, abide in any way
And so, good fool, I say
Adieu.

Exit Samantha.

DEBBIE FINE:

Bye. She's weird. I'm going to spill this.
HIMMER: Who goes there?
DEBBIE FINE:

A bone picker
A fool, a mad girl
I've been called all things
And all in the last five minutes.
PRENTICE: We greet you.
DEBBIE FINE: Hi.
HIMMER: I smell something sweet and sour.
PRENTICE:

Silence! Don't defile sacred memory.
This girl mourns the recent dead
That crowd our once playful streets
And make of every path an alley
Toward our dim necropolis.
HIMMER: What's in the glass?

DEBBIE FINE: Elixir.

HIMMER:

Elixir vitae? Serum of eternal life,
Quintessence of being and true nectar of the gods?

DEBBIE FINE:

I don't think so.
If I got the story right
You drink this and turn into a pile of bones.

HIMMER:

Then it is hemlock, drink of Socrates
And those who can stomach no more
The burlesque of tragedy—give it here,
I will gulp down its contents,
And of Despair—Wisdom's foul fiancée—
I will wave goodbye.

PRENTICE:

Stop, good friend!
Kind Maiden, pay no attention to my friend's broken ravings
For his father, the King,
has lost his reason
and he, good son, seeks to follow.
Or better yet—lend your glass to me—
I upon reflection wish to drink.
My palate is dry of this world
and its brief menu of judgments,
fake piety and ill intent.

HIMMER:

You mimic me, good friend
to shame me but I cannot be
shamed in a time so shameful
nor can I tame a wild desire
to be free of disgraceful company,
the company of our generals
and heads of state
who munch lives for breakfast
and tell us to fast,

that taxes and insane edicts
will improve our souls.
I bid you, Wise Woman, hand me your
    foolproof medicine, I have an ache in
    my heart so wide armies cross there
    and are perished—hand me this lucky juice.

PRENTICE:

This way, Holy Daughter of Man, the drink is claimed.
This way and it is half swallowed—it is mine.

HIMMER:

Over here, I tell you, it is only a straw I lack.
Lend it here and with head thrown back,
Sweet Sybil, I drink it black.

DEBBIE FINE:

Well, make up your minds
I haven't got all day.
Why don't you have half a glass each?

PRENTICE:

It is a potion too weak.
Neither would die and we would both lie
With bellyaches, complaining of the great cold.

HIMMER:

Miss, let me tell you
Although perhaps you know,
We have lost the war.

DEBBIE FINE: No.

PRENTICE: Yes.

DEBBIE FINE: No, it's not true.

HIMMER:

It is, and the Spartans march toward the city as we speak
And rather than fall at the hands of our victors
    better we should drink eternity no matter
    how bitter the aftertaste—
Waitress, the drink.

PRENTICE:

It is mine.

274

I too defy the Spartans
And know that when they arrive
We will be put in captivity
Tortured then and held to
Die slow agonized deaths
Spat at and jeered on
A death most infamous
Deserted by all gentleness.

HIMMER:

Well spoken my close friend,
I cannot without fairness
Take relief from the lady's goblet
We will have a duel
And the winner drinks all.
We will use our arms
And wrestle standing
While we can still stand.
The lady will be our referee.
Let us begin at once
And end the day.
Foot to foot
Arm to arm
Clamped fist to clamped fist
The loser takes the survivors to lunch.
Let it commence!

Himmer and Prentice arm wrestle standing up, struggling back and forth, fairly evenly matched although Prentice must work harder to keep the match.

DEBBIE FINE: All this for a little elixir?

Enter Jacob Blank: as an old man in a slightly tattered toga. He is unobserved by the arm wrestlers.

JACOB BLANK:

Did I hear the word elixir?

My mouth waters to taste the word more loudly.
'Tis like champagne I'm told, better.
No champagne hangover, is it true, honey?

DEBBIE FINE:

I wouldn't know,
I'm only holding it for a friend.

JACOB BLANK:

A familiar alibi,
Come on, give us a kiss.

DEBBIE FINE:

Fresh!
Be warned, I'll alert my friends
And they'll punch you.

JACOB BLANK:

Why side with them,
I'm younger and better looking.
Come on now, one harmless little kiss couldn't hurt.

DEBBIE FINE:

All right then, have it, if it will stop you asking.
There!

JACOB BLANK:

Oh! I am transported.
A kiss divine. I always get what I ask for.
Now a sip of that elixir!
Tell me, where did you purchase it?

DEBBIE FINE:

I didn't purchase it, I got it
From a goddess, I think, and
I'm told to collect bones with it
And make more dead.

JACOB BLANK:

A clever ploy to hoard her booty.
Clever girl, sell me your treasure
If you will for I feel so fine today
I wish to drink elixir
And live this young and happy, oh, forever.

276

Here, take this sack of gold.
I have a kingdom somewhere,
It is yours but for a swallow
Quick before it cools
Quick before the contest is over for these fools.

HIMMER: I have won!

PRENTICE:

You have lost by winning
And by winning lose.

JACOB BLANK: Athletes, I toast your Olympian triumph! *(He drinks)*

PRENTICE:

It is the King
And he drinks the poison.

JACOB BLANK: It is elixir.

HIMMER: Father, it is poison.

DEBBIE FINE: It is elixir.

HIMMER:

It is poison
It is poison
It is poison.

JACOB BLANK:

Already I go lightheaded
Oh what a clever goddess it is who brews elixir
We must give up all other worship and worship only her.
I lose a step—
I trip—
The elixir works
I live forever
Eternal youth, good health and the envy of my peers.

Enter Patrick.

PATRICK:

Be alerted, the Spartans are at the gate
To take more captives for their hate—

HIMMER: Get a doctor—get a doctor! Now, quickly go, get a doctor!
My father is poisoned.

Patrick exits running. Samantha enters having heard some of the commotion.

HIMMER: Dear Father, it isn't elixir you've drunk but poison I intended for myself, if we don't hurry you will die.

DEBBIE FINE *(At Jacob Blank's side)*: Darling.

PRENTICE: Mr. Blank.

JACOB BLANK:

I don't die

I go to—to—

away from—

on a journey somewhere—

far from the poison world.

HIMMER:

If anything, I envy you, kind King,

You leave a city in ruin

For a city always new.

I join you there so soon.

JACOB BLANK:

How quick the transportation system is,

How efficient: everyone with a single ticket in his hand,

The other free to wave.

Patrick enters, out of breath.

PATRICK: Someone is coming. A doctor.

JACOB BLANK:

Don't be spoilsports, good friends,

Wish me good journey—

SAMANTHA: He's dying. Oh, Mr. Blank.

HIMMER: Dad, it's me Himmer, I want to say good-bye.

JACOB BLANK:

Himmer, your mother wanted to call you Himmel.

Himmel means heaven, I go there now.

She liked my poems, where are they now?

Everyone wish me good journey!

278

HIMMER: Good journey.

PRENTICE: Good journey.

SAMANTHA: Good journey.

DEBBIE FINE AND PATRICK: Good journey!

JACOB BLANK:

I woke up this morning and what did I see?
The end of me. The end of me.

HIMMER:

I woke up early early this morning
And what did I see?
The end of me, the end of me, the end of me.

END OF PLAY

HARRY KONDOLEON's *plays include* Christmas on Mars, The Fairy Garden *and* The Vampires; *he is also the author of a novel,* The Whore of Tjampuan. Zero Positive *was first performed on April 16, 1988 at the New York Shakespeare Festival's Public Theater.*

Photographer ROBERT MAPPLETHORPE*'s work has been shown in more than two hundred exhibitions since 1973. The exhibition "Robert Mapplethorpe: The Perfect Moment," which originated at the Institute of Contemporary Art in Philadelphia in 1988, has gone on to Chicago, Washington, D.C., Hartford and Berkeley; the show is also scheduled for Cincinnati and Boston. Mapplethorpe was forty-two when he died of AIDS, on March 9, 1989.*